Publications of the
CENTRE FOR RENAISSANCE AND REFORMATION AND STUDIES

Essays and Studies, 49

SERIES EDITOR   KONRAD EISENBICHLER

Victoria University
in the
University of Toronto

Umberto Grassi

Bathhouses and Riverbanks: Sodomy in a Renaissance Republic

Toronto
Centre for Renaissance and Reformation Studies
2021

CRRS Publications
Centre for Renaissance and Reformation Studies
Victoria University in the University of Toronto
Toronto, Ontario M5S 1K7, Canada
Tel: 416/585–4465 Fax: 416/585–4430
Email: crrs.publications@utoronto.ca Web: www.crrs.ca

The CRRS gratefully acknowledges the generous financial support it receives for its publishing activities from Victoria University in the University of Toronto. In the case of this volume, Dr. Grassi's research has received funding from the European Union's Horizon 2020 Research and Innovation Programme under the Marie Sklodowska-Curie grant agreement No 795514 (Project SPACES). Dr. Grassi thanks the History Department of the University of Maryland, College Park, for supporting the publication of this volume. The book is the result of Dr. Grassi's research activities. It reflects only the author's view and the Research Executive Agency is not responsible for any use that may be made of the information it contains.

Library and Archives Canada Cataloguing in Publication
Title: Bathhouses and riverbanks : sodomy in a Renaissance republic / Umberto Grassi.
Names: Grassi, Umberto, author. | Victoria University (Toronto, Ont.). Centre for Renaissance and Reformation Studies, publisher.
Series: Essays and studies (Victoria University (Toronto, Ont.). Centre for Renaissance and Reformation Studies ; 49.
Description: Series statement: Essays and studies ; 49 | Includes bibliographical references and index.
Identifiers: Canadiana (print) 20210197315 | Canadiana (ebook) 20210197390 | ISBN 9780772721983 (softcover) | ISBN 9780772722003 (PDF)
Subjects: LCSH: Sodomy—Law and legislation—Italy—Lucca—History. | LCSH: Sex customs—Italy—Lucca—History.
Classification: LCC KKH4216 .G73 2021 | DDC 345/.455302536—dc23

Cover image:
Benedetto da Milano, from cartoons by Bartolomeo Suardi known as Bramantino, "February" (detail), ca. 1504–1509. Civiche Raccolte Artistiche, Castello Sforzesco, Milan. https://www.milanocastello.it/en/content/bramantino (by permission).

Typesetting and cover design:
Iter Press

Contents

ACKNOWLEDGMENTS

Behind the pages of this book there is a large part of my life as a researcher. I started working on the sources of the Office of Decency in Lucca for my MA dissertation, and subsequently made of this investigation the subject of my PhD at the University of Pisa. The PhD thesis was awarded the "LGBTQ Studies Prize" of the Maurice group in Turin, which resulted in its publication in Italian in 2015. I am now working as a Marie Skłodowska-Curie global fellow based at the PoliTeSse (Politics and Theories of Sexuality) Research Centre of the University of Verona, with the History Department of the University of Maryland as a partner institution. In the framework of this new project, I have been able to revise the original Italian manuscript and work on a restructured and historiographically updated version of my first book.

It would be impossible to acknowledge all the people that helped me in the various stages of this work. I am grateful to historian, journalist, and gay activist Giovanni Dall'Orto, who first told me about the existence of the archival series of the Office of Decency in Lucca, suggesting to the young and excited student I was at the time to engage in the arduous but gratifying work of this research. I thank Prof. Adriano Prosperi for entrusting me with this enterprise, first as an MA and then a PhD thesis supervisor. I learned the craft of the historian from him, and I could not have been luckier to have such an extraordinary mentor. With her great scholarship — and humanity — Prof. Daniela Lombardi was an invaluable point of reference for me while I was a PhD candidate in Pisa. Dr. Michael J. Rocke has generously shared his knowledge of Renaissance homoeroticism with me since I was a young student embarking on this field. Simonetta Adorni-Braccesi accompanied and guided me into the labyrinthine history of Lucca's religious dissent with a generosity and commitment that has no comparison. Prof. Helmut Puff introduced me to the latest developments in the international historiographical debate on queer and sexuality studies. Prof. Simoma Cerutti hosted me during a two-month stay at the École des Hautes Études en Sciences Sociales (EHESS) in Paris, during which I had access to the invaluable resources of the Bibliothèque Nationale de France. Archivist Sergio Nelli introduced me to the Archivio di Stato in Lucca, and encouraged me when, as a young student, I first stumbled on the apparently unreadable hand of a sixteenth-century notary.

I thank my Marie Skłodowska-Curie supervisor Prof. Lorenzo Bernini for his support during the implementation of my project — of which the current book is only a secondary, but relevant deliverable — and my co-supervisor Prof. Philip Sorgel for his incomparable hospitality during the outgoing phase of my fellowship in the USA. I am grateful to Francis Gordon for translating my convoluted Italian prose into a smooth and readable English. I also thank the CRRS copyeditor Vanessa McCarthy and the director of the Essays and Studies series Prof. Konrad Eisenbichler for their meticulous revision of the volume. Simone Ragagli, a friend and expert in Lucchese religious history, has been of invaluable help during the final revision of the typescript. When, due to the restructions imposed on travels to contain the Covid19 pandemic, I was not able to go back to source material and bibliography, he provided me with his support at a distance with great generosity and irreplaceable competence.

I owe a debt of gratitude to the incredible staff at the Department of Human Sciences at the Università degli Studi di Verona and the Department of History at the University of Maryland, who helped me deal with the thousands of problems a scholar faces when migrating abroad. I sincerely thank you all for your patience and support during these years.

UMBERTO GRASSI

A Note on Terminology

The terminology used to describe sexual acts, feelings, and desires has changed dramatically over time. At any given moment in history, it has been shaped by current gender constructs and religious beliefs, and influenced by social, economic and cultural factors. Historical subjects dealt with sexual matters differently according to circumstances and codes of communication. People did not talk about sex in the same way when they were in a brothel as when they were writng a literary work, a theological or medical treatise, or a law code. "Sexuality" is a modern construct, born with human and social sciences, and "gender" is an even more recent category. A great deal of work has been done by historians to untangle the complex problems that arise when dealing with these issues from a diachronic perspective. This historiographical debate is inextricably tied to the contemporary developments in gender studies and has profited of the contribution of scholars coming from a wide range of disciplinary fields. While I will deal with the debate on the history of sexuality and homosexuality in the introduction and chapter 7, here I limit myself to some introductory remarks about the use of the words "homosexuality" and "homosexual." It is well known that these terms were coined in the nineteenth century and, although overlapping in many ways, they do not coincide with previous constructs, like sodomy or sex "against nature." In order to avoid anachronisms, I do not use these terms interchangeably. However, I do use "homosexuality" when I compare modern and premodern constructs, as well as when I explicitly refer to the field of study of the "history of homosexuality." "Homosexual" is never used as a noun to refer to a person's identity, but only as an adjective, as a synonym for adjectival forms loike "same-sex" or "male-male" (i.e.: "homosexual intercourse," "homosexual desire" and so on). The same cautions have ben adopted in using the terms "heterosexual" and "heterosexuality," which, is important to emphasize, are not transhistorical and universal categories either, being even more recent constructs than "homosexual" and "homosexuality" and, we shall not forget, modeled on them. That said, as I will argue more broadly in the course of the volume, the fact that I use this terminology carefully does not imply that I assume that, before the creation of the term homosexuality, same-sex intercourse was exclusively a sinful act that did not influence the way in which same-sex attracted women and men perceived themselves as individuals and members of a community.

This interpretation was crucial to the "acts-identity" debate (whose terms will be explained later in the book). As we will see, although extremely insightful and productive, this binary has long been overcome in historical studies.

A Note on Transcriptions

In the book there are lengthy quotations from sixteenth-century judicial proceedings. They are reported in translation in the body of the text, with the Tuscan vernacular original in the footnotes. As far as the original is concerned, I modernized the punctuation (reducing the overuse of commas and introducing semicolon and full stops to break escessively long sentences). I also simplified the spelling, substituting the latinazing form "ti" (for the sound "tsi") with the current transcription "zi" (e.g.: "offitio" — "offizio"). I erased some archaic uses of the consonant "h" (e.g.: "anchora" — "ancora," "huomo" — "uomo"). In general, spelling was not standardized at the time, and the transcritptions of the notaries were often inconsistent throughout the reports. For this reason, I decided to modernize some words for sake of fluency and readability. For instance, while the consonant "s" was sometimes used instead of the "z" in syllables which, in modern Italian, always sound "dz" (like "ragazzo," which was then spelled both in the form "ragazzo" and "ragasso"), I decided to standardize these instances adopting the the modern spelling. You will find direct speech often reported in the cites. In these cases, I added the inverted commas, which were not used in the original documents. However, I only did that when there was an actual direct speech in the source, that is, when judges, defendants or witnesses were reported in the first person (e.g.: he said, I do not want — wich becomes: he said "I do not want"). I want to make clear that I never romanticize the original reports by changing the reported speech into a direct speech.

INTRODUCTION

This book provides a thorough investigation into the activity of the Office of Decency (*Offizio sopra l'Onestà*), a state magistracy focused on regulating sodomy in the Republic of Lucca between the fifteenth and the seventeenth century. This archival collection contains one of the largest assemblages of documents on (mostly) male-male sexual interaction in Italy after those bequeathed by the two other major secular courts established to regulate the "nefarious sin" of sodomy, the Venetian Committee on Sodomites (*Collegium Subdomitarum*), whose records were examined by Guido Ruggiero for his *Boundaries of Eros* (1985) and Gabriele Martini (Il «vitio nefando», 1988), and the Florentine Night Officers (*Officiali di Notte*), scrutinized by Michael Rocke for his *Forbidden Friendships* (1996).[1] The material preserved in the State Archive in Lucca offers yet another vantage point for observing the complex interactions between institutional dynamics, social practices, and the multifaceted cultural meanings of unreproductive sexual behaviour in Italy, this time in one of the last republican city-states on the peninsula.

The study builds on the example of a tradition that focused on criminal sources to uncover the history of past homosexualities. After Boswell's ground-breaking study *Christianity, Social Tolerance and Homosexuality* (1980), which prominently relied on literary and theological sources, a social-history approach mostly based on judicial archives dominated this field of research, with Bray's *Homosexuality in Renaissance England* (1982) marking a turning point. Studies on the Italian peninsula have generated some masterpieces in this field, thanks to the commitment of brilliant historians and the richness of documents stored in the Italian archives. Some city-states in Italy had specific tribunals devoted to the monitoring of sodomy, which resulted in the collection of an invaluable source material. The institutional policing of sodomy was most extensive in Venice, Florence, and Lucca. For a long time Ruggiero's study on the Venetian archives and, above all, Rocke's analysis of the Florentine sources marked the highest achievements in the history of past homoerotic desire, at least until the impact of queer studies revolutionized our approach to this matter. This book aims to complete this

---

[1] A revised version of some parts of the introduction to the original Italian version of this book was published in a previous article in English that I have used extensively in the first part of these introductory remarks; see Grassi, "Acts or Identities."

virtual "triad" by bringing to light the activities of the third major institution governing sodomitic practices in Renaissance and Counter-Reformation Italy, the Office of Decency in Lucca.

A lot has happened since Rocke's *Forbidden Friendships* was published in 1996. Many new theoretical insights have changed the ways we approach the study of past sexualities, especially homoerotic desire. Most of the innovative shifts have, however, taken place through the exploration of a different set of sources from those that inspired the first, prolific wave of inquiry into male-male sexual desires and practices. The challenge of this book is to re-open a dialogue with a line of research that was partly interrupted more than a decade ago, with a strong belief that this approach still has much to offer researchers and readers. While engaging with new methodologies that have transfigured our understanding of past sexualities, this study also endeavours to respond to some of the issues left open by past scholars in their own terms, believing that they are still relevant to present-day scholarship.

Since the 1990s, the polemics about the "social construction" of homosexual identities that monopolized the historiographical debate on the history of homosexuality have been overtaken by a more nuanced approach to the issue. This dispute revolved around the appropriateness of projecting onto the past categories such as "homosexuality" and, even more radically, sexuality per se. Boswell was aware that terms such as "gay" and "homosexuality" required careful use when referring to past societies.[2] His book, however, became emblematic of what was later defined as an "essentialist" approach by those who, inspired by the Foucauldian assumption of the nineteenth-century medical invention of homosexuality, embraced a "social constructionist" methodology. This crystallized opposition proves to be specious when we return to the roots of Boswell's and Foucault's original positions. It is worth noting that the latter wrote a short review for the back cover of the 1981 paperback edition of *Christianity, Social Tolerance and Homosexuality*, stating that the book was "a truly groundbreaking work," and that Boswell revealed "unexplored phenomena with an unfailing erudition." As Carolyn Dinshaw has underlined, Boswell's work influenced Foucault's reflections. In a 1982 interview, the French philosopher stated that the term "gay," as it was used by Boswell, was a "useful instrument of research" insofar as it focused more on consciousness and on "what one makes" of an experience, than on the

---

[2] Boswell, *Christianity, Social Tolerance, Homosexuality*, 41–59.

problem of desire and its supposed "naturalness."[3] Didier Eribon had already pointed out that even though Foucault strongly refused to view homosexuality as a changeless anthropological category, he nonetheless admitted that some permanent features — namely, the subject's self-consciousness of diversity — did exist.[4] Although he criticized those who connected Timarchus and Michelangelo along a continuous history,[5] Foucault also asserted that the awareness of same-sex sexuality went far beyond individual experience and produced a sense of belonging to a social group that dated back to antiquity.[6] The terms of the "social constructionist" versus "essentialist" debate therefore suppose a woodenness in Foucault's theoretical approach that is completely alien to his methodology.

Nevertheless, this dispute had the merit of prompting research that contributed to an impressive advancement in our historical knowledge of past sexual epistemologies. The most powerful input to the debate came from queer theorists at the beginning of the 1990s. Unlike their predecessors, they did not focus on what had come before, but rather on what happened from the nineteenth century onwards. Whereas historians, wishing to restore the radical otherness of the past by refusing to use contemporary categories of interpretation, contrasted previous categories with a supposedly "modern" — and homogeneous — homosexual identity, queer theories tried instead to deconstruct precisely the latter. In *Epistemology of the Closet* (1990), Eve Kosofsky Sedgwick asked what are we referring to when we speak of homosexuality "as we know it today."[7] She listed many differences that break the boundaries dividing hetero- and homo-sexuality, questioning why humanity has been split into two apparently unconnected groups based on a preference for partners from the same or the opposite sex, while many other binaries could have been established.[8] This provocative argument led historian David Halperin, a former radical constructionist in his *One Hundred Years of Homosexuality* (1990), to review his previous approach when he came to write *How to Do the History of Homosexuality* (2002). Whereas Sedgwick denounced the instability and incoherence of "homosexuality" as a descriptive category, Halperin tried to understand the historical roots of its contradictions: all (and often

---

[3] Carolyn Dinshaw, "Touching on the Past," 67–68, with reference to O'Higgins, Foucault, "Sexual Choice, Sexual Act."

[4] Eribon, *Réflexions*, 454, with reference to Foucault, *Dits et Écrits*, 4.292.

[5] Eribon, *Réflexions*, 453, with reference to Foucault, *Dits et Écrits*, 4.316.

[6] Foucault, *Dits et Écrits*, 4.320.

[7] Kosofsky Sedgwick, *Epistemology of the Closet*, 44.

[8] Kosofsky Sedgwick, *Epistemology of the Closet*, 22–27.

conflicting) interpretative models through which same-sex relations had previously been interpreted were channelled into the present-day concept of homosexuality, thus determining its complexity.[9] The perception of male homosexuality, he stated, is still strongly influenced by past categories such as effeminacy and pederasty, as well as ancient models of male companionship. While *kinaidia* (a Greek word that defined sexually receptive and effeminate men) clearly denoted a specific identity, others, such as pederasty, referred to behaviours that could have been enacted transversally — to use contemporary categories — by hetero-, bi- or homo-sexual people.[10]

Notwithstanding Halperin's effort to harmonize queer criticism and a "historicist" approach, some scholars engaged in the project of "*queering history*" started to question the effectiveness of his "historicism." As Carla Freccero pointed out in 2006, while the Foucauldian genealogy of sexuality criticized the creation of identity through the multiplication of taxonomies, Halperin actually projected into the past this pernicious "modern" attitude that queer theorists are *de facto* trying to deconstruct.[11] Furthermore, since time itself was targeted by some of the most radical representatives of the "queer galaxy" (such as Lee Edelman), the relation between queer theories and history has become far more complex. The idea of a continuous, future-oriented time that compels one to sacrifice the present for the sake of society and in the name of reproduction is considered in this perspective as one of the most successful achievements of heteronormative societies.[12] Carla Freccero, Jonathan Goldberg, and Madhavi Menon,[13] among others, have taken up this challenge and tried to conceive history without a chronologically ordered and continuous timeline.

Valerie Traub, however, criticized their methodological proposal and defended diachrony against the accusation that it is a mere reproduction of "heteronormative" models. She asserted that while the formal procedures of a diachronic method cannot be exempted from ideology, they must not be confused with ideology itself. If history and historiography have become "teleological, heterotemporal, or straight," this is due to "analytic and material processes" that deserve to be understood and historicized.[14]

---

[9] Halperin, *How to do the History of Homosexuality*, 12.

[10] Halperin, *How to do the History of Homosexuality*, 104–109.

[11] Freccero, *Queer/Early/Modern*, 31–50.

[12] Edelman, *No Future: Queer Theory and the Death Drive*.

[13] Goldberg and Menon, "Queering History," 1608–1617.

[14] Traub, "The New Unhistoricism," 32.

In the English-speaking academic world, these debates have taken place mostly in the framework of a cultural historical approach that has profitably privileged literary and visual sources over extensive and quantitative surveys of criminal archives.[15] In my opinion, however, these incredible achievements have favoured an attitude of relative indifference towards those on the lowest ranks of the social ladder. Given their inability to produce written sources, the lives, desires, and struggles of these social actors are barely accessible when historians direct their attention away from judicial documents. This is one of the reasons why I am compelled to look back at the criminal archive, although with a different perspective. A recent brilliant example that moves in this direction is Zeb Tortorici's *Sins Against Nature: Sex and Archives in Colonial New Spain* (2018), a book that challenges traditional approaches to criminal sources by exploring trials for "sins against nature" in the early modern Spanish colonies. Tortorici explores the colonial archive by relying on queer theories and the flourishing new literature on the history of emotions. The feelings and anxieties of those who engaged in behaviours ranging from same-sex intercourse to bestiality, masturbation, and profanation of sacred images are explored along with the emotions of those who controlled them and recorded their experience, experiences brought back to life through the historian's desire.[16]

It is not by chance that such a brilliant contribution has come from a scholar working on Iberian empires. The historiography on sexuality in Spain, Portugal, and their colonies has indeed been extremely productive in the last few decades. Some authors have been receptive to stimuli from the field of

---

[15] The list is endless (though special mention goes to the works in Series Q, published by Duke University Press), but see Goldberg, *Queering the Renaissance* and *Sodometries*; Dinshaw, *Getting Medieval*; Burger, Kruger, *Queering the Middle Ages*; Pugh, *Queering Medieval Genres*; Kłosowska, *Queer Love in the Middle Ages*; Mills, *Seeing Sodomy in the Middle Ages*.

[16] The problems raised by the archive have long been problematized in studies on gender and sexuality. Foucault's *Archaelogy of Knowledge* and Derridda's *Archive Fever* have been influential texts in this field of research. Arondekar's *For the Record*, focused on the Indian colonial archive, represents a theoretical milestone in the relation between the historian, the archive, and the history of sexuality. For a contemporary perspective on how feminist archives are created and the emotional involvement of those exploring them see Eichhorn, *Archival Turn*. On the affective and the erotic dimensions of writing queer history see Freeman, *Time Binds* and, with a gaze oriented to the past, Dinshaw, *Getting Medieval*.

queer theories.[17] Others, although still largely based on more traditional approaches to religious and secular criminal sources,[18] have nevertheless been able to move in a direction that goes against the grain of certain established paradigms in the history of premodern male homosexualities. One of the most compelling conclusions drawn from the analysis of innumerable Iberian and Latin American sources is the close relationship between male effeminacy and a sexually receptive role in homosexual intercourse, evident in popular environments as well as among the elite since the late sixteenth century.[19] Furthermore, historians of the peninsular and the colonial Iberian world have brought to light the existence of large networks of sodomites that constituted veritable semi-clandestine cultures, especially in urban environments like Seville, Lisbon, and Mexico City.[20] These examples completely undermine the once well-established thesis of Randolph Trumbach, who hypothesized that a homosexual identity characterized by phenomena of gender inversion and the construction of extensive networks of homoerotic sociability first emerged in late-seventeenth- and eighteenth-century Northern Europe. This was said to replace an earlier premodern paradigm largely featuring the model of classical pederasty, where adults in positions of power exercised their authority over their subjects in a lower position by engaging in penetrative sexual acts with both females and young males.[21]

The sources presented here constitute further proof that this interpretative model does not give an accurate picture of past sexual lives. While there are many cases in Lucca where young boys were abused by adults, many others show young people involved in a lively homoerotic culture in which partners were not separated by a large age gap and sexual role was not determined by age or social status. Reciprocity rather than inequality seems to be

---

[17] Blackmore and Hutcheson, *Queer Iberia*; Garza-Carvajal, *Butterflies Will Burn*.

[18] For a solid archival research based on Inquisitorial sources see Bennassar, "Le modèle sexuel" and Monter, *La otra Inquisición*.

[19] Among many examples, see Carrasco, *Inquisición y represión sexual*, 101; 107–108; 135; Mantecón Movellan, "Beyond Repression," 104. For similar examples in the Colonial world see Vainfas, "The Nefarious and the Colony," 346; Garza-Carvajal, *Butterflies Will Burn*, 68–71 (on the same Mexican cases see also: Gruzinski, "Ashes of Desire"); Tortorici, *Sins Against Nature*, 110–115.

[20] For Seville, see Perry, "The 'Nefarious Sin'"; Mantecón Movellan, "Los mocitos de Galindo" and "Beyond Repression." For Lisbon, see Mott, "Pagode português." For Mexico City, see Garza-Carvajal, *Butterflies Will Burn*, 131–183; Gruzinski, "Ashes of Desire."

[21] Trumbach, *Sex and the Gender Revolution*, "London Sapphists" and "The Transformation of Sodomy."

a habitual pattern among same-sex-attracted young men in Lucca. Between the 1550s and 1560s, the judges uncovered extended networks of sodomites aged between 15 and 25 who habitually met up on riverbanks not far from the city walls on hot summer days. Interestingly enough, none of them reported rape or violence (a pattern that frequently emerges from the sources analyzed by Marina Baldassari in her study on early modern Rome).[22] This clandestine sociability was characterized by a high degree of flexibility, sexual versatility, and promiscuity. With their focus on youths as a specific sector of society, these cases shed light on the role of homosexual behaviour in constructing the performances of masculinity among young people in the Early Modern Period.

As Tortorici has pointed out, it is crucial for historians to understand how the archive was constituted, what interests it served, and what anxieties it embodied. In this analysis, silences and blind spots are as relevant as the elements emphasized by the source material. Unlike the Spanish and colonial documents mentioned above, the archives of the Office of Decency are unforthcoming when it comes to recording the emotional dimensions of homoerotic relationships. Cases where violence against young boys or female partners occurred were much more extensively reported than those that described consensual acts of sodomy between — mostly young — peers. The latter cases were often resolved by recurring to forms of expedite justice, allowing a speedy solution to the proceedings and frequently resulting in a steep but not unaffordable fine. This attitude was reflected in a long series of very brief proceedings where notaries succinctly took note of names, ages, professions, numbers of partners and sexual encounters, and the role played during intercourse by the defendants (that is, whether they were "active" or "passive," to use the terminology employed by those who wrote the reports). These dozens of cases, however, are completely overshadowed by the lengthy reports regarding cases of abuse of minors and, especially, heterosexual sodomy, which were instead extensively debated in the courtroom. This difference in the ways in which information was archived has led me to the conclusion that, at least to a certain extent, consensual homosexual intercourse among young people was considered a minor offence. In order to realize this and to understand the predominance of versatility among these groups, however, I had to carry out the quantitative analysis of many cases that were less thoroughly documented, creating a database and analyzing the aggregate

---

[22] Baldassari, *Bande giovanili*.

data. In doing this, I adopted a methodology that was crucial to early studies on the history of sexuality and can still open new perspectives if implemented wisely. While curiosity about the emotional dimensions of the construction of the archive directed my observations to elements that received less attention, the only way to make this silence speak was to reconstruct the series of information that would otherwise have been too incoherent to be interpreted.

Conversely, the scarcity of information about the emotional life underpinning these cases has prompted the adoption of a qualitative approach that builds on the results achieved in the last few decades in the field of the history of emotions.[23] Thanks to the methodological insights from this prolific scholarship, the present study resists the tendency to analyse strategies of regulation and the spread of homosexual practices in Renaissance societies through reference to an outdated "hydraulic model." This term refers to both psychological theories and common-sense views that understand emotions as "fluids" that fill the sensing subject. These fluids are believed to exert pressure that requires release, calling for constant surveillance in order to avoid its socially destructive potential. Historians can now benefit from new scientific achievements in the study of emotions, which, together with feelings, are no longer understood as autonomous from "reason." We now focus on discerning the complex interactions between intellect, will, wishes, and feelings. Emotions are not independent from the monitoring self; they can be cultivated, polished, and chosen, as well as controlled.[24] This book explores what kind of cultural constructions and social performances favoured the diffusion and relative acceptability of homosexual behaviour among the young; it refrains from considering the relationship between institutional surveillance and social practices in terms of "repression" and "control," preferring to use "regulation" and "negotiation" as a theoretical framework to understand these dynamics. This is not a way to deny the existence of conflict, nor the fact that the occasional recourse to the death penalty is a powerful reminder of

---

[23] The history of emotions is now established as one of the most influential disciplines in the field of historical studies. Since the pioneering works by Peter and Carol Sterns ("Emotionology"), William Reddy (*Navigation of Feeling*) and Barbara Rosenwein (*Emotional Communities*), many major studies have been published summarising the main theoretical acquisitions in this productive research sector with extensive bibliographies: Matt and Stearns, *Doing Emotions History*; Plamper, *History of Emotions*; Broomhall, *Early Modern Emotions*; Corbin, et al., *Histoire des émotions*; Broomhall, et al., *Cultural History of the Emotions*; Broomhall and Lynch, *Routledge History of Emotions*.

[24] Solomon, *True to our Feelings*, 142–149.

the extent to which the policy on sexual mores was viewed as a serious affair. It is an invitation to create an even more complex notion of the interaction between norms and desires, one of the most important achievements in this field of research since the impact of Foucault's *History of Sexuality*. Foucault denied the "repressive hypothesis," that is, that sex had long been repressed in the West, suggesting instead that the increasing focus on sexual desires by religious institutions triggered a proliferation of discourses that led to "sexuality" being placed at the very core of individual identity. The "repressive hypothesis" stimulated strategies of sexual liberation as a polemical response that, in Foucault's perspective, fundamentally missed the point that it is the idea itself of sexuality as the primeval centre of the self that deserves critical analysis.[25] The Foucauldian perspective, largely embraced by studies on the history of sexuality, did, however, create excessive dependence on the kind of normative discourses that Foucault privileged in his analysis (theology, law, and medicine). Without denying their significance, these disciplines, relevant to the history of epistemology, coexisted with a wide range of other explanations of sexual desires and practices.[26] The focus of emotion scholars on the coexistence of different sets of emotional regimes in different groups within the same society has favoured a more complex and multifaceted approach to the issue. In his *Navigation of Feeling* (2001) William M. Reddy emphasized the creation of emotional refuges in the midst of societies that exert excessive control on the emotional performances of their members. Barbara Rosenwein, however, in her *Emotional Communities* (2006) and *Generations of Feeling* (2016) highlighted how this model is still excessively indebted to a hydraulic understanding of emotional life, stressing at the same time that Reddy's paradigm, far from being universally applicable, was almost exclusively suited to complex societies at a developed stage of state formation. Her proposal to shift the attention of emotion scholars to 'emotional communities' was an invitation to analyze the emotional performances of the multiple formal and informal groups that constituted larger social bodies.

This approach, however, is possible only when we have access to source types that are not available in cases like the present study. As far as we know, unlike other early modern Italian communities such as Venice and Florence, Lucca has less cultural artifacts that explicitly celebrated homosexual desire.

---

[25] Foucault, *Will to Knowledge*, 17–49.

[26] See, for example, Spector, Puff, and Herzog, *After the History of Sexuality*; Chiang, *Revisiting the History of Sexuality*.

In this context, the interpretative framework of Monique Scheer's reflection on emotions as social practices has proven particularly valuable to understand the construction of the homoerotic sociability of Lucca. Drawing on Bourdieu's theories on socially apprehended habitus, this approach also helps to solve some conundrums of the acts/identities debate, allowing historians to grasp the depth of the consequences of repeated acts in the construction and interiorization of social values.[27]

In a few cases, however, the notaries recorded words and sentences that explicitly allude to the emotional life of the witnesses and defendants. Although scattered, these hints provide the opportunity to grasp the quality and intensity of the emotional life of the social actors involved in the judicial proceedings. Even before the rise of the history of emotions as an independent field of research, emotions and feelings had been a core element of the history of the family, so that the conclusions drawn by a generation of scholars in medieval and early modern families in Europe affected our understanding of past emotional performances. This historiographical tradition devalued the ability of early modern people to feel and express care and love for their spouses, children, and relatives. In the upper classes, patrimony and family alliances oriented the choice of partners, while for peasants and urban paid workers the family was essentially considered a unit of production. From the late 1970s onwards, these characteristics were interpreted as the main reasons for the low emotionality of family relationships, a detachment that the high child mortality rate was supposed to have increased by discouraging the creation of deep bonds between parents and children.[28] All these assumptions have gradually been scaled back by more recent scholarship;[29] the belief that the modern nuclear family is the only place where feelings of love and affection are allowed to grow has revealed its pervasively western-centric and liberal undertone.[30] This research takes a further step in this direction. Rather than studying the history of homoerotic relationships in contrast to the history of the family, I have integrated the analysis of the two areas, attempting to understand how emotional performances in the respective domains influenced one another. As we will see in Chapter 7, this perspective allows us to paint a

---

[27] See below, Chapter 7. Scheer, "Are Emotions a Kind of Practice?"

[28] See especially the foundational work of Ariès, *Centuries of Childhood* and Stone, *The Family, Sex and Marriage*.

[29] See, for example, Ozment, *Ancestors*.

[30] Particularly significant in this direction are the recent contributions by Barclay, *Love, Intimacy and Power*; Barclay, et al., *Death, Emotion and Childhood*.

far more nuanced picture of past emotional lives, where homoerotic feelings could find space within the heterosexual family and where other affective bonds, like friendship and mateship, intertwined with parental networks along a continuum rather than constituting mutually exclusive alternatives.

As mentioned above, the affective dimension of homoerotic bonds can be grasped only by paying attention to details, gaps, and blind spots in the archive. Conversely, extensively reported cases of heterosexual sodomy and abuse perpetrated against children and teenagers constitute an invaluable source when we try to expand our knowledge of the life conditions of both adolescents and women. It is surprising that, despite the manifest concerns expressed by the proliferation of decrees and laws that aimed to regulate the interaction of children and adolescents with adults, youngsters did not benefit from any particular protection when exposed to the threat of a criminal conviction for sodomy. Although they were given lenient penalties, children and teenagers never enjoyed full immunity (unless they spontaneously denounced their partners). It is, however, even more interesting to note that they were not considered mere objects, but active subjects of desire by the judges, who attributed a sexual agency to them that sounds disconcerting to modern readers.

The tendency to blame the victims of abuse seems to be at play also in cases of heterosexual sodomy, which further reveals the extent to which the law worked as an extension of patriarchal power in sexual matters. It was, however, easier for women than for male teenagers to mobilize their social networks to obtain the aid they needed to accuse their aggressors; their reported cases allow an in-depth exploration of these episodes of community support. Of course, it is not surprising that heterosexual sodomy frequently emerges from the sources in cases of violence. In contrast to homosexual relationships, which were prosecuted anyway, consensual heterosexual partners could enjoy much more freedom to experiment when they were away from prying eyes. The only instances of consensual anal sex between a man and a woman prosecuted by the Office of Decency are related to the regulation of prostitution, a category that, as we will see, was increasingly monitored during the sixteenth century. The conditions of women and adolescents in relation to their aggressors seem to share some common features. On some occasions, it is quite likely that members of both categories tried to use the accusation of sodomy as a trump card to challenge the overbearing authority of male protectors, using the instrument of criminal accusation as a pathway to freedom from an abusive gendered power that both society and the law tended to make almost unassailable.

As a case study, Lucca also offers a fresh perspective on the history of religious dissent in its complex relationship with sexual nonconformity. In the context of the religious conflicts that shook Italy after the outbreak of the Reformation, Lucca's hidden but notorious pro-Calvinism offers a unique opportunity to analyze the role played by the regulation of sexuality in the religious crisis of the sixteenth century. While research on radical dissent, libertinism, and atheism have dealt with the connections between sexual licence and criticism of the dogmas of the Catholic Church — and, more broadly, institutionalized religion —,[31] sexual themes have often been overlooked in the study of the "Italian Reformation" and the spread of Calvinism in the peninsula. The collection of data stored in the Office of Decency archives allows us to scrutinize the sexual policy of a ruling class that stood out for its Reformed and pro-Calvinist leanings.

Furthermore, this rich case study offers a vantage point to critically re-engage with categories like "confessionalism," "social discipline," and confessionalization that for decades dominated scholarship on state formation and institutional reforms in periods of religious turmoil.[32] The religious crisis affected the way in which Lucchese society related to the surveillance of sexual mores, which conversely influenced the pattern of persecution of religious dissent. Although increased papal repression in the second half of the sixteenth century forced Lucca into the fold of Catholic orthodoxy, heresy continued to proliferate. The City Council managed to keep the Church's inquisitorial tribunals away from the small, independent state and maintained religious order in its territories by founding a secular tribunal devoted to the control of religious disputes. As demonstrated in reports drafted at the time, Lucca's Office of Religion was shaped along the lines of the Office of Decency.

In the midst of the religious turmoil of the second half of the century, both Catholics and pro-Protestants seem to have used the accusation of sodomy as a political tool to discredit their adversaries. This attitude reflected

---

[31] See Grassi, "Sex and Toleration"; Cryle and O'Connell, *Libertine Enlightenment*; Darnton, "Sex for Thought"; Hunt, *The Invention of Pornography*; Cavaillé, *Les déniaisés*. Many examples are analyzed in Barbierato: *Inquisitor in the Hat Shop*; for some of the most relevant among them see 14, 29, 54–55, 102, 104, 187.

[32] For the relevant bibliography on social discipline and confessionalization, see below, Chapter 9.

a long-standing tradition that, without conflating the two categories, saw unreproductive sexuality as a stable attribute of the stereotype of the enemy of Christian society.[33] Sodomy was considered a practice that implied a more or less conscious rejection of the order inscribed by God in nature, a violation of the reproductive purpose of sexuality, and a behaviour that clouded the light of natural reason.[34] However, it seems that secular institutions in Lucca chose to embrace a mediating policy and protect their citizens from defamation, avoiding the association between sodomy and heresy in the trials held by the Office of Decency. At the same time, they engaged in an exhausting struggle with the ecclesiastical hierarchy to protect their own privileges and independence from Rome. As a crime of mixed jurisdiction, sodomy was one of the bones of contention in the skirmish between the government and the local Church. The wearying clash between religious and civil institutions gave rise to a public discourse — reminiscent of the much more influential and widely recognized case of Venice — that anticipated many of the familiar themes of eighteenth-century jurisdictionalism.[35] The thorough analysis of these conflicts from the perspective of the regulation of sexual mores not only offers a fresh view on the previously studied political history of this small republic, but also shows the benefit of a close reading of local dynamics in order to interpret the historical shifts brought to the scene by both the Reformation and the Catholic response to it. Moreover, it helps to understand this conflict within the wider framework of a long-term process of Christian renewal. While for decades much emphasis was placed on the alliance between State and Church in the extension of an increasingly bureaucratized control of individual consciences, the case of Lucca further proves what has already been highlighted by a new generation of scholars of post-Reformation Europe.[36]

---

[33] Boswell, *Christianity, Social Tolerance, and Homosexuality*, 283–286; Goodich, *The Unmentionable Vice*, 7–10; Puff, *Sodomy in Reformation Germany and Switzerland*.

[34] This is especially due to the influence of Thomas Aquinas on subsequent Christian (especially Catholic) moral theology. His contribution is, however, far more complex than the reception of his work in western Christianity: Boswell, *Christianity, Social Tolerance, and Homosexuality*, 303–332; Jordan, *The Invention of Sodomy*, 136–158; Todeschini, "'Soddoma e Caorsa.'"

[35] On the Lucchese republican model as *ante litteram* jurisdictionalism, see Ragagli, "La Coscienza di una Repubblica" and "L'Inquisizione della Repubblica." For an original reassessment of the widely studied issue of the conflict between Venice and the papacy, see De Vivo, *Information and Communication in Venice*.

[36] On the Reformed world, see Rublack, *Reformation Europe*; for Catholicism, O'Malley, *Trent and All That*. Further bibliography below, Chapter 9.

Church and State constantly negotiated their respective areas of influence, often with violent clashes, while civic and religious institutions were characterized by deep internal fractures.

The Reformed ideals of the ruling classes marked the pinnacle of the civic religion model that Lucca had embraced since the later Middle Ages, a model that strongly influenced the institutional stance on sexual nonconformity, including containment strategies. Lucca provides an example of how the model of civic religion could resist the centralizing efforts of post-Tridentine Catholicism after exposure to Reformed ideals. Interestingly enough, those members of the ruling class who were more open to stimuli from the European Reformation acted in continuity with a past where lay people contributed to the administration of the sacred in a climate of communal participation.[37] The bureaucratized reform of religious matters stemmed from the part of the local Church that was more responsive to the efforts of the religious hierarchies, warmly (and belligerently) supported by the Roman Curia. The outbreak of the Reformation thus facilitated the growth of ideas that would be crucial to the future evolution of mature jurisdictionalism. This process occurred, however, in a context where religion was still a vital element in the political and social life of the community, looking back to a past tradition that aimed to resist the attempts at centralization that historiography has qualified as "modernizing" forces in European history.

This is particularly clear in the policy on sexual mores. The Office of Decency embodied an approach to the social regulation of sexual morality that was typical of late-medieval disciplining strategies, which started to be called into question after the Council of Trent. In fact, before the disciplining efforts made by the local bishop to implement the Tridentine decrees, the intense scrutiny of sexual mores partly reflected the desire to address social habits that were deeply rooted in spite of religious interdictions. Comparative analysis of the special tribunals in Venice, Florence, and Lucca reveals that the way sexual morality was dealt with in the two Tuscan cities was substantially different from the strategies employed in La Serenissima: while judges in Venice tended to inflict a few exemplary punishments, those in Florence and Lucca, where judicial prosecutions were more widespread, generally imposed minor sentences. Both strategies, however, prove that the increased surveillance of sexual nonconformity went hand in hand with certain forms of social tolerance. Sodomy had to be policed, but its eradication appears to have been

---

[37] For an overview, see Terpstra, "Civic Religion."

not only impossible, but even undesirable. The case of Lucca allows us to examine the interaction between spoken and unspoken rules, social habits, and
religious injunctions. Religious beliefs were the cement of society as a whole.
When it came to sexual mores, the tendency to mediate between repression
and toleration did not express a conflict between religious fundamentalism
and "proto-secular" views but reflected a different understanding of religion
in relation to society. The ability to live with the complexity of the social body
by governing it from within emerges as one of the distinguishing features of
pre-Tridentine Catholicism. Conversely, after Trent, religious authorities encouraged common people to increasingly participate in the sacramental life,
favouring a process of internalization of the moral injunctions of the Church
that shifted the balance from the social repercussions of personal actions to
the internal tribunal of the soul.[38]

The re-evaluation of marriage that occurred after the Reformation, af-
fecting both the Protestant and the Catholic worlds, certainly influenced the
way in which society and institutions dealt with sexual nonconformity. Any
form of non-marital relationship and non-reproductive sexual intercourse
was placed outside the spectrum of social acceptability from then onwards.
When there was a binary opposition between sexual abstinence and marital
status, there was more room for negotiation with out-of-wedlock sexual experiences. The more Protestants and Catholics glorified marriage, along with
the role of marital sex, the less other forms of desire and affection could be
allowed to flourish.[39]

While Lucca defended its institutional independence from the Roman
Curia, it considered a change in the regulation of sexual mores a price worth
paying to soothe the aggressive intentions of Rome. New laws determined
more severe treatment of the matter, along with some substantial adjustments
to the activities of the Office of Decency. The approach featuring many trials

---

[38] The thesis of the "turning inward" of Christianity from a religion centred on communal life to one focused on the internal court of the individual conscience was brought
to the fore of historical studies by Bossy, *Christianity in the West*. It was at the core of the
first volume of Foucault's *History of Sexuality* (*The Will to Knowledge*). The role of the
Roman Inquisition in facilitating this process, with its reliance on sacramental confession
as a means to collect information, was explored by Prosperi, *Tribunali della coscienza*. On
the impact on society of the internal reorganization and bureaucratization of the Catholic
Church in Italy, see Prodi, *Papal Prince* and *Disciplina dell'anima*.

[39] Wiesner-Hanks, *Christianity and Sexuality* 145–246 and Lombardi, *Storia del
matrimonio* 115–130. For further bibliography on post-Tridentine sexuality see below,
Chapters 10 and 12.

with relatively lenient penalties — a form of vigilance that aimed to reduce excesses rather than extirpate the "problem" — gave way to more focused repression with consequently more severe punishments. While, as we have seen, until the late 1560s judges often recurred to expedite justice (a sort of abbreviated negotiation that frequently resulted in a fine), from the following decade onwards cases started to be examined in greater detail with more witnesses summoned and increasingly long reports produced. Moreover, the focus progressively shifted from homosexual to heterosexual sodomy, pushing homosexual desire out of the public sphere. An issue that institutions and society were able to deal with cautiously thus turned into an "unspeakable" crime, a secret and embarrassing reality that had to be ignored in order for it to cease to exist.

This change in sexual paradigms, however, sowed the seed of reactive discourse. Some cases reported in the Office of Decency records document the tendency of both the government and common people to resist Church interference through their most intimate life choices. As at the end of the sixteenth century the Office shifted towards the surveillance of heterosexual sodomy, these manifestations of popular discontent were mostly related to practices of heterosexual misconduct, especially prostitution, fornication, and concubinage. Although the judges were looking for proof of consummated anal intercourse, defendants and witnesses provided a wealth of extra information regarding their thoughts on extra-marital sex, living together like husband and wife without benefit of clergy, engaging in open relationships, and having sex with prostitutes. The documents offer insights into the life experiences of many women and men living on the fringes of society who were able to adapt the moral norms divulged by the Church to their needs by relying on various forms of social acceptance, group support, and couple solidarity.

In a handful of cases, lower-class people took the freedom of self-determination in matters of sexual mores to its most radical conclusions, leaning towards blasphemous attitudes that prompted a brutal reaction from the Officers. In these cases, the trope of humane and divine *crimen laesae majestatis* was crucial to justify the resulting virulently repressive attitude. Used by the secular institutions to claim authority over sex at the expense of the Catholic Church, the freedom of self-determination was also critically re-appropriated by some individuals who, although unaware of legal theories, probably understood that sexual prescriptions were used by the elite (both ecclesiastical and secular) to keep people under control.

What is exceptional in Lucca is that male-male sodomy was excluded from the picture in cases where sexual nonconformity combined with politically subversive attitudes. Unlike many other examples that have emerged in criminal sources across Italy (and elsewhere in Europe), in Lucca the embodiment of the enemy of society — prone to lust and heedless of divine and political authority — was not someone who engaged in male homosexual intercourse[40] but a male rapist practising heterosexual sodomy. I am inclined to believe that this distinctive feature reflected the interests of the prosecuting institutions rather than the social configuration of radical dissent in Lucca. The republican city-state seemed to be concerned with regulating homosexual behaviour but refused to use it instrumentally in political and religious conflicts. This is partly the result of the discretion of a small city-state that was accustomed to avoiding scandals and not airing its dirty laundry in public, as well as a reflection of the persistent influence of the civic-religion model on the life of the small republic. Male-male sodomy, which society was no longer able to deal with, was thus pushed into the closet. However, it was spared the strong condemnation that institutions elsewhere expressed by associating it to radical religious dissent. This was probably another example of the attempt to mediate between a civil-religion model inspired by principles of moderation and the rigours imposed by post-Tridentine Catholicism to the regulation of sexual desire.

---

[40] For further bibliography on the demonization of the sodomite during the religious turmoil of the sixteenth century, see below, Chapter 8.

Institutional Control

CHAPTER 1

THE OFFICE OF DECENCY: THE REGULATION OF SODOMY IN LATE MEDIEVAL AND EARLY MODERN ITALY

On 28 February 1570, a young man, Alessio di Lorenzo, made a statement before the Office of Decency in Lucca. Although his exact age is not known, he was probably young in years, given that at the end of the trial the magistrates punished him with a sentence usually reserved for minors. It is certain, however, that he came from the countryside and earned his living selling waffles (*cialdoni*) around the city. Right from his first interrogation he confirmed the version of events provided by his accuser, Nicolao di Lommoro, who had been tried a few days previously. Nicolao had approached him on the pretext of buying some waffles and led him into the wooden shack where he slept. Then, after closing the outside door, he seduced him, armed with weapons of persuasion:

> "I want you to do me a favour and don't say no," and when asked "what favour?", he said "you can imagine what it is." When he answered "no Sir, I'm not in the habit of doing that," Nicolao replied "you have to do it for me in any case, as I want to give you a pair of trousers and a pair of stockings, [...] but don't say anything to anyone," and so he consented and [Alessio] was sodomized by him.[1]

This was not a new occurrence; the same scene had already played out with Orazio, a shoemaker from Modena, who had also promised him a gift

---

[1] "'voglio tu mi facci un piacere et non dichi di no' et dicendoli: 'che piacere,' disse: 'te lo puoi immaginare,' et esso rispose: 'messer no, non ci sono avezo,' et Nicolao rispose: 'me l'hai da fare ad ugni modo, che ti voglio dare un paio di braconi et un paio di calzette, [...] ma non dire cosa alcuna a persona,' et così li consentì et [Alessio] lo sogdomitò." ASL, Onestà 1, 1570, fol. 13^r.

of stockings, bought him sweets, and given him a *grosso*.[2] Orazio's persuasive strategy also alluded to sex as a "favour." However, unlike the other defendants, Orazio was not from Lucca and, according to Alessio's account of his courtship, expected a Lucchese to be particularly obliging to this type of "favour":

> "I want you to do me a favour, *I know that you are gentlemen in Lucca* and do favours [...] you've done them for others and I want you to do this for me" [...] and he approached him, pulled down his trousers, and sodomized him once.[3]

Was there really a common belief that Lucca was a den of sodomites? The city certainly shared in the same bad reputation for sodomy that all of Tuscany had throughout the Italian peninsula and indeed Europe. In 1425, the Franciscan preacher Bernardino of Siena thundered from the pulpit that "every time sodomy is mentioned [...] there is a putrescent stench in the mouth," the "stench of this entire land of Tuscany" had already reached God and was "before the devil."[4] From the fourteenth century onwards, preachers described Florence as a veritable Sodom and Gomorrah. Its notorious debauchery was known even across the Alps, leading Germans to coin the ironic neologisms *Florenzer* and *florenzen* to refer to sodomites and their sexual activity.[5] While Tuscany represented the apex of sodomy, the entire peninsula also aroused strong suspicions. In the sixteenth century, the Venetian patrician Girolamo Priuli believed that the price paid by the Republic of Venice in the Italian Wars was divine punishment for the corruption of its moral values and, above all, for its tolerant attitude towards this sin.[6] Even

---

[2] A small silver coin.

[3] "'voglio che tu mi facci un piacere, *so che in Lucca sete galanthuomini* et fate de piaceri [...] ne hai fatti a delli altri voglio che mi facci questo a me' [...] et se li accostò et li mandò giù i calzoni et lo sogdomitò una volta." ASL, Onestà 1, 1570, fol. 13ᵛ. Emphasis added. Here and henceforth all translations are my own, unless otherwise indicated.

[4] "ogni volta si ricorda la soddomia [...] la bocca è fracida di puzza [...] puzza di tutto questo paese di Toscana [...] dinnanzi al dimonio"; Bernardino da Siena, *Prediche volgari*, 4.2, 270–290, "Del *peccato contro natura*" (1425). On the preacher and his condemnation of sodomy, see Rocke, "Sodomites in Fifteenth-Century Tuscany."

[5] Goodich, *Unmentionable Vice*, 83–84.

[6] Priuli, *I diarii*, 4: 30; 33–36, cited in Davidson, "Sodomy in Early Modern Venice," 67.

in the following century, the Scottish traveller William Lithgow noted in his memoirs that the beastly practice of sodomy:

> for beastly Sodomy, it is as rife here as in Rome, Naples, Florence, Bullogna, Venice, Ferrara, Genoa, Parma not being exempted, nor yet the smallest Village of Italy: A monstrous filthinesse, and yet to them a pleasant pastime, making songs, and singing Sonets of the beauty and pleasure of their Bardassi, or buggerd boyes.[7]

The issue of 'public reputation' played a pivotal role in the complex legislative process that led the authorities in Lucca in the mid fifteenth century to establish the special magistracy of the Three of Decency (*Tre sopra l'Onestà*), subsequently called the Office of Decency (*Offizio sopra l'Onestà*). In a law passed on 22 April 1381, the city's rulers had already ascertained that there were men in the city unconcerned about their salvation — described as "perverters of the law" (*legem pervertentes*) — who had been prompted by a "diabolical spirit" (*spirito diabolico*) to indulge in the sodomitic vice, persuading boys and young men to tarnish themselves with what was, in their eyes, a heinous sin. The 1381 text continued by expressing the consternation of the legislators over the consequent potential damage to the good name of the Republic, highlighting their commitment to punishing delinquents with exemplary severity in order to dissuade reprobates from persisting in their bad habits and, thereby, to avoid God's condemnation. To remedy this extremely regrettable situation, the General Council — the Republic's main legislative body — conferred the Chief Tax-Collector (*Maggiore Esattore*) and the Custody Captain (*Capitano di Custodia*) with the power to "probe and investigate" the actions of the "delinquents and seducers in the aforementioned crime."[8] The *ad hoc* committee (*Balìa*), whose authority would end the

---

[7] Lithgow, *Totall Discourse*, 38. The passage is discussed in Davidson, "Sodomy in Early Modern Venice," 65.

[8] "inquirere et investigare [...] delinquentes et seductores in dicto crimine"; ASL, CG 7, 480 (22 April 1381). The Capitano di Custodia was a member of the Podestà's family and was invested with many responsibilities in the supervision and safekeeping of the city and the surrounding area. He carried out nocturnal patrols, conducted surveillance against gambling and possession of prohibited weapons, and assembled the popular militia if necessary. He was also head of the gatekeepers and guardians of the city and villages. See ASL, CG 5, 285–288 (1375–76). The delegation of power to the Captain of Custody in 1381 has been studied by Imbasciati in her MA dissertation, *Lucca e la repressione dell'omosessualità*.

following Kalends of May, was granted granted the right to "punish, sentence, and fine" guilty parties "according to its free will and in a way befitting its discretion."[9] Although in the following decades there was no follow-up to this special provision, it already contained the fundamental principles that would guide the Republic's future measures against the spread of the 'unmentionable vice.' It was also one of the first examples of delegated *inquisition*, a distinctive feature of the Lucchese judiciary, whereby the General Council exercised the power to suspend ordinary jurisdiction over criminal justice in matters of significant public and political interest. Thus, in exceptional circumstances, certain cases could be taken over and delegated to specific judges — professional magistrates or ordinary citizens — who seemed best suited to serve justice more effectively.[10] Over the following centuries, this principle of the special delegation of powers became the cornerstone of many government initiatives that were, with increasing frequency, launched to tackle the most delicate political and social emergencies.

This impromptu nature characterized the foundation of Lucca's Office of Decency, a tribunal of three citizens appointed to investigate and scrutinize the crime of sodomy (the first officers were elected on 8 March 1448). Initially established to operate for only one year, the Office did not instantly assume strictly codified responsibilities or a fixed structure. Rather, it was immediately granted the same jurisdiction over criminal justice as the Consiglio Generale.[11]

This marked the beginning of a surge in legislative provisions, with sexual behaviour as one of the most frequently recurring criminal matters in the Council's pronouncements.[12] An addendum to the Statutes of 1 June 1448 modified the wording of the oath taken by the Podestà; when taking office, he now had to pledge his firm commitment to investigate the "detestable crime of sodomy" with the utmost diligence, trying and sentencing the culprits as required by law.[13] The proliferation of laws enacted over the following decades resulted in a somewhat contorted procedure; there was a fundamental

---

[9] "punire, condemnare et multare [...] pro sue arbitrio voluntatis et ut sue discretioni videbitur convenire"; ASL, CG 7, 480.

[10] Adorni-Braccesi, "La magistratura delle Cause Delegate," 273. See Montauti, "Le cause Delegate."

[11] ASL, CG 16 (8 March 1448).

[12] See Salerni, "Una repubblica cittadina," 349–369.

[13] "detestabile vitium sodomiae"; ASL, Statuti 10, aggiunte, fol. 257ʳ (27 June 1448).

underlying conflict that saw legislators torn between adopting public punishments — thereby using the deterrent of disgrace — and favouring secret resolutions — so as not to tarnish the city's good name. In the meantime, the duties of the Officers of Decency were defined more clearly, while the system of punishments for offenders became increasingly complex.[14] This formative period ended in 1539 with the final drafting of the Statutes (which remained in force until they were abolished in 1806 by Napoleonic decree).[15] The magistracy was finally given a fixed structure in Chapter 107 of Book IV, which was dedicated to criminal matters, under the heading "On the punishment of sodomites" ("Della pena de sodomiti"). The Palazzo del Podestà was to be its headquarters, while the Podestà, his court, and the Capitano del Contado were required to provide "work, support, and help" ("officio, favore e aiuto") whenever requested to do so, on pain of ten gold florins in the event of non-fulfilment. The Officers were provided with a notary to draft the minutes of their meetings, which had to be held at least once a week. Every session was paid,[16] while unjustified absenteeism was punished with a fine. Laws were also passed to protect the Officers' safety,[17] and Officers who were struck, injured, or insulted could identify and punish offenders without holding a regular trial, a testament to the degree of arbitrary power the Council bestowed on them.[18]

Lucca was neither the first, nor the only city to entrust the regulation of sexual nonconformity to a tailor-made magistracy. Indeed, throughout the Quattrocento, legislators in many places responded to concerned voices denouncing the spread of the sodomitic vice by increasing the number of measures against it and tightening the grip of judicial surveillance over it. As we know from the pioneering studies of Guido Ruggiero and Michael J. Rocke, by 1418, thirty years before Lucca's first Onestà, the Republic of Venice already had founded the Committee on Sodomites (*Collegium Subdomitarum*), while in 1432, Florence established the Night Officers (*Officiali di Notte*). Although our sources never refer directly to these precursors, the Lucchese

---

[14] Salerni, "Una repubblica cittadina," 349–369.

[15] *Statuto 1308*, prefazione prima (Salvatore Bongi), xx–xi.

[16] The payment was two *bolognini*.

[17] Insults and offences against the officers were punished with sentences similar to the penalties inflicted on those who offended the Podestà, while those who threatened them were fined one hundred florins, a sum liable to limitless increase depending on the seriousness of the circumstances.

[18] *Statuti della citta di Lucca*, Chap. 107.

institution was clearly indebted to them, not only in terms of its structure but also, and above all, in its similar judicial practice. While Venice saw few trials but applied extremely harsh sentences, both Florence and Lucca hosted a substantial number of judicial proceedings but applied relatively mild punishments.[19] In Venice, between 1450 and 1550, the average annual number of defendants was around five, compared to roughly two hundred and twenty in Florence. Some fifteen or sixteen thousand people were tried in Florence between 1432 and 1502 (the year in which the magistracy of the Night Officers was abolished), with more than three thousand convicted (approximately forty-three a year).[20]

Although complete trial records in Lucca start only in 1551, we do have an index of names that allows us to draw some estimates for the period from 1539 and 1551. Having considered certain methodological precautions,[21] it can be hypothesized that, between 1539 and 1551, around five hundred and seventy-one people went on trial and ninety-six were convicted (almost certainly a flawed estimate), while the more reliable sources record that from 1551 to 1599 three hundred and sixty-eight people out of a total of five hundred and ninety-six defendants were convicted. These statistics are far from negligible if we bear in mind that, in the mid-sixteenth century, Lucca's population was around twenty thousand and that, in the seventeenth century, it grew steadily, reaching almost thirty thousand.[22]

The Office of Decency had a well-structured system of punishments. From the first medieval draft of the Statutes to the 1539 version, including the bewildering number of reforms passed in the fifteenth and sixteenth centuries, legislators increasingly took into consideration offenders' subjective

---

[19] Canosa, *Storia di una grande paura*, 7–10.

[20] Rocke, *Forbidden Friendships*, 47.

[21] The use of this index requires a degree of circumspection because it is not clear what criteria were used to draw up the lists or whether they contain the names of those under investigation, of suspects, or of convicts. It was sometimes possible to compare lists made after 1551 with the complete trial transcriptions, and in most of these cases the names on the lists correspond to those on trial. However, as there is not always a two-way correspondence between the data sets, the information should not be used too casually. Nevertheless, some names are accompanied by a clear indication of their sentences, which I have subsequently verified by consulting the volumes of the "Sentences and Banishments" ("Sentenze e Bandi") in the Podestà archives, and found that the information was often consistent.

[22] Adorni-Braccesi, «*Una città infetta*», 7.

circumstances. After the first statutory collection in 1308, in which the crime was punished by a fine of three hundred *lire* followed by permanent banishment,[23] penalties were tightened in 1331 with the introduction of the death sentence for those over the age of eighteen.[24] Thereafter, however, there was a gradual softening of sentences as the extent of the Office's control increased; on 8 February 1458, the death penalty was abolished.[25] Although it was reintroduced shortly afterwards,[26] it was far less likely to be applied because now it was part of a provision that took account of many variables to determine the degree of the offender's culpability. The system of punishments then settled into the form assumed in the 1539 statutes (Table 1), thereby providing the referential framework for the Office's work, at least in the period that can be studied with the available documentation.

There were strong similarities between the criminal justice system in Lucca and its equivalent in Florence, where the laws had already been reconfigured in 1432 when the Night Officers were established. Although in Lucca more importance was given to the factor of age and in Florence to recidivism, both cities adopted an extremely similar template that imposed incremental penalties.[27]

Nevertheless, there is a significant difference between describing the body of laws that regulated court proceedings and assessing the consistency between legislative provisions and actual judicial practice. In the strict Venetian justice system, the severity of the laws was frequently waived; in the sixteenth century, the number of death sentences started to drop as the punishment was replaced by other harsh penalties, such as life imprisonment or permanent banishment, mostly imposed on those sentenced *in absentia*.[28]

In Lucca, too, the sentences most frequently imposed by the Office of Decency were milder than those imposed by the law, although judges largely respected the system by considering youth to be an attenuating circumstance and by considering multiple convictions to be a reason for progressively increasing the penalties. Table 2 helps us to understand the discrepancy in Lucca between the laws in force and their practical application, as well as the consistency with which officers implemented their arbitrary power. Defendants

---

[23] *Statuto del 1308*, 230.

[24] ASL, Statuti 4 (1331), Book I, Chap. LCIII.

[25] Salerni, "Una repubblica cittadina," 349–369.

[26] ASL, CG 18, 149–154 (21 July 1458).

[27] Rocke, *Forbidden Friendships*, 51–52.

[28] Martini, *Vitio nefando*, 69.

could almost always decide how to pay their debt to justice, choosing between corporal punishment, a fine, imprisonment, or banishment. Although it is not always possible to identify these choices in the records, in the vast majority of cases (three hundred and forty-two) the convict's decision was specified in a brief note. We find, for example, that corporal punishment accounted for 17.8% of sentences possibly because it was frequently a mandatory sanction for the youngest offenders, with no other alternative offered. When the convicted had a choice, we find that 32% chose banishment to "purge" their crime and 27.4% opted for a fine. Only 16.6% preferred imprisonment in the Sasso prison; these were often the poorest convicts, those who could not afford to pay a fine.[29]

In Lucca there were few cases of recidivism. In these instances, the severity of the law was also seen in the chambers of the Palazzo del Podestà. On 21 October 1550, the "Sentences and Banishments" of the Podestà features a list of sixteen people accused of committing sodomy in the city "time and time again" from 1545 onwards.[30] Minors were punished with twenty-five or fifty "lashes of the belt" (*cinghiate*) depending on the case, while culprits aged between eighteen and thirty were fined fifty gold florins with the addition, not the alternative, of a year's banishment. Two of these — Jacopo di Lucca and Baldassarre di Girolamo dal Fabbro — already had a conviction against their name, so their fines were doubled to one hundred gold florins. The worst fate, however, was suffered by their peer, Bastiano Stiabuzzotti; after his third conviction, his doom was sealed by the blunt phrase, noted down separately by the notary: "let him be burnt with fire until he is dead"[31] Such a severe sentence was not pronounced again until the 1580s.

In Lucca, Florence, and Venice, the magistracies appointed to prosecute sodomy had extremely similar relationships with the political authorities. Because they were a direct emanation of the government, they were granted extraordinary (and arbitrary) powers. However, as we will see, certain significant differences between the three political systems influenced the composition

---

[29] For their part, the Florentine Night Officers only imposed financial penalties. Michael Rocke suggested that economic interests lay behind the extension and scope of control exercised by this magistracy in the city. At a time of crisis for the state coffers, a self-financed magistracy had the advantage of not weighing on public accounts, instead helping to increase revenue through the collection of fines. Rocke, *Forbidden Friendships*, 53.

[30] "più e più volte"; ASL, Podestà, Sentenze e Bandi 264, fol. 268[r-v].

[31] "Igne comburi ita quod moriatur"; ASL, Podestà, Sentenze e Bandi 264, fol. 199[r-v].

and activity of the special tribunals they established to police sexual noncon-formity. As far as Lucca is concerned, we have already seen that the Office of Decency was a mouthpiece of the General Council and delegation. The Venetian Committee on Sodomites (*Collegium Subdomitarum*) originated as an internal committee of the Council of Ten, a magistracy established in the wake of the 1310 Querini-Tiepolo conspiracy that had posed a serious risk to the survival of republican institutions. While initially set up as a political police force invested with specific responsibilities to prevent and contain any form of attack against the security of the state, over the following centuries the Council's jurisdiction expanded significantly as a result of its speed and dis-cretion. As the embodiment of a gradual attempt to exert oligarchic control, it prompted several jurisdictional conflicts with other magistracies.[32] It is no coincidence that the Council managed to guarantee full control over sodomy following a 1418 jurisdictional conflict. This came after years of disputes with ordinary magistrates, above all with the Lords of the Night (*Signori di Notte*), who continued to claim authority over the regulation of sexual mores. The Council of Ten had first asserted jurisdiction over the matter during a 1406 scandal involving many nobles and some churchmen.[33] After years of bitter controversy during which the Lords of the Night were accused of corruption and breach of duty, on 6 April 1418 the Council of Ten managed to dispos-sess them completely by founding the Committee on Sodomites (*Collegium Subdomitarum*).[34]

In Florence, because the governing oligarchy directly controlled the ap-pointment of the Night Officers from the start, officers were elected from only a restricted circle selected by the Signoria and the Council. Regular electoral procedures were not allowed until 1446, but even then the choice was still limited since the magistracy remained under the close control of the political and social elite. Five members had to belong to the seven major guilds, thus representing the interests of the city's leading merchants, bankers, and profes-sional and manufacturing classes, while just one member had to belong to one of the fourteen minor guilds of craftsmen and shopkeepers.[35]

The mechanisms of justice in the little Republic of Lucca were quite dif-ferent, reflecting not only the special nature of the political system, but also

---

[32] Martini, *Vitio nefando*, 26.

[33] Ruggiero, *Boundaries of Eros*, 109–145

[34] Ruggiero, *Boundaries of Eros*, 134.

[35] Rocke, *Forbidden Frienships*, 48.

the customs and usages established to exercise power in the "peaceable and popular state" ("pacifico et populare Stato"). First, unlike in Florence, Lucchese corporations were devoid completely of political weight and representation despite their influence on the internal organizational structure of the world of work.[36] Second, because appointments were controlled by the oligarchy, there was no need to forcefully restrict official's eligibility. Indeed, although the mechanism of elections — both for the main bodies (the General Council and the Elders)[37] and the minor offices — was devised to favour the rotation of individual members, the system was structured so that control remained in the hands of the mercantile oligarchy even with changes in government. As Marino Berengo observed, although the General Council featured one of the broadest levels of involvement in Italy with a hundred councillors present during deliberations, it was widely known that the concentration of power in the hands of a few families, and this constituted a problem.[38] Indeed, all political life in Lucca revolved around twenty-four families (*casati*),[39] with a balancing system that prevented any one family from gaining more power than the others.[40] Holding almost half of the Council's seats, these families also employed great strategic expertise to guarantee a certain degree of representation for a large number of 'second-level' families, thereby neutralizing their subversive potential.[41]

The composition of the Office of Decency was a precise reflection of the distribution of power in the city's main political bodies. Out of the one hundred and forty-one citizens who served as court officers from 1545 to 1591, fifty-eight (41%) came from the *casati*, the twenty-four most politically represented families. They were joined by members of 'second-level' minor families, who first had entered the government during the initial decades of

---

[36] Berengo, *Nobili e mercanti*, 7–8.

[37] The General Council (*Consiglio Generale*) was Lucca's main legislative body (see Glossary).

[38] Berengo, *Nobili e mercanti*, 31.

[39] The twenty-four families were: Poggi, Arnolfini, Bernardi, Trenta, Burlamacchi, Cenami, Guinigi, Balbani, Guidiccioni, Tegrimi, Rapondi, Bernardini, Martini, Franciotti, Turrettini, Vellutelli, Del Portico, Mei, Nobili, Pini, Micheli, Serfederighi, Sergiusti, Serdini. Berengo, *Nobili e mercanti*, 28n.

[40] The Poggi Uprising, which was suppressed and led to the expulsion of that important *consorteria* (clique) from public life in the city, was the only episode of this type. Berengo, *Nobili e mercanti*, 83–99.

[41] Berengo, *Nobili e mercanti*, 128.

the century: the Sanminiati[42] (1511), Boccella[43] (1526), Lamberti[44] (1528), and Mazzarosa[45] (1529). Other minor families gained access to political representation only after the 1531 Straccioni Uprising, among them the Menocchi[46] (1532), Orsucci[47] (1532), and Sinibaldi[48] (1532) families.[49] Indeed, the political repercussion for the "comfortable" (*comode*) middle-class families that were behind the anonymous violent revolt of weavers that broke out in 1531 was their inclusion in the ruling class in a secondary role.[50]

However, the involvement of the mercantile-noble class in the work of the Office of Decency was not limited to serving as judges. They also often appeared in the dock. As a matter of fact, the defendants who appeared before Italian magistracies that regulated sodomy always encompassed a broad social cross-section. As mentioned above, before the founding of the Committee on Sodomites (*Collegium Subdomitarum*) in Venice in 1418, jurisdiction over sodomy had been transferred from the Lords of the Night to the Council of Ten following a scandal involving several patricians and

[42] Ludovico Sanminiati was an Officer in 1548: ASL, CG 42, Riformagioni Pubbliche, 573 (9 November 1547); and in 1565: ASL, CG 51, 355 (23 November 1564).

[43] The Boccella family was widely represented. Giovanni Maria was elected as a member of the Office of Decency in 1550 (ASL, CG 44, 553, 19 November 1549), while Giuseppe was elected three times in the second half of the century: in 1570 (ASL, CG 56, 415, 30 November 1569); in 1581 (ASL, CG 66, 612, 23 November 1580); and in 1590 (ASL, CG 74, 833, 9 December 1589).

[44] Girolamo in 1550 (ASL, CG 44, 553, 19 November 1549); Nicolao in 1562 (ASL CG 50, 761, 17 November 1561); Pietro in 1571 (ASL, CG 57, 475, 20 November 1570); and Antonio in 1577 (ASL, CG 63, 437, 26 November 1576).

[45] Fabio Mazzarosa served as one of the Three of Decency in 1572 (ASL, CG 58, 509, 2 December 1571).

[46] Vincenzo, officer in 1585 (ASL, CG 70, 457, 7 December 1584).

[47] At the end of the century, responsibility for prosecuting the "nefarious sin" was awarded to Giovanbattista in 1585 (ASL, CG 70, 457, 7 December 1584) and to Jacopo in 1588 (ASL, CG 73, 392, 7 December 1587).

[48] Vincenzo in 1559 (ASL CG 73, 392) and Augusto in 1580 (ASL, CG 65, 451, 23 November 1579).

[49] Thanks to Alessandro Ragagli for providing me with the list of *Riformagioni* that announced the annual elections of the Office. My source for the dates on which the families first entered the ruling class, is ASL, Libro d'oro, chapter *Del tempo in cui ciascheduna famiglia cominciò ad havere de' Signori*, 30–31.

[50] Berengo, *Nobili e mercanti*, 117–146. The protests were triggered by the reform of the statutes of the Court of Merchants (Corte dei Mercanti), which considerably reduced the weavers' freedom to produce and sell on their products without going through the control and intermediation of the powerful controllers of major trading.

anonymous commoners. Other types of sixteenth-century sources (legislative texts, sermons, private diaries, and writings by polemicists) document rising concerns over the corruption of the Venetian ruling class. For example, the patrician Girolamo Priuli wrote in his diaries: "What should I say and write, most learned *lectores*, about the Venetian Patricians and Senators, seasoned in age, full of wisdom, with a white beard, who were so immersed and suffocated by this Gomorrean sin?"[51]

In Florence, between 1478 and 1502, five hundred and three members of the most influential families (about 12% of the total) appeared in court to answer charges of sodomy. Rocke restricted his survey to a select group of a hundred and ten lineages recognized as the cream of the Florentine elite, and observed that, in this case the vast majority of cases (ninety-one) had at least one member[52] who previously had been involved in a sodomy trial before the Night Officers or the Eight of Ward (*Otto di Guardia*). Court officers proved to be more reluctant to hand down sentences in such cases. In 1494, this prompted the indignation of an anonymous critic, who accused them of convicting the poor and acquitting the powerful.[53]

Lucchese sources allow us to trace the social background (through the indication of a family name or profession) of around one thousand one hundred people involved in Office proceedings in varying capacities (as suspects, defendants, or witnesses). These include three hundred and thirty-three people from the mercantile ruling class,[54] including about sixty from

---

[51] "Che debbo io dire et scrivere, sapientissimi lectores [...] dei Patritzi et Senatori Veneti, provecti di etade, pieni di sapienzia, cum la barba canuta, che in questo sgomorreo vizio errano tanto immersi et suffochati?"; Priuli, *I diarii*, 4:35–36; the passage is commented by Romano Canosa in *Storia di una grande paura*, 137.

[52] There were eight from the Adimari family and five from the Alberti family. The Altoviti, Bardi, and Capponi families accounted for ten, four, and six defendants respectively, along with eight members of the Cavalcanti family, four Frescobaldis, and three Guicciardinis. Not even the Medicis, with nine defendants, escaped accusation. There were four from the Pandolfini and Peruzzi families and five from the Soderini and Strozzi families, along with six, nine, and twelve defendants from the Pucci, Ridolfi, and Ruccellai families, respectively. Rocke, *Forbidden Friendships*, 141–142.

[53] Rocke, *Forbidden Friendships*, 145.

[54] We are rightfully somewhat reticent to use the term 'noble' (and similar words, like 'noble class', etc.) to describe the Lucchese oligarchy; in sixteenth-century Lucca, the definition was still uncertain because the governing class became noble only over the course of the century. Even before the social figure of the merchant and man of government in Lucca became more rigidly defined, the late transition can be seen — in principle and only at a verbal level — in the gradual shift in sixteenth-century notarial deeds from using the

the twenty-four main *casati* and an equal number from the upwardly-mobile families that entered government after the 1531 Straccioni Uprising. Unfortunately, it is not easy to determine the magistrates' stance towards them; even their sentences are difficult to examine since the majority of those from rich or privileged families included in the sources (two hundred out of the three hundred and thirty-three) appear in the index of names in the sixth volume, suggesting that they were officially charged but offering little detailed or reliable information. If, however, we consider the mostly complete trial records from the other volumes, we find that the conviction rate for upper-class defendants was around 40%. Although this figure is not negligible, it is well below the average conviction rate of 82% calculated from the total sample of defendants. The elite in the "peaceable and popular state" of Lucca, therefore, were aided and abetted to some degree by the court officers when their sentences were formulated, although there was never a guarantee of full impunity. Instead, they were always vigilantly monitored by the magistrates, themselves part of the same political ruling class. As we will see, especially in the third part of this book, this attitude echoes the commitment of the Lucchese ruling classes to watch over the decency of public affairs, a commitment that reflected their particular cultural and religious values.

In addition to merchants, it was possible to trace the professions of a further seven hundred and fifty-one suspects (see Table 3). The most striking features are the broad social cross-section and the wide spectrum of professional figures. The only imbalance is the predominance of textile workers, but this disparity reflects the prime role played by silk production in the Lucchese economy. Not only were weavers the largest and best organized category of workers, but they also had the closest ties to the governing mercantile class, which supplied them directly with raw materials and was responsible for selling their finished products. Around this well-structured group of textile workers there was a more varied assortment of spinners, shoelace makers, shearers, and cloth dyers,[55] while the margins of the Lucchese economy and guilds were populated by builders and woodworkers, also well represented in Office sources. Leather workers, involved in at least twenty-one cases (with six convictions), were slightly further up the Lucchese social hierarchy than other artisans, and their workshops were extremely active in the export trade.

---

appellative "civis et mercator" to using "nobiles viri." We must thus be cautious whenever we use the term 'noble.' See Berengo, *Nobili e mercanti*, 256–257.

[55] Berengo, *Nobili e mercanti*, 66–70.

However, it is never clear in notarial deeds whether the term *coriarius* was used to refer to a simple leather worker craftsman or to an entrepreneur who also marketed his leather products.[56] Alongside these tradesmen there are defendants employed in the service sector, such as butchers (*beccai*), cheese-makers and vendors (*caciaiuoli*), tailors, physicians, and bakers. However, the list could be extended even further to include apprentices, labourers, mattress makers, humble pedlars (*rivendugliori*), and the composite miscellany of occasional workers associated with the skilled professions who offered their services for a few years, months, or even weeks, whether to pay off a debt, to meet a temporary need, or to fill dead time between work in the fields. Finally, there are beggars and paupers always ready to carry out small tasks in exchange for a few coins, a piece of bread, a hunk of cheese, or a glass of wine. In some respects, they were in a similar position to the substantial ranks of household staff and servants from the Versilia and Garfagnana areas who served in palaces owned by elite Lucchese families. Since they did not sell, own, or buy anything, official sources bear only faint traces of their existence. However, despite the unfortunate circumstances surrounding their frequent appearances in the documents of the Office of Decency, often with dramatic accounts of abuse, this research has enabled their memory to be transmitted to posterity with new dignity.

With regard to Florence, the data collected by Rocke paint a very similar picture to the one that emerges from the Lucchese archival materials, which document some 350 different jobs and professions. The most striking similarity is the high concentration of workers in the textile and clothing sector, in keeping with the composition of the Florentine job market and economy. As in Lucca, there are also small-scale local tradesmen and those who produced food or offered services (barbers, handymen, odd-job men, engravers), as well as members of the clergy and the notarial professions, construction workers (including carpenters), servants and — to a lesser extent — peasants.[57]

This broad social cross-section allows us to debunk two myths. First, there is the age-old idea that links sodomitic behaviour — above all, homosexual intercourse — to the moral dissolution, weakness, and financial well-being, often instinctively associating it with the moral decadence of the ruling and privileged classes.[58] The second myth consists in the romantic idealiza-

---

[56] Berengo, *Nobili e mercanti*, 73–74.

[57] M. Rocke, *Forbidden Friendships*, 134–147 and chart on 249.

[58] See Toscan, *Carnaval du language*, 194–216; Rocco, *Alcibiade*, 50.

tion of the figure of the "homosexual" that positions him at the margins of society in a broad category with all the outcasts of medieval and early modern society such as beggars, lepers, prostitutes, and witches.[59] In fact, the sources demonstrate that, in historical terms, it is not possible to outline a fixed 'social profile' of the sodomite; even in condemnatory rhetoric, the most horrifying aspect of the 'unmentionable sin' was its potential ubiquity and socially transversal shift.[60] In the second part of this book, we will see the extent to which Lucchese sodomitic networks were characterized by a high degree of cross-class mingling. Sometimes, sexual relationships were affected by tensions that pitted groups divided by rank and age against one another, which led to the instrumental use of sex as a means to reinforce hierarchies. At other times, the opposite could also be true, with anal sex, above all among men, taking the form of social revanchism. At still other times, the blend resulted in a loosening of social boundaries, whose potentially subversive nature was regarded with discomfort and fear by political institutions.

While sodomy was not confined to any particular social environment, it was not the exclusive prerogative of urban centres, either. Although the criminal sources used to reconstruct the topography of the 'nefarious sin' in medieval and early modern Europe are mostly from city courts, they also document its spread in the rural world.[61] In this way, while urban clusters provided the necessary framework for flourishing homoerotic cultures, the sources reveal that abandoned shacks in the countryside could also become meeting places for homosexual encounters. However, the lack of sources makes it difficult to gain knowledge of sodomitic sociability in rural areas. Instead, increasing judicial surveillance in urban centres led to an accumulation of sources that provide a valuable resource for historical research.

Despite the intrinsically biased nature of the sources themselves, the Lucchese documents highlight the fact that sodomy was not an exclusively urban practice. In 1560, five men from Acqua Calida took part in an orgy in a hut; one of them then went to Lucca to report it to the Office, which investigated and then acquitted everyone.[62] In 1572, two youths and an adult from Vorno raped a boy in the countryside near Massaciuccoli; in this case,

---

[59] See for example McCall, *Medieval Underworld*, 199–209.

[60] There have often been fraught relations between 'universalizing' and 'minoritizing' views of homosexual desire and homoerotic attraction. See below, Chapter 7, 147–148.

[61] There is a striking example of persecution in the Dutch countryside in the eighteenth century in Boone, "Those Damned Sodomites."

[62] Onestà 1, 1560, fols. 16^r–17^r.

all three were convicted.[63] Another sexual assault, again against a child, occurred in Marlia in the winter of 1578.[64] In 1582, three inhabitants of Valle
Buia were convicted of homosexual sodomy.[65] Eleven years later, a father
reported a sexual assault against his ten-year-old son in Collodi, in the vicari-
ate of Villa Basilica, where he lived with his family. The defendant, a young
apprentice from the nearby village of Pariana, was acquitted after a long
period of imprisonment and harsh torture.[66] The different types of criminal
actions in these cases thus ranged from child abuse to consensual sex between adults, behaviours that are now generally associated with significantly
different moral values.[67] However disappointing as it may sound to a modern
reader, at the time such acts were grouped together under the umbrella term
of "sodomy." This complex relationship between legal categories and sexual
behaviours will be examined in the second part of the book.

---

[63] Onestà 2, 1572, fols. 76r–77v.

[64] According to what appears in the records of a trial held the following year. Unfor-
tutnately, all traces of the trial's conclusion have been lost. Onestà 2, 1579, fols. 23r–27v.

[65] Onestà 3, 1582, fols. 21r–23r.

[66] Onestà 3, 1593, fols. 59r–64v.

[67] In conservative discourse, however, pedophilia and homosexuality continue to be
closely associated. This is often the result of religious propaganda, often from the Catholic
Church, whose upper echelons are notoriously culpable of covering up widespread child
abuse.

CHAPTER 2

JUDICIAL PRACTICE

Criminal matters received increasing coverage between the thirteenth and fourteenth centuries, with dedicated sections in the statutes of almost all Italian communes. The expansion of criminal jurisdiction was a fundamental political tool in the redefinition of the power structure and was used strategically across the board. It was employed by political communities either to defend a system based on broad political representation or to move towards the status of a principality. Justice — above all, criminal justice — assisted both the political affirmation of new social and family groups and the validation of the new power structure. The increase in special magistracies in cities like Lucca and Florence (and the expansion of their jurisdiction to include crimes against morality) was one of the main instruments in this affirmation process. In the fifteenth century, there was a concerted public attack on social practices and behavioural habits that contravened the general system of values and moral codes of the *civitas*, such as 'unlawful' sexuality, harassment of clergy, extravagance, gambling, blasphemy, and corruption of public officials. One of the main aspects of this profound process of transformation was the establishment of active justice through the development of *ex-officio* procedures that were put in place of reactive justice that, instead, aimed to settle conflicts within the community. While the control of everyday habits by judicial institutions was a tangible sign of the extension of state jurisdiction in practical terms, in theoretical terms legal thinking provided intellectual validation for the new forms of power. The main task of notaries, clerks, and officials was to reinforce the certainty of state authority in the eyes of subjects.[1]

The accusatory procedure, which could be initiated by any citizen, featured a judge who acted as (at least in theory) an impartial arbitrator and was characterized by publicity and orality. Conversely, the inquisitorial procedure (*inquisitio*) was the result of an *ex-officio* initiative by a magistrate who managed every step of the process, including the collection of evidence, and who ordinarily acted as both prosecutor and judge.[2] Because the accusatory

---

[1] Zorzi, "Justice," 498–501.
[2] Dezza, *Accusa e inquisizione*, 4–5.

procedure required a plaintiff who often asked for fair compensation, it was adopted for 'private' crimes that, by their very nature, were not considered a destabilizing influence on the public and social order of the state. On the other hand, the *inquisitio* was used for 'public' crimes committed against God, the state, or public interest.[3]

As far as the persecution of sodomy was concerned, the Lucchese Statutes allowed the Office of Decency to conduct both types of procedure. This dual-channel structure was not, however, restricted to these magistrates; it could be used for almost every type of crime in the Lucchese justice system and its many constituent offices. The fourth part of the Statutes — the section on criminal law, entitled "Punish the Evil" ("punire i maleficii") — opened with an introductory chapter bearing the unambiguous heading "On proceeding against delinquents" ("Di procedere contra gli delinquenti") and provided a general outline of the laws that regulated the prosecution of criminal offences. After obliging judges to prosecute crimes under their jurisdiction with the utmost zeal, the first principle allowed each judge to proceed "by way of accusation or *inquisition*, and *ex-officio*, and with or without a denunciation by consuls".[4]

Despite the options available, the Lucchese justice system generally tended to favour inquisitorial procedure.[5] What was distinctive about the Officers of Decency was the total arbitrariness of their power, along with the suspension of all laws protecting the accused or those under investigation (normally provided for in the Statutes for other crimes). Indeed, they were allowed

> every authority [...] in examining, investigating and prosecuting. *They shall not be restricted either by any laws or statutes, but may*

---

[3] Martini, *Vitio nefando*, 74. See below (Chapter 12, 229–226) for an analysis of the relationship between sodomy and political treason in late medieval and early modern law.

[4] "tanto per accusa, quanto anchora per inquisizione, et per officio, et con dinuncia de consoli, et senza dinuncia"; *Gli Statuti della città di Lucca*, Book IV, Chap. I.

[5] It was even specified in the next passage that the *inquisitio* should not be stopped if accusers suddenly appeared after a procedure had started; the accusatory procedure would have saved them from investigations if they were involved in the crime. Even more revealing in this sense is the next passage, which allowed the suspension of an accusatory procedure in order to undertake an inquisitorial procedure in all cases and at any moment if the judge felt it necessary to investigate the accuser to check for any complicity in the reported crimes. *Gli Statuti della città di Lucca*, Book IV, Chap. I.

proceed [...] omitting all solemnity, and substantiality of the law and statutes [...] as their discretion will see fit, in such a way that *any method and means may be lawfully used* by the aforementioned Office to obtain a *summary judgement* of the truth.[6]

This "summary judgement of the truth" was ultimately characterized by approximation and randomness. Not surprisingly given this lack of fixed regulations, it was not always possible to understand whether cases were launched as inquisitorial or accusatory procedures, or a combination of the two. However, the great majority of the cases were intiated by the Office in the form of an inquisitorial proceeding. When denunciations by an injured party occurred, it was often to report a rape. In some cases, the parents of abused children appeared as the plaintiffs. In March 1552, a weaver from Val d'Ottavo, Giovanni Tomei, went to the Palazzo del Podestà to seek justice for "Giovanni Paulo, his son of around nine years old", whose abuse had been discovered along with the symptoms of a sexually-contracted infection.[7] In other cases, female rape victims came forward to demand justice for the maltreatment they had suffered. Instances of self-denunciation (often combined with the reporting of others) were instead more frequent. Out of five hundred and forty-seven defendants (taken from a huge sample of data selected from the most reliable sources[8]), around one hundred appeared before the court of their own accord to confess and denounce their partners at the same time in order to enjoy impunity (*in animo conseguendi impunitatem*). The 1539 Statutes regulated the procedure, ensuring that complete remission of guilt would be granted only if there had been no previous information about crimes committed by the person "reported or accused in this way."[9]

The procedural records clarify the reason for this specification; leaks were not infrequent and, on more than one occasion, suspects had already been informed that they were under investigation before being summoned

---

[6] "ogni autorità [...] in ricercare, investigare et procedere, et non siano stretti da alcune leggi, over statuti, ma possano procedere [...] omissa ogni solennità, et sustanzialità di ragione et statuti [...] come alla discrezione loro parrà, in modo che licito sia al ditto Officio ogni modo, et via per haver la verità summaria." *Gli Statuti della città di Lucca*, Book IV, Chap. 107. Emphasis added.

[7] "Giovanni Paulo suo figlio di età di anni nove in circa"; Onestà 1, 1552, fol. 11ᵛ.

[8] The years from 1551 to 1556, 1560, 1568, 1570, the period between 1572 and 1574 (inclusive); then from 1577 to 1582, 1585, 1588–89 and 1591–92.

[9] "così dinunciato over accusato"; *Gli Statuti della città di Lucca*, Book IV, Chap. 107.

to the Office to respond to charges. This made it possible to pre-empt a summons by disclosing personal involvement in the offence, which guaranteed exemption from punishment. Aware of this option, the Officers took harsh measures when statements by self-confessed criminals seemed mendacious, even resorting to "rigorous examination" (*rigoroso examine*), that is, torture. Nevertheless, this rigour was not always observed and impunity was sometimes granted to offenders already accused in previous depositions.[10] In a minority of cases, however, the Officers did convict "those appearing spontaneously" (*sponte comparentes*) who had partially hidden the truth in the information they provided or who were revealed to have made a false statement on the basis of other testimonies.[11]

Accusations came under less scrutiny in Florence, where the Night Officers — also without any specific legal training and not bound to comply with the laws that regulated the formal procedures of ordinary courts of justice — boosted their operations through ample use of secret denunciations that were often anonymous (known as *tamburatio* or *notatio secreta*) and did not require the accuser to provide any evidence. They were sometimes delivered by hand, but were mostly dropped into special boxes (*tamburi*) installed around the city and surrounding area.[12] The boxes were opened at least once a month and the denunciations transcribed into registers. To encourage the community to act, the Night Officers were also required to reward those who lodged a denunciation with a quarter of the fine paid by anyone convicted. They also had to guarantee full anonymity.[13] As far as Venice is concerned, following a deliberation of 18 August 1462, the Council of Ten took harsh measures to limit false accusations of sodomy. As in Florence, but unlike in Lucca, denunciations "without a signature" (*senza sottoscrizione*) were permitted. It was not until a 1647 reform that the Venetian legal system adopted a more cautious stance towards this instrument of accusation, restricting its use to a few carefully deliberated cases not including sodomy.[14] Even before this date, however, the Committee on Sodomites (*Collegium Subdomitarum*)

---

[10] Onestà 1, 1552, fol. 16^v (Belgrado di Nicolao Altogradi).

[11] "sponte comparentes"; Onestà 1, 1568, fols. 4^r and 12^r (Chimento di Francesco Chimenti).

[12] In the second half of the fifteenth century, the Officers placed such boxes in the churches of San Pier Scheraggio and Orsanmichele, the Florentine cathedral, and in Prato, Pistoia, Pisa, Empoli, and Arezzo.

[13] Rocke, *Forbidden Friendships*, 49.

[14] Martini, *Vitio nefando*, 78–80.

was the most diligent of the institutions in question, supplementing the passive task of receiving denunciations with tireless investigative work.[15]

Magistrates in Lucca also took the initiative through active crime prosecution; they did not always wait for denunciations or self-denunciations, and occasionally used spies and covert scouts.[16] Magistrates used *targetti*[17] to conduct their investigations on a more constant basis and make arrests (during the period studied these were Desiderio, Vincenzo da Gattaiola and Paulino da Gattaiola). On more than one occasion defendants began their depositions by recounting the moment when they were apprehended and taken to prison by one of them.[18] At the start of a trial in 1592, Vincenzo da Gattaiola stated that he and the Bargello had raided the room of the *mazzieri*[19] at around four after sunset and caught two men naked, both of whom were arrested. He had heard about their long-standing relationship and secret meeting places through the "public rumour and notoriety" circulating among the *mazzieri* and *targetti* at the Palazzo dei Signori.[20] In other instances, the suspects had sometimes tried to bribe one of the servants at the Office of Decency to avoid being denounced.[21]

Given the ease of transmission of venereal disease and the frequent ruptures resulting from anal rape, hospitals were a good starting point when

---

[15] Ruggiero, *Boundaries of Eros*.

[16] Their contribution to judicial proceedings was not regulated by the statutory provisions, but the records contain some traces of their work. Sometimes the notary Piero Pieraccini noted down in the trial registers the expenses and takings of the Office, and, on 20 August 1556, the Officers ordered the clerk to give the notary ten florins so that he could pay Giovanni, "a covert scout" ("uno esploratore segreto"), for the charges against Lorenzo di Francesco da Menabbio. There are similar instances in a note written soon afterwards, which speaks of remuneration for a "secret spy" ("spia segreta": Onestà 1, 1556, fol. 77ʳ), and another payment of ten *scudi* is recorded at the end of the 1560 trial records; Onestà 1, 1560, unnumbered folio.

[17] See Glossary.

[18] Among others, see Onestà 3, 1585, unnumbered folio (Bernardo di Agostino Ghivizzani di Lucca, 4 October).

[19] See Glossary.

[20] "*pubblica voce et fama*"; Onestà 3, 1592, fol. 10ʳ.

[21] Onestà 3, 1593, fol. 79ʳ. The Florentine Night Officers also used spies and secret informers with a similar role to their Lucchese counterparts, which is, however, more clearly defined in sources. In general, they collected the charges before the Officers opened proceedings; they were salaried, although, like the accusers, they also benefitted from a quarter of the fine imposed on the defendants if they were found guilty; Rocke, *Forbidden Friendships*, 49–50.

looking for suspects. Indeed, it was during a visit to the "hospital of the incurables" (*spidale delli incurabili*) that one of the *targetti* from Gattaiola found "a certain Chiara, a former wet nurse for Ser Lorenzo Capini, who told him that a man named Paulo de' Carletti had damaged her rear parts."[22] In Venice, barbers (the 'general practitioners' of the early modern period) were obliged to report anyone seeking treatment for suspect "ruptures" (*rotture*) of the posterior.[23] Although in Lucca the *Libri chirurgorum* (collections of the reports that physicians treating those wounded by blows or weapons were obliged to present to the justice system) do not contain accounts of cases of sodomy, barbers and surgeons constantly supported investigators. Indeed, the only sure evidence was often the presence of lacerations in the rectum of those under scrutiny.[24] In March 1519, when Margherita denounced her husband for forcibly sodomizing her on numerous occasions, she backed up her statement by referring to her many visits to a surgeon, Messer Fortunato Serafini, for treatment. When questioned, however, he repudiated her claim, stating that, despite her frequent complaints, he had never found any rupture or effusion of blood.[25] The outcome of this medical consultation was probably one of the key elements in the reconstruction of evidence in the case, leading shortly thereafter to the acquittal of the accused husband.[26] It cannot be ruled out that a male solidarity network might have played a role in discrediting the reliability of the woman.

Venereal disease was sometimes also an important factor in the establishment of facts. At least, this is what the Officers claimed in a case involving Jacopo di Bastiano del Bastaio, a thirteen-year-old syphilitic defendant who had accused his alleged aggressor; the Office suspected the latter's innocence precisely because he bore no tangible signs of the disease. The accuser then referred to treatment that the purported rapist had received from a surgeon. However, when questioned, the surgeon denied providing any such assistance.[27]

---

[22] "spidale delli incurabili [...] una Chiara già balia di Ser Lorenzo Capini la quale gli ha detto che uno de' Carletti nominato Paulo, l'ha guasto le parti drieto"; Onestà 3, 1582, fol. 15ʳ.

[23] Ruggiero, *Boundaries of Eros*.

[24] Onestà 3, 1591, fol. 2ᵛ, deposition of Caterina da Menabbio. On the relations between doctors and judges in sodomy cases in Lucca, see Hewlett, "French Connection."

[25] Onestà 3, 1591, fols. 4ʳ–5ʳ.

[26] Onestà 3, 1591 fol. 9ʳ⁻ᵛ.

[27] Onestà 2, 1574, fol. 14ʳ.

The lack of medical evidence led to an almost immediate acquittal; they did not even proceed with torture "as there is not sufficient evidence."[28]

If the receptive partner bore no injuries from the sexual relations, the only way to prove that a crime had been committed was through third-party testimonies or confessions by offenders. In Florence, besides confession, concurrent statements by two eye witnesses (*de visu*) were also admitted as conclusive evidence, as was one statement by an eye witness supported by two testifiers "of public repute" (*de pubblica fama*), or, simply, four of the latter.[29] We have seen above that reputation also played a role in Lucca in guiding investigations and provided adequate grounds for launching a trial. Unlike in Florence, however, in practice it never constituted sufficient evidence for a conviction, regardless of the number of testimonies collected; in Lucca, confession, as opposed to rumour, was the only admissible evidence and no punishment was ever imposed without it.

Mendacious accusations were sometimes made and, although not the order of the day, cases of bribery were by no means the exception. Those accused often defended themselves by claiming that they had been slandered and denounced out of spite. On 27 October 1556, Geronimo di Jacopo Bizzarri, a citizen of Lucca, appeared before the Officers to denounce himself, confessing that he had committed acts of sodomy with Caterina, a prostitute from Genoa. After almost a month during which Caterina was imprisoned and interrogated to no avail, Geronimo withdrew his initial statement, saying that Caterina's harassment had driven him to the desperate act of self-denunciation; besides tormenting him, "she brought many accusations against him to the Palazzo del Podestà". On hearing of this defamation, "and having been told about it by many and that he would consequently be banished, as it seemed that he had been greatly wronged without any fault on his part, choking with rage he came as stated above [...] to accuse her." He stated that "in truth nothing happened, and he only did it out of fury."[30]

In a similar case from November 1592, after being caught contradicting herself several times, a young woman, Margherita, admitted that she had falsely accused Marco Durante, one of the Bargello's attendants, of sodomy

---

[28] "non essendoci indizi bastevoli"; Onestà 2, fol. 15ᵛ.

[29] "de visu"; "de pubblica fama"; Rocke, *Forbidden Friendships*, 50.

[30] "portò di lui molte accuse a palazzo"; "et essendoli riferito questo da molti et che perciò riceverebbe bando, parendoli ricevere gran torto, senza sua colpa, suffocato dalla collera venne come di sopra [...] ad accusarla"; "in verità non è cosa nessuna, et solo lo fece per la collera"; Onestà 1, fol. 71ʳ⁻ᵛ.

because "he wished me ill and wanted to report me." Although the young woman had already confessed to accusing Ser Jacopo Bruschi only because she had been paid to do so, it seems that she was telling the truth about Durante; during his interrogation, he confirmed that his initial accusations had been based on suspicion alone. It is interesting to note, however, once again underlining the lack of 'integrity' in the justice system, that Durante did not act out of personal interest but to help Gattaiuola, the Office's secret informer, "earn something [...] because we were friends."[31]

Physical threats sometimes stopped people with information or those directly involved from making a denunciation to the Office. A victim of homosexual rape stated that he had waited a year to come forward and then withdrawn his statement several times during the trial for fear of threats made by his rapist; shortly after the crime, the alleged rapist "found him at the Pozzo Torelli and told him that he would kill him unless he retracted".[32] In the same way, when the Magnificent Lords Vincenzo Sinibaldi and Ser Rocco da Sesto ordered fourteen-year-old Giovanni di Leonardo dalla Cuna "to tell the truth about whether he was sodomized by anyone and by whom", he replied "that he is afraid that he will beat him up."[33]

When it came to torture, the Officers adopted a relatively 'protective' stance. As a result, it was employed only in the most complex procedures that featured persistent, stubborn denials of involvement. The most frequently used method of torture in Lucca and, indeed, in sixteenth-century Italy was the *strappado*.[34] During the first phase, called 'verbal threat of torture' (*terrizione verbale*),[35] the accused "is asked to tell the truth about the aforementioned matters because there is other evidence against him [...], otherwise it will be necessary to resort to rigorous examination."[36] This was followed by 'physical threat of torture' (*terrizione reale*),[37] inflicted by leading the accused to the designated place, undressing him, tying his hands behind his back with

---

[31] "mi voleva male et mi voleva far accusare"; "guadagnare qualcosa [...] perché eravamo amici"; Onestà 3, 1592, fols. 47ᵛ –48ᵛ.

[32] "lo trovò al pozzo Torelli et li disse che l'ammazzerebbe se non disdiceva"; Onestà 1, 1560, fol. 13ᵛ.

[33] "di dire la verità se è stato sogdomitato da nessuno et da chi"; "che ha paura che colui li dia delle botte"; Onestà 1, 1568, fol. 5ᵛ.

[34] Fiorelli, *Tortura giudiziaria*, 1:196.

[35] Fiorelli, *Tortura giudiziaria*, 1:238–239.

[36] "interrogato che vogli dire la verità delle cose soprascritte perché ci sono altri indizi contra di lui [...], altrimente bisognerà venire a rigoroso essamine"; Onestà 2, 1572, fol. 8ʳ.

[37] Fiorelli, *Tortura giudiziaria*, 1:239–240.

a rope, and interrogating him further. The transition to the implementation of torture was never wholly arbitrary and the Officers of Decency were careful to employ it with caution. They always remained faithful to the spirit of the Statutes, which stipulated in general that "no officer dare, or presume, to have anyone tortured, or prove anything [...] unless he first has legitimate evidence and if it emerges [...] he may proceed with the usual torture *with all moderation*."[38]

In one case in 1577, after the Officer ordered the accused to be bound, "seeing that he was in danger due to a wound under his arm, he ordered for cube torture to be used instead",[39] which consisted of pressing an ankle between two concave iron cubes.[40] On another occasion, a man who was about to be subjected to "rigorous examination" was asked directly whether he had any physical impairment. When he replied "that he had a ruptured vein in his chest", the surgeon who had treated him before his arrest was questioned and confirmed the man's inability to endure the *strappado*; then, even after his confession of guilt, the Officers had the good judgement to have him imprisoned "in a more pleasant place."[41] During the same proceedings, a thorough medical examination was conducted before the torture of another man under investigation, leading once again to the suspension of the interrogation after a swelling in his groin was diagnosed.[42]

A forced confession under torture was considered invalid in almost all criminal and procedural law treatises unless it was later confirmed by the defendant.[43] A ratified confession had the same value as a spontaneous confession,[44] whereas an unconfirmed admission of guilt was valid only as partial evidence, although it could still lead to a conviction if accompanied by other forms of proof.[45] In any case, judges were authorized to carry out only the maximum number of torture sessions permitted by local law, after which

---

[38] "nissuno officiale, ardisca, over presuma, provare alcuno agli tormenti, o attestare cosa alcuna [...] se non consterà prima degli indicii legittimamente, et apparendo quegli [...] possi procedersi a gli consueti tormenti, *con ogni moderazione*"; *Gli Statuti della città di Lucca*, Book IV, Chap. 43. Emphasis added.

[39] "vedendo che per una ferita sotto il braccio pativa pericolo, ordinò che fosse posto in alternativa al tormento del dato"; Onestà 2, 1577, fol. 6ʳ.

[40] Fiorelli, *Tortura giudiziaria*, 1:197–198.

[41] "che ha rotto una vena nel petto"; "in un fondo più piacevole"; Onestà 3, 1588, fol. 8ʳ.

[42] Onestà 3, 1588, fol. 9ᵛ.

[43] Fiorelli, *Tortura giudiziaria*, 105–106.

[44] Fiorelli, *Tortura giudiziaria*, 117–124.

[45] Fiorelli, *Tortura giudiziaria*, 115.

the accused had to be acquitted due to insufficient evidence.[46] As a result, resistance to torture — seen as "purgation of the evidence"[47] — frequently led to release.

Judges in Lucca clearly also entertained the suspicion that a confession obtained through torture was a form of extortion, given that they made a point of asking "whether the statement was made because it was the truth or in order to leave prison."[48] There was only one occasion on which a defendant refused to confirm his confession: a policeman (*birro*), Muzio da Ascoli, was accused of having sodomitic relations with a female prostitute whom he had maintained for a period of time; at the end of his tether, after being allowed to sit down and confessing, he said

> "Gentlemen, are you happy?"; and when asked what he wanted to infer, he replied: "Torturing me, one of your servants, like this for the sake of a whore […] being forced to say what I did not do, I'd even say that I killed due to the torture."[49]

The Officers responded that "nothing but the truth is required from him"; to which Muzio replied, "I don't want any more *strappado*, what I said is true and I did it and it is the truth, and I said it because it is the truth."[50] The following day, however, Muzio refused to confirm this statement because "the torture made me say it", but as soon as the magistrates' assistants led him back to the *strappado* chamber, he capitulated once and for all and confirmed his statement,[51] thereby signing his own death sentence.

---

[46] Fiorelli, *Tortura giudiziaria*, 125–135.

[47] "purgazione delli indizi"; Fiorelli, *Tortura giudiziaria*, 135–142. See also Langbein, *Torture and the Law of Proof.*

[48] "se quanto ha detto l'ha detto per la verità o per non uscirsi di prigione"; Onestà 3, 1582, fol. 17ᵛ.

[49] "signori sete contenti?"; et dettoli che cosa vuole inferire, rispuose: "per una puttana darmi questi tormenti, a un vostro servitore […] essere forzato a dire quello che non ho fatto, per i tormenti che dirò anche d'havere ammazzato." Onestà 4, 1595, fol. 19ʳ.

[50] "da lui non si vuole altro che la verità"; "non vo' più corda, è vero quanto che ho detto et l'ho fatto et è la verità et l'ho detto perché è la verità"; Onestà 4, 1595, fol. 19ᵛ.

[51] "il tormento me l'ha fatto dire"; Onestà 4, 1595, fols. 19ᵛ–20ʳ. We will return to this case in Chapter 12.

CHAPTER 3

HEAVENLY ANXIETIES AND WORLDLY COMPROMISES

In fifteenth- and sixteenth-century Italy, military setbacks, political crises and natural scourges such as famine and plague were all seen as God's punishments, serving as warnings to communities whose decadent moral behaviour had flaunted divine laws. In Florentine legislation, the 'sin against nature' was directly associated with the occurrence of serious natural calamities. The historian Bernardino Segni (1504–1558) wrote that in 1542 Duke Cosimo I promulgated two extremely harsh laws against blasphemy and sodomy that were supported by the clergy, out of fear that the destruction caused by the Mugello earthquake and the storm damage done to the dome of the cathedral were omens of imminent disaster.[1] The 1381 legislation passed by the Lucchese government granting the *Capitano di Custodia* the power to prosecute sodomy explicitly stated that its aim in dissuading reprobates from persisting in their habits was to avoid disgracing the good name of the city in the eyes of men and to evade God's punishment and condemnation of the community.[2]

In the Middle Ages and Early Modern Period, profession of faith and public life were inextricably intertwined. Religion was one of the main pillars used to build and maintain urban communities;[3] it formed the hub of the organization of the entire social structure. Even the annual timeframe was influenced by the liturgical calendar and its recurring feast days, processions, and celebrations.[4] In this context, public rituals provided an extremely important element of cohesion in the community.[5] It was vital for community members to create a supernatural protection network as a symbolic defence of the city, a sacred fortification. To this end, every city strengthened its identity by establishing its own form of worship, entrusting its fate to a patron

---

[1] Rocke, *Forbidden Friendships*, 232–233.

[2] ASL, CG 7, 480.

[3] Niccoli, *La vita religiosa nell'Italia moderna*, 42.

[4] Niccoli, *La vita religiosa nell'Italia moderna*, 15–18.

[5] On the role of ritual in city life, see Trexler, *Public Life in Renaissance Florence* and *Church and Community*; Trinkaus, Oberman, *The Pursuit of Holiness*.

saint who provided the earthly community with heavenly protection and mediation.[6]

Lucca was a notable exception in this sense. Its Christocentric religiosity was based on worshipping the cross and passion of Jesus rather than an individual saint. This religiosity was expressed most notably in the cult of the Holy Face, a reputedly ancient wooden sculpture of Christ crucified that was kept in the cathedral, long held by locals to be the authentic symbol of the city.[7] It was also expressed in the cult of the Holy Cross. Lucca's wealthiest and largest confraternity, whose members included the most eminent citizens and many of the ruling elite, was in fact dedicated to the cult of the Holy Cross. Founded in the thirteenth century, the first of many confraternities established in Lucca between the thirteenth and fourteenth centuries, it focused on a wide range of charity work, such as distributing food to the poor, managing the hospital of San Luca, and assisting those sentenced to death.[8] Like other brotherhoods (both in Lucca and elsewhere), after an initial surge of devotion its mainly penitential character was gradually toned down to offer charity and assistance to the weakest members of the urban community, as well as to provide reciprocal support and self-help to its own members.[9] Confraternal associations played an essential part in organizing the social relations of their members, while at the same time encouraging ties of solidarity between classes. Though with varying levels of privilege, they strengthened the individual sense of belonging to the community and offered a strong collective identity. They also made an effective contribution to the social policing of public morality, both externally through their work

---

[6] Niccoli, *La vita religiosa nell'Italia moderna*, 45.

[7] From the fourteenth century onwards, participation in the procession of 13 September, the eve of the feast of the Holy Cross, was regulated by an increasing number of proclamations and laws; attendance became compulsory on pain of hefty fines. Besides this form of coercion, the government also took the opportunity to show citizens the compassionate face of justice by granting an amnesty for minor offences on the day (Adorni-Braccesi, «*Una città infetta*», 27–28).

[8] Berengo, *Nobili e mercanti*, 359–360. On the role played by confraternities in comforting convicts sentenced to death, see Terpstra, *The Art of Executing Well*.

[9] This gradual redirection of energies was facilitated by the work of the mendicant orders, who seized the opportunity for spontaneity by steering it and pressing to stabilize and formalize groups into recognized associations, organized and integrated into the context of civic life. See Niccoli, "Istituzioni ecclesiastiche e vita religiosa," 116. For a description of the phenomenon in medieval Lucca, see Savigni, "Le confraternite lucchesi" and Andreucci, "Momenti e aspetti del moto penitenziale."

and internally by monitoring the behaviour of their members.[10] Even in 1602, after stipulating the sanctionable obligation to confess and take communion[11] and reiterating that "the companies are instituted to do good, and to shun evil",[12] the Statutes of the Confraternity of the Madonna della Stiava, founded in Lucca in 1498, stated that they would offer no possibility of doing penance and receiving forgiveness to those tarnished by the terrible sin of sodomy, clearly regarding them as being without redemption. Instead, they would punish those convicted by removing their names and all references to them from the registers.[13] The confraternities were thus invested with great responsibility in the widespread transmission of Christian values in society, both by helping to make the community more closely knit and governable and by dispelling the fear (perceived as real at the time) that rampant impiety could trigger divine wrath.

The idea of collective responsibility for sin assumed an increasingly prominent role in fifteenth-century preaching. Even more moderate preachers concluded that while individuals were punished for their own faults, there was nothing to stop them from either receiving an expiatory punishment for the sin of another or being chastised together with the latter if they tolerated or approved of the wrongdoing in question. This apprehension was powerfully echoed by preachers in pulpits and squares in cities at salient moments of the liturgical year. Political authorities in Italian communes reserved the right to select ministers for the major preaching cycles of Lent and Advent

---

[10] For a wider view of confraternities in late medieval and early modern Europe, see Eisenbichler, *Companion to Medieval and Early Modern Confraternities*; Pastore, et al., *Brotherhood and Boundaries*; Terpstra, *Lay Confraternities*.

[11] "le compagnie sono instituite per far bene, et fuggire il male"; ASL, Capitoli della Confraternita della Madonna della Stiava, Chap. 13.

[12] ASL, Capitoli della Confraternita della Madonna della Stiava, Chap. 21.

[13] "And because the Lord God hates the sin of sodomy and we must also detest it, we order that if any member of our Company should fall into this sin, against God's wishes, he shall be considered *ipso facto*, and without any further statement, removed from the Company without any hope of ever returning, and the Prior will be obliged to have him struck off our Table" ("Et perché è molto in odio al Signore Dio il peccato di Sodomia, et ancora deve essere detestato da noi, comandiamo, et vogliamo che se alcuno di nostra compagnia incorresse in tal vizio, che Dio non voglia, s'intenda *ipso facto*, et senz'altra dichiarazione, privo della nostra Compagnia senza speranza di mai più tornarvi, et il Priore sia obbligato farlo cancellare dalla nostra Tavola"). ASL, Capitoli della Confraternita della Madonna della Stiava, Chap. 22.

and the mendicant orders supplied well-qualified and highly charismatic candidates.[14]

The weight of these preachers' words can partly account for the foundation of the three 'sister' magistracies in Lucca, Venice, and Florence to prosecute the 'nefarious sin' of sodomy. However, other aspects of 'civic religion'[15] are equally valid in explaining why, given the level of engagement, a policy of widespread, but relatively moderate, containment was adopted in Lucca and Florence, whereas extremely cautious sentencing was implemented in Venice despite its harsher penalties. A careful examination of the evidence reveals that communal institutions played a mediatory role between anxiety over purity, millenarian fears, and the need to 'govern reality.' While the political use of religion led to the exclusion and persecution of any expression of nonconformity in public and private behaviour, at the same time the extensive involvement of lay associations in the management of religious life and the intertwining of the spiritual, political, and civic realms created fertile ground for a form of 'down-to-earth' religiosity that sought compromises, also in terms of governing sexual morality.

The attitude towards prostitution is an enlightening example in this respect. Starting in the second half of the thirteenth century, the governments of Christian Europe — from great sovereigns to city councils — started to designate special places for the practice;[16] municipal brothels were established in many central and southern Italian cities between the fourteenth and fifteenth centuries. Lucca was one of the first, followed by, among others, Venice in 1360, Florence in 1403, and Siena in 1421. There are various reasons why prostitution was transformed from an activity on the margins of legality into a public concern regulated by the political authorities, with certain factors playing a more or less influential role than others in determining institutional choices in different contexts. In some cases, the establishment of a brothel (*postribulum*) may have been a response to citizens' complaints about the unchecked spread of prostitution in city streets.[17] It is also possible that increased control over health and hygiene played a role, as the practice could be monitored (and stopped) during times of pestilence, just as commercial

---

[14] Niccoli, "Istituzioni," 114.

[15] For a summary of the concept see Terpstra, "Civic Religion."

[16] Berengo, *Europa delle città*, 638–645. See also Canosa, Colonnello, *Storia della prostituzione in Italia*. For a deeper analysis of the phenomenon of prostitution in its relation to the practice and regulation of sodomy see below, Chapter 5.

[17] Berengo, *Europa delle città*, 641.

gatherings and group dances were banned.[18] The regulation of prostitution was also influenced by economic factors since once it was legalized it became a taxable profession boosting the communal coffers.[19] The income from prostitutes was first entered into the registers of the Lucchese Chamber in 1349, while the first rental contract documented in the public records is dated 1351.[20]

The approach of the mendicant orders was also fundamental in this respect. While on the one hand they implemented an iron fist policy by urging the faithful to embrace morally righteous conduct (especially when the liturgical year or certain traumatic events made penitence and change necessary), on the other hand their mercy was extended as much towards 'women of ill repute' as those whose poverty prevented them from accumulating a sufficient dowry for marriage. In their own way, prostitutes were a necessary element for maintaining social peace, so the mendicant orders viewed them as a testimony to the misery of the human condition because of their destitution and the humiliation they endured. They were thus accepted to the extent that they provided an outlet for desires that society had to deal with; in Nîmes, they even took part collectively in the Ascension Day procession.[21]

While there are no accounts of such levels of acceptance in Lucca, the integration of prostitutes is documented in the records. On 19 August 1440, they were granted permission to leave their brothel whenever they wanted and move freely to anywhere in the city, enjoying rights equal to those of any other class of citizen.[22] A few years later, in 1456, a council ruling (*riformagione*) entrusted the Office of Decency not only with managing the revenue from prostitutes but also with protecting them and guaranteeing their safety while carrying out their work.[23] When the government decided to establish the magistracy of the Protectors of Prostitutes (*Protettori delle Meretrici*) in 1534 — the most significant measure taken in the interests of public women —, the Standard-Bearer of Justice (*Gonfaloniere di Giustizia*) said in the General Council that, despite their necessary role in limiting damage in

---

[18] Rossiaud, *Medieval Prostitution*, 8.

[19] Berengo, *Europa delle città*, 641.

[20] Bongi, *Bandi lucchesi*, 373–388.

[21] Rossiaud, *Medieval Prostitution*, 68. We will return to this crucial point in Chapter 5. See there for further bibliography.

[22] Bongi, *Bandi lucchesi*, 373–388.

[23] ASL, CG 17, 809 (27 October 1456).

any city, they were subjected to all kinds of abuse and insults in Lucca, underlining that this was a result of the spread of sodomy.[24]

Some years earlier, in 1511, Venetian prostitutes had allegedly complained that sodomy was responsible for a dearth of customers, meaning that
they could no longer earn a living,[25] while a Florentine law of 1403, by which
the Capitano del Popolo and the Esecutore di Giustizia undertook to build a
public brothel, opened with a resolution to prosecute and punish sodomites.[26]
In his analysis of a medieval proclamation (*bando*) on the protection of prostitution, Salvatore Bongi — the most erudite and diligent of the nineteenth-
century Lucchese archivists — stated that, in the context of the promiscuity
that ensued after the plague, magistrates started to view 'public women' in a
better light because of the proliferation of sodomy. Indeed, prostitution was
actually approved of and safeguarded under pretence of imposing order and
restrictions.[27]

This tolerant attitude, which took shape from the desire to regulate, but
not eradicate, sexual practices condemned by Christian morality, was justified
by considerations of social order that were linked to the characteristic demographic and economic structure of urban societies between the Middle Ages
and the Early Modern Period. When David Herlihy and Christiane Klapisch-
Zuber analyzed data from the 1427 Florentine land registry (*catasto*) in their
now seminal historical study, they focused on the fundamental role played by
the possession of property in the formation of families. Men who wanted to
undertake careers as merchants, bankers, or jurists in the city needed time to
accumulate sufficient wealth to create a new household suited to their social
status. As a result of the economic considerations and prestige associated with
marriage, which formalized both a family tie and a strategic alliance for urban patrician families, the selection of a spouse was researched carefully and
sometimes at great length.[28] With regard to Lucca, as we have already seen,
mercantile families not only played a pivotal role in transmitting property but
also constituted the heart of the political system. Kinship formed the basis

---

[24] Bongi, *Inventario*, 1: 213.

[25] Martini, *Vitio nefando*, 20.

[26] Rocke, *Forbidden Friendships*, 30–31: "in line with the typical medieval belief that
prostitution served a positive social function, civic leaders might have tacitly assumed
that furnishing men with an abundant supply of professional whores with whom to satisfy
their sexual desires would help to keep them away from boys and to channel their erotic
impulses in more acceptable directions."

[27] Bongi, *Bandi lucchesi*, 373–388.

[28] Herlihy and Klapisch-Zuber, *Tuscans and Their Families*, 202–231.

of the electoral mechanism, allowing the main families to maintain control over the representative bodies. Experience in public life weighed heavily in reinforcing the deep-rooted sense of the family unit. Marriage was a means to cement alliances within the ruling class and the dowry system offered an opportunity to circulate huge amounts of capital. Nevertheless, over the course of time the burden of the dowry came to be seen as a growing threat to the protection of property; the value of dowries rose so much that legislative provisions were required to alleviate the situation. In the 1530s, wealthy Lucchese families still gave daughters an average of one thousand ducats for their dowries and two hundred for their trousseaus, amounts that rose constantly and had already increased by 25 percent by the middle of the century.[29] This issue did not affect only the highest social classes; workers were also forced into lengthy waits before they were able to shoulder the burden of a family. Consequently, those in the lowest ranks of the social hierarchy often had no choice but to remain unmarried. Although apprenticeships — official or otherwise — started at an early age for the poorer classes, learning a trade was unlikely to guarantee sufficient short-term income to reach subsistence level.[30]

The result of late marriage (especially for men) — a common element in urban societies in Western Europe during the late Middle Ages and the Early Modern Period — was that for structural reasons sexual desires could not be expressed 'legitimately' in conjugal union. Because many young men, from the top echelons of the political and economic elite to the broader base of the poor and the disenfranchised, were forced to remain unmarried for at least fifteen years after reaching sexual maturity, prostitution and male-male intercourse provided easy outlets.[31]

This type of functional explanation is useful for understanding the institutional rationale. Although government sources never used these precise terms, social and demographic history studies have helped us grasp the practical reasons that might have determined certain political choices, primarily the relative toleration of sodomitic behaviours and other sexual nonconformities. At the same time, however, such 'mechanistic' reasoning cannot be adopted to comprehend, or even worse, to 'explain', individual behaviour. Although behavioural models and social expectations were conditioned by

---

[29] Berengo, *Nobili e mercanti*, 40–41.
[30] Berengo, *Nobili e mercanti*, 76–82.
[31] Herlihy and Klapisch-Zuber, *Tuscans and Their Families*, 222–223.

the social and economic context, a simple utilitarian logic does not tell the whole story. We will now venture into a more elusive grey area, exploring the backstreets, squares, markets, and walls of Lucca, as well as move out through the city gates into the surrounding countryside. In this new terrain, the focus will be on meanings that can be derived from the nuances of spoken and unspoken cultural and social values and the paradigms that shaped emotional performances at the time, rather than on explanations exclusively stemming from institutional logic.

SOCIAL PRACTICES AND EMOTIONS

CHAPTER 4

MALE SAME-SEX DESIRE AND AGE GROUPS

The documents produced by the Office of Decency are a valuable source for reconstructing the everyday life experiences of the men and women summoned before the civil tribunals in sixteenth-century Lucca for transgressions of sexual morality, particularly the 'nefarious sin' of sodomy. The number of prosecutions makes it possible to carry out quantitative analyses, evaluating the aggregate data regarding the age of defendants and their sexual partners, who were often mentioned during trials but were not always formally investigated by the Officers.[1] From the 1570s onwards, the richness of detail added to transcriptions of court proceedings by notaries allows us to enter the qualitative realm and reconstruct the emotional lexicon of the same-sex relationships described in the sources. This aspect, which emerges clearly in the analysis of the case involving the nobleman Girolamo Nucchelli, discussed below, will be examined in greater depth in Chapter 7.

The quantitative analysis of trial sources from the 1550s and 1560s has allowed for the reconstruction of sodomitic sociability patterns. In the first wave of modern historiography based on criminal sources, the pederastic model was considered the privileged way for same-sex desire to be expressed in the premodern Christian West.[2] As we have already seen in the introduction, this paradigm, which found its most rigid systematization in the works of the influential historian Randolph Trumbach,[3] was revised thanks to the influence of new scholarship, especially queer history and research based on the investigation of Iberian sources.[4] As we will see, in Lucca pederasty was not

---

[1] The following quantitative survey will thus refer to individuals implicated — not necessarily tried — in court proceedings.

[2] Especially in Rocke, *Forbidden Friendships*, and Bray, *Homosexuality in Renaissance England*.

[3] Trumbach, "London Sapphists"; *Sex and the Gender Revolution*; "The Transformation of Sodomy."

[4] For a critical evaluation of the historiographical debate on premodern homosexualities, see above, "Introduction," and below, Chapter 7 and "Conclusions."

the only dominant paradigm in the economy of homoerotic desire. Similarly, the negotiation of male homosexual relations did not take place exclusively within the framework of a rigid division between receptive and insertive roles (which was long considered a constitutive feature of age-structured sodomy). Versatility, both with the same long-term partner and with different partners in subsequent encounters, was not an exception in the sexual culture of Lucchese sodomites. This holds true especially in regard to relationships between young boys and adolescents. The lesser frequency of such accounts in documents from other historical social contexts (such as Florence) is probably due to the lack of interest in equal relationships between young men shown by institutions elsewhere. Because the Lucchese sources do not allow us to follow the experiences of these individuals in later life, it is impossible to determine whether they were cases of juvenile exuberance that were later replaced by other forms of sexual behaviour in adulthood. Nevertheless, this sociality seems to take shape as a well-defined group culture; even though the relevant sources are somewhat barren, providing no access to the subjective perceptions of those prosecuted, the analysis of these social networks seems to define relatively closed groups whose members were bound by close relationships featuring a high degree of sexual promiscuity.

We can determine the age of 590 people involved in proceedings of the Office of Decency (see Table 4). The aggregate data is divided into age groups in accordance with the categories established by Lucchese law (under fourteen, fourteen–eighteen, eighteen–thirty, thirty–fifty), with the death penalty automatically prescribed only for anyone older than fifty.[5] This partition is consistent with the age-old subdivision of the stages of a man's life that was widely shared in medieval and early modern Italy and had its roots in Isidore of Seville's *Etymologiarum* (vol. 2, l. xlii), subsequently absorbed into the *Decretum Gratiani*. Isidore (c. 560–636) subdivided the phases of a man's life by establishing a succession of age brackets to which he attributed specific features and faculties. The first stage was infancy (*infanzia* in vernacular Florentine), identified as the 'reasonless' age. Infancy lasted until age seven, when it turned into childhood (*puerizia*), the time when, according to Roman Law, children started to develop a certain degree of legal accountability. There was a specific

---

[5] For a better understanding of the statistics, when analysing the praxis of the Office of Decency (which, as we will see, substantially diverges from the laws) I have divided the eighteen–to–thirty age group into two parts at age twenty-five. This is because charges were brought much less frequently against the under-twenty-five years old in the Lucchese sources. For the statutory laws, see above, Chapter 1.

age bracket that identified the transition from childhood to adolescence, which ranged from ages fourteen to twenty-eight (*adolescenza*). At this stage, young men were considered prone to sexual impulses and anti-social behaviours. Adolescence was then followed by the stage of youth (*gioventù*), which stretched until the age of fifty. It was only then that men were believed to acquire *gravitas*, that is, the mastery over their passions that finally turned a youth into a wise and trustworthy adult. This age of maturity was believed to last until seventy, which was the beginning of extreme old age.[6] Although reflected in contemporary literature, the clarity of Isidore's partitions was complicated by the manifold ways in which the terms *fanciullo*, *adolescente*, and *giovane* overlapped in Tuscan common usage. These categories were extremely ambiguous so it is often difficult for historians to understand which stage of life documents of the time referred to when using them. Although they don't name the age brackets, in Lucca the Statutes seem to attempt to clarify this intricate picture by introducing a distinction within the group that corresponds to Isidor's adolescence. In the Lucchese criminal code, the latter is slightly extended, ranging from fourteen years to thirty, instead of twenty-eight, and it is divided into two categories: from fourteen to seventeen and from eighteen to thirty. This more nuanced attitude seems to codify a distinction we can perceive in the artistic representation of the biblical figure of David, who, despite been characterized as an adolescent, it was represented as an androgynous teenager, probably aged less than eighteen, in Donatello's statue and as an older, fully developed young adult in Michelangelo's sculpture.[7]

We have already seen that this framework was essentially followed by the Office of Decency, which imposed much more moderate punishments on younger men than what was decreed in the Statutes. It is not entirely clear, though, which criteria were used by legislators to establish the boundaries of these age classifications. In their general provisions for dealing with criminal offences, the 1539 Statutes decreed that — apart from cases of homicide and *lèse-majesté* and without prejudice to the administration of corporal punishment — sentences for the under-sixteens had to be mitigated by a 25% reduction. Young children and those "close to childhood" could not be "held accountable for any crime in any way" and could neither be tried nor punished.[8]

---

[6] Taddei, "Puerizia, *adolescenza* and *giovinezza*," 16–20; Eisenbichler, *Boys of the Archangel Raphael*, 18–21.

[7] I thank one of my reviewers for suggesting this evocative parallel.

[8] "prossimi d'infanzia"; "in modo alcuno tenuti di alcun delitto"; *Statuti della città di Lucca*, Book IV, Chap. 58. On childhood, liability, and sexual infractions, see below,

In the case of sodomy, however, punishments were imposed on fourteen-year-olds (having reached sexual maturity and marriageable age), while the under-fourteens suffered corporal punishment (in practice) from age ten onwards.

Table 4 provides an immediate overview of the groups predominantly involved in legal procedures, with the majority of defendants aged between fifteen and twenty-five (62.5%). Boys in the ten–to–fourteen age bracket accounted for approximately 10%, while adults (twenty-five–to–thirty) constituted 7.6% of the total sample. Regarding the extremes of the age range, the youngest group accounted for only 3.4%, while the over-forties were present to an almost negligible degree.

In its (male) homosexual form, sodomy assumed vastly different meanings depending on the age group that practiced it. In Florence, sodomization was one of the ways in which a young man was initiated into the virtues of masculinity by an insertive adult who temporarily transformed him into an object of pleasure. The expression of homoerotic desire was frequently based on a clear distinction of roles, a strong intergenerational hierarchy, and precise power relations. Homosexual behaviour was not, therefore, part of a minority culture but a central element of the dominant male culture that showed relative indifference to the sexual object when the positions of power between the penetrator and the penetrated were respected. The transition to full maturity was identified with the assumption of the insertive role and the (possible) persistence of a bisexual orientation that saw young men as potential objects of pleasure as much as women.[9] This paradigm is strongly reminiscent of Classical Antiquity[10] and, generally speaking, is a model that featured (over long periods) in many premodern societies.[11]

Chapter 6.

[9] Rocke, *Forbidden Friendships*, Chaps. 3 and 5.

[10] Dover, *Greek Homosexuality*; Bernard, *Homosexuality in Greek Myth*; Cantarella, *Bisexuality*. There is an excellent summary in Lear, "Ancient Pederasty." Important reflections are made by Foucault, *The History of Sexuality*, vols. 2–3, and Halperin, *One Hundred Years of Homosexuality*. On pederasty in the law, see Cohen, "Law, Society and Homosexuality" and Winkler, "Laying Down the Law." There is a critical rereading of the theme of love for young men in Davidson, *Greeks and Greek Love*. See also the recent collection of essays by Cantarella and Lear, *Images of Ancient Greek Pederasty*. On the Roman world, see Williams, *Roman Homosexuality*. For an overview of sexuality in the classical world see Golden, Toohey, *A Cultural History of Sexuality in the Classical World*; Skinner, *Sexuality in Greek and Roman Culture*; and Hubbard, *A Companion*.

[11] In addition to Rocke, see, among many others, Bray, *Homosexuality in Renaissance England*; Hergemöller, *Sodom and Gomorrah*; Berco, "Social Control"; Puff, *Sodomy in*

With regard to Lucca, there are as many similarities as differences with the Florentine model described by Michael Rocke. In our case study, we were able to determine age and sexual role in two hundred and fifty-nine cases. The processing of the data from this sample provided some partly unexpected results; for example, a younger age did not always correspond to a receptive role. While this correlation prevailed among the under-tens, there was more variation in the eleven–to–fourteen age bracket: although the majority played a receptive role (twenty out of thirty-six), a significant number had reciprocal relations or assumed different roles in different relationships (twelve) and a minority were accused only of acts of insertive (three) or heterosexual (one) sodomy. There was greater flexibility among defendants aged between fifteen and seventeen, with an almost perfect balance between those assuming insertive (twenty-four), receptive (twenty-nine), and versatile (twenty-one) roles. In addition, there were two cases of heterosexual sodomy. Over the age of eighteen, there were more similarities with the Florentine model, with 85% assuming an insertive role, a percentage that remains almost unvaried until the age of thirty, although some cases of reciprocity were documented in the twenty-six–to–thirty age bracket. In both Florence and Lucca, the transition to full maturity between the ages of thirty and forty was shown by definitive identification with an insertive role. Nevertheless, the members of this age group are a significant minority among defendants in court proceedings (see Table 4). Only one man over forty was convicted for relations with younger insertive partners.[12]

Although age difference was an intrinsic aspect of homosexual sodomitic relationships, the gap was not as large as studies on premodern homosexualities seem to suggest.[13] It was possible to determine the difference in age between partners in eighty-nine relationships. By further narrowing

Reformation Germany and Switzerland.

[12] See below, 76–83.

[13] It is also possible to draw several conclusions from this sample. Only eighteen of these relationships were consummated between peers who were, in most cases (thirteen), aged between fifteen and seventeen. In a relative majority (twenty-three) of the remaining seventy-one cases, one of the two partners was aged between fifteen and seventeen, while the other was between eighteen and twenty-five. Eleven were relationships in which one of the two partners was aged between eleven and fourteen, and the other between fifteen and seventeen; seven of those in the eleven–fourteen group had a partner in the eighteen to twenty-five bracket. For the remainder, two men aged between twenty-six and thirty had relations with young boys aged between eleven and fourteen, while five had relations with adolescents between fifteen and seventeen. For the over-thirties, only one had relations

the sample, seventy-one cases were identified in which sources were explicit about the age difference and the sexual role of at least one partner. Of these, twenty-four were reciprocal relationships — a significant figure — while the role distribution in the remaining forty-one cases reflected the age hierarchy.

With regard to the punishment of these behaviours, Lucca differed from Florence, where insertive partners accounted for almost all of the convictions (96.6%). The clearer distinction of roles was certainly influential there, as receptive partners — mostly under-eighteens — benefitted from the mitigating legal circumstances for young defendants. In Lucca, however, only 57% of those convicted were insertive, while the others were divided in varying proportions between receptive (18.8%), those who switched roles with their partners (8.3%), those who assumed different roles at different times in different relations (10.4%), and, finally, those sentenced for heterosexual sodomy (5.3%, both men and women).

In Lucca no age group was completely exempt from conviction because the formula that left the punishment of minors under the age of fourteen to the discretion of the *Podestà* (*ad arbitrium potestatis*) meant that, in practice, corporal punishment was administered to children as young as ten. About half of the eleven–to–fourteen-year-olds were sentenced to be flogged, while 29% were given either a fine of approximately six *scudi*, one month in prison, or one year in exile. Many exceptions, however, also illustrate the way in which magistrates sometimes acted arbitrarily in these trials. For example, the fourteen-year-old son of a Lucchese cheesemonger was sentenced to choose between either a fine of eight *scudi*, twenty-five lashes, one month in prison, or one year in exile after confessing to one "reciprocal" relationship, even though it had been consummated two years earlier when the defendant was only twelve years old.[14] A similar sentence was given to his peer, Andrea di Cecco di Bernardino, found guilty of repeated relations, sometimes simultaneously, with six or seven people.[15] Conversely, when Borromeo di Bernardo Borromei, who was around thirteen years old, confessed to relations with eleven partners, he was initially punished with a fine of twelve and a half *scudi*, an unusually high penalty, subsequently reduced to eight *scudi* in consideration of his young age.[16]

---

with a fourteen-year-old minor; likewise, only one man over forty sodomized a youth aged between fifteen and seventeen.

[14] ASL, *Offizio sopra l'Onestà* 1, 1553, fol. 28ᵛ. He chose exile.

[15] Onestà 1, 1553, fol. 23ʳ.

[16] Onestà 2, 1579, fols. 59ʳ–62ᵛ.

Adolescents aged between fifteen and seventeen were mostly punished with one year of exile, commutable to a fine of six *scudi* or one month in prison (38.3%). A significant number, however, opted for corporal punishment (26%), while 10% received lighter sentences because of mitigating circumstances that are not always clear. On the other hand, a further 10% were sentenced to stricter punishments of a year and a half of exile, while one defendant — admittedly a repeat offender — was exiled for two years in 1548.

For the eighteen–to–twenty-five age bracket, 66.6% were sentenced to the equivalent of a year's exile, while a much lower percentage (16.6%) received lesser punishments. To this we can add those who received relatively mild corporal punishment (a negligible percentage) and those given far more severe sentences (although the latter were always repeat offenders). Between the ages of twenty-six and thirty, 65.2% had to choose between a fine of twelve and a half *scudi*, a month in prison, or a year in exile. A sizeable number (21.7%), however, also served a sentence of four years' banishment or an equivalent punishment.[17]

Therefore, despite the fact that legislators and judges in Lucca focused on age as a potentially aggravating or attenuating circumstance, there was effectively no 'age of innocence' to enable exemption from criminal conviction. At the same time, our sources show that there were no significant differences in the ways that sexually insertive and receptive individuals were sentenced.

As in Lucca, the situation in Venice was more nuanced than in Florence. Although the justice system in La Serenissima punished "actives" (*agenti*) with greater severity in a similar way to Florence, some asked for the death penalty to be introduced for passive consenting individuals, too (above the age of twenty for men and eighteen for women). At the same time, they advocated banishment for minors, believing that the spread of the 'sin' in the city was precisely a consequence of the relative impunity enjoyed by women and sexually receptive sodomites (*pazienti*), who were punished less severely than their insertive partners.[18] These measures were rescinded in 1516 when new legislation was approved that guaranteed impunity to youths who reported receptive adults. In his diaries, Marin Sanudo writes that he heard a public proclamation in the Rialto area denouncing the fact that "in this city there are men in their thirties, forties, fifties, and sixties who have themselves

---

[17] To calculate these data, I worked with a sample of two hundred and forty-six defendants between 1539 and 1592 whose age and sentence could both be identified.

[18] Canosa, *Storia di una grande paura*, 131–132.

sodomized", noting the amused reactions of foreigners, who "laughed about it, saying that old men let themselves be worked over." At the same time, Sanudo expressed intense concern for his city's reputation ("thus this news will travel all over the world"), a veiled criticism of the lack of political tact on the part of the Council of Ten in its failure to show a level of discretion befitting the good name of the Republic.[19]

Despite the significant differences among these cities, disgust for the passivity of the adult male is a common feature of every situation studied thus far. In Lucca, in January 1572, seventy-two-year-old Girolamo Nucchelli confessed to having "engaged in the sin of the passive sodomite"[20] with many young men from the city and the surrounding area. Among them was Luviso, whose father Baldassare, a high-standing politician from the important Guidiccioni family, had been elected to the Council of Elders twelve times between 1540 and 1571.[21] Nucchelli was also invested with great responsibilities, including a spell as ambassador at Duke Cosimo's court in Florence. In 1538, he sent dispatches to the General Council when Cosimo was suspected of having supported an attack on a group of merchants from Lucca by fifty armed horsemen who stole their valuable cargo of silk.[22] Almost thirty years later, in 1567,[23] he served the Republic once again when he was elected — ironically enough — to the Office of Decency.[24] In 1572, at the time of his trial, Nucchelli was working "in the tax office" of the Republic,[25] which is where he had met the young Luviso Guidiccioni.

Luviso's deposition reports that the seduction began when Nucchelli mischievously alluded to the physical prowess of Luviso's brother, Count Guidiccioni,[26] during a countryside stroll: judging by his success with women,

---

[19] "in questa città alcuni di anni 30, 40, 50 e 60 i quali si fanno sodomitar"; "ridevano, dicendo li vechi si fano lavorar"; "siché per tutto il mondo anderà questa nova"; Sanudo, *I diarii*, vol. 12, cols. 386–387. This passage is cited in Canosa, *Storia di una grande paura*, 135–136.

[20] "usato il vitio sogdomitico patiendo"; Onestà 2, 1572, fol. 15^r.

[21] ASL, ATL, 111.

[22] Berengo, *Nobili e mercanti*, 169.

[23] This was a year for which there was no documentation in the Office archive apart from two names noted in an index without any specification about whether they were defendants or only suspects. See Onestà 6, unnumbered folio.

[24] ASL, CG, Riformagioni Pubbliche, 53, 464 (26 November 1566).

[25] "in Offizio alla gabella"; Onestà 2, 1572, fol. 2^r.

[26] Luviso's brother was a surrogate Elder in 1575, while he held the position regularly in 1579, 1582, 1585, and 1588. ASL, ATL, 111.

Girolamo said to Luviso, he must have had "a nice animal [between his legs]" and "you must also have the same because you have a fine nose". When Luviso replied evasively, Nucchelli asked him if he could prove it, but the young man declined, saying he was ill.[27] Although he was well aware that the older man frequently enjoyed sexual relations with younger men,[28] Luviso continued to spend time alone with him and received increasingly explicit requests.[29] Despite having heard that the elderly defendant had "a completely festering and rotten arse riddled with haemorrhoids" as a result of his sexual habits,[30] Luviso confessed to a friend that he wanted to "do that business to him" but was warned to be careful since "it was a mortal sin."[31] Given his confession, it seems that Luviso did not heed this advice. Taking note of his admission of guilt, the Officers used a previously unknown degree of verbal force in asking a man convicted for the first time why he had done it, "considering that [Nucchelli] was disgusting and [...] had a festering arse."[32]

It was, however, the appearance of another defendant that cast new light on Nucchelli's amorous relations and raised the suspicion that the young men who readily ceded to his requests were motivated by financial interests. After publicly denouncing Nucchelli in order to obtain immunity for himself, the young Paolino di Agostino di Minucciano repeated his accusations to the old man's face and described how Nucchelli "had encouraged him and had kept asking him, [saying that] he wanted to do it and be sodomized, [until] he was misled into error and so he sodomized him."[33] Collapsing in tears, Nucchelli declared that on many occasions he had helped Paolino financially then, turning in tears to the youth, said: "Paolino, think of your soul. If I gave you money, you know full well what for, these are favours that I did for you and your father, which do not deserve to be repaid in this way."[34]

---

[27] "un bel pezzo d'animale"; "anchor voi dovete avere il simile perché havete un bel naso"; Onestà 2, 1572, fol. 2[r-v].

[28] Onestà 2, 1572, fol. 3[v].

[29] Onestà 2, 1572, fol. 2[v].

[30] "il culo tutto marcio et guasto et pieno di morice"; Onestà 2, 1572, fol. 3[v].

[31] "et farli quella faccenda"; "era peccato mortale"; Onestà 2, 1572, fol. 4[r].

[32] "atteso che [...] era schifo et [...] haveva il culo marcio"; Onestà 2, 1572, fol. 4[v].

[33] "ma incitandolo detto Girolamo et richiedendolo più volte che nelo volesse fare et sogdomitarlo fu forzato cascare in errore seco, et così lo sogdomitò"; Onestà 2, 1572, fols. 5[v]-6[r].

[34] "rispuose piangendo Paolino pensa all'anima tua, e sai bene se io ti ho dato denari per che causa te li ho dati, son questi i piaceri che io ho fatto a te e a tuo padre, non meritano queste et simil cose"; Onestà 2, 1572, fol. 9[r].

The youth admitted that the man had provided him with financial assistance. On one occasion, when he had been imprisoned "for stone throwing," he had sent word "to beg the esteemed Girolamo Nucchelli to come to his aid with some money"[35] and was given a *riccio* (a coin). After his father confirmed his testimony, Paolino then revealed that Nucchelli had offered twenty-five gold *scudi* to keep him quiet about their relationship.[36] Although Nucchelli initially denied this attempted bribery, admitting only that he had given Paolino "money many times and that he had done so seeing him in need, and that he provided honest services, as men are accustomed to doing for one another,"[37] in the end he cracked and confessed (before torture) that Paolino and four other young men had sodomized him on many occasions. After swearing on the Scriptures that he had stated the truth, Nucchelli threw himself at the mercy of the Officers: "And knowing I have sinned greatly in all these matters, I ask God and your lordships to pardon him as much as one can implore for the love of God."[38] He also added the (hardly credible) justification that he had not pursued pleasure but merely sought relief for the haemorrhoids that afflicted him. This time, the Officers did not adopt the usual procedure of "negotiating a settlement" (*comporre la pena*, that is, agreeing to a reduced sentence with the defendant), but referred the case to the Podestà "so that he will be punished and convicted according to the penalties of the Statutes,"[39] which, in his case, prescribed the death sentence.

About a month later, Nucchelli wrote a petition to the General Council of Lucca in which he begged to be pardoned for his misdeeds, pleading not to have to pay for his mistakes with his life.

The afflicted and unhappy servant of your Magnificent Lordships and this Magnificent and honourable Council, Girolamo Nucchelli, pleads with tears in his eyes and with due reverence,

---

[35] "per certa sassaiuola"; "a pregare lo spettabile Girolamo Nucchelli che lo volesse soccorrere di qualche denaio"; Onestà 2, 1572, fol. 9ʳ. The episode is confirmed by an intermediary between the two, fol. 9ᵛ.

[36] Onestà 2, 1572, fol. 13ʳ, 14ʳ.

[37] "più volte denari et che ne li dava vedendolo in bisogno, et che li faceva de' servizi […] honesti, che soglino far li homini l'uno all'altro"; Onestà 2, 1572, fol. 13ᵛ.

[38] "Et di tutte queste cose cognoscendo di havere gravemente errato, et ne domanda perdono a Idio et alle signorie vostre et quanto può si raccomanda per l'amor di Dio"; Onestà 2, 1572, fol. 14ᵛ.

[39] "perché lo punischi et condanni in le pene delli Statuti"; Onestà 2, 1572, fol. 16ᵛ.

explaining that he finds himself in danger of miserably losing his life for the mistakes that he made. He has since asked to be pardoned for them by our Lord God many times, so he now asks for pardon for them from your Magnificent Lordships, and this Magnificent and hon. Council, only wishing to say that everyone should pray that his divine Majesty does not raise his hands from his head, because without his safekeeping every man is liable to commit any sin, which is what happened to the present supplicant, who bereft of divine assistance, fell into this ruin. Knowing that I deserve punishment and not knowing what to say except that he entrusts himself to the bountiful compassion and mercy of your Magnificent Lordships and this magnificent and hon. Council, may they offer that which most pleases them in that way it is given from his merciful and just hand, which he will consider to be best for his soul. He will also pray to God to grant strength to support him with the patience which befits a truly contrite sinner, and with his whole heart he entrusts himself to them, wishing them every happiness.[40]

The outcome was the commutation of the death sentence to life imprisonment on the condition that he find guarantors to secure the payment, within four days, of a five hundred gold *scudi* fine. If he did not, the Podestà was invited to apply the statutory laws and execute him. Nucchelli clearly managed to do so, because a brief note in the margins of the deliberation

---

[40] "L'afflitto et infelice servitore delle Magnifiche S. V. et di questo Magnifico et hon. Consiglio Girolamo Nucchelli, con le lacrime agli occhi, et con la reverenza che debbe, supplicando espuone, ritrovarsi in pericolo di perder miseramente la vita per l'errore da lui commesso, del quale si come n'ha più volte domandato perdono a Nostro Signore Iddio, così hora ne domanda venia alle Signorie vostre M., et a questo Magnifico et hon. Consiglio, et non vuol dire altro se non che ciaschuno ha da pregar sua divina Maestà che non gli levi le mani di capo, perché senza la sua custodia ogni huomo è sottoposto à commettere qualsivoglia delitto, come è intervenuto a esso supplicante, che derelitto dal divino aiuto, è incorso in questo precipizio, et conoscendomi degno di castigo non sa che dirsi, se non che si rimette nella molta pietà et misericordia delle S.V. M. et di questo magnifico et hon. Consiglio, che le diano quello che più le piaccia che in che modo le venga dato dalla sua pietosa et giusta mano, reputerà che sia per meglio de l'anima sua, et pregherà Idio che conceda forze di sopportarlo con quella pazienza che a ben contrito peccatore si conviene, et con tutto il cuore se le raccomanda pregandoli ogni felicità." ASL, Podestà, SB 286, 1572, fol. 140ʳ.

reports that he was allowed to leave prison two years later, in 1574, to spend the rest of his life under house arrest.

Nucchelli's case is useful not only for understanding the disdain directed at transgressions of the unwritten rule that prescribed an exclusively insertive role for adults, but also for revealing interesting details about the sexual behaviour of young men. One of the factors that Luviso di Baldassare Guidiccioni invoked as a mitigating circumstance, beyond his desire to swindle money from Nucchelli (which he admitted in the end), was his wish to prove his youthful vigour by showing the old man his erection.

> Under interrogation, Luviso stated that approximately six or eight months after being cured he was called by Girolamo while passing his house. The latter was at the corner, or, rather, at the door of his house. Luviso entered his house and went to find something to drink. Because they had drunk, Girolamo said to him, "Let us retire to the bedroom," and so they went into his bedroom on the ground floor. Lying back on the bed, Girolamo asked him "If you would like me to see your thing, it will please me," and Girolamo began to unbuckle his codpiece for him. Seeing this desire, Luviso quickly unbuckled himself […] and showed him his member. Fondling it himself, Luviso could not make it erect, so Girolamo added "Let me fondle it a little" and placed his hands on it and fondled it but did not make it erect. He touched Luviso's face with his hands and, seeing that he was not going to become erect, said "Let us save this for another time" and left.[41]

Luviso decided to resort to apothecary remedies to tackle his impotence:

---

[41] "Item interrogato disse che dopoi, 6 o 8 mesi in circa essendo risanato passando esso Luviso da casa di esso Girolamo che era in sul canto, o, vero uscio di sua casa, chiamò esso Luviso, et entrò in casa sua, et fece trovare da bere, et poi che hebbeno beuto Girolamo li disse, 'ritiriamoci un poco in camera,' et così andorno in una sua camera terrestre et appoggiatosi al letto esso Girolamo gli disse 'hora se voi volete che io vedi un pogo il vostro coso, mi farete piacere,' et esso Girolamo li cominciò a sfibbiare la brachetta, et esso vedendo questa sua voglia si sfibbiò […] et li monstrò il membro, et maneggiandolo esso Luviso da se, non lo poteva far arrissare, allora Girolamo soggiunse 'lassatelo un po' maneggiare a me' et ci puose su le mani et maneggiatolo alquanto non fu modo di farlo arrissare, et li toccò un poco con le mani il viso et vedendo che non si li voleva arrissare, disse detto Girolamo 'riserviamoci a un'altra (volta)' così si partì." Onestà 2, 1572, fol. 2ᵛ.

seeing that he could not become aroused *and wanting to get it hard as a young man*, he went to see Gianbattista [Savona] in Vanni's apothecary shop. He asked him for a drug that would give him an erection, to which Gianbattista said that if he returned in two or three days he would give him a good drug for that purpose, which he did. Luviso took it two or three times but it had no effect on him. He returned to tell Gianbattista that it had not worked at all for him and he also used garlic [...] which had no benefit for him.[42]

On seeing this failure, Girolamo deliberately wounded the pride of the object of his desire by teasing him about the weakness of his attributes:

and when he used the said garlic, if he remembers correctly on 11 May, he returned one day to Girolamo's bedroom, to whom he said "You know that I took a drug and garlic to make me erect, but nothing was of any use to me." Girolamo lay on the bed and Luviso placed his hand on his codpiece at Girolamo's request and loosened it to reveal his penis. Luviso fondled it but did not become erect in Girolamo's presence and Girolamo said to him "You have no backbone."[43]

Luviso's final justification for his actions was his desire to allay Nucchelli's suspicions about his 'flaccidity.' "As a young man", Luviso felt obliged to satisfy Nucchelli's desires: "When interrogated about his intentions when

---

[42] "vedendo che non si arrissava et *desideroso pur come giovane che si li arrissasse* andò a trovare Gianbattista [Savona] in bottega di Vanni speziale et gli disse che li desse qualche lattovare da farnelo arrissare, il quale Gianbattista disse che ritornasse da lui fra dui giorni o 3 che li darebbe un lattovare buono per ciò et così ne lo diede, et esso Luviso lo prese in 2 o 3 volte ma non li operò cosa alcuna, et ritornò a dire a Gianbattista che non li aveva operato cosa alcuna, et li adoperò anchora uno aglio [...] che non gli fece benefitio alcuno." Onestà 2, 1572, fols. 2^v–3^r. Emphasis added.

[43] "et dimentre che adoperava detto aglio se bene si ricorda di maggio il 11, ritornò un giorno in camera di detto Girolamo, al quale disse 'sappiate che ho avuto un lattovare et uno aglio per farmi addrissare la faccenda, et nulla mi ha giovato,' allora Girolamo appoggiato al letto detto Luviso mise mano alla brachetta sua a richiesta di Girolamo et la sciolse mostrandole il cotale, et esso Luiso maneggiatoselo da se stesso senza si li arrissasse in presenza di Girolamo, et esso Girolamo li disse 'voi sete debile di stiena.'" Onestà 2, 1572, fol. 3^r.

he committed these acts with Girolamo, he responded that since Girolamo had immediately asked to see his erect penis, *being a young man* he would gratify him if asked to do it."[44]

This was not a naïve or arbitrary way to build a defence. Indeed, in legal terms being a youth justified a modified or even mitigated sentence. In law, ceding to one's passions — first and foremost love — was generally regarded as a weakening of the will (with less personal responsibility as a result).[45] Young men were believed to be particularly liable to this weakness. Paolino di Agostino also demonstrated an inability to resist Nucchelli's solicitations, saying — if only to exonerate himself — that he had not been able to control his will despite the disgust caused by the old man: "under interrogation, he said that after that time he did it on many more occasions at the supplication of Girolamo, who encouraged him a lot and gave him money. *Therefore, as a young man*, he sodomized him many times in response to Girolamo's many pleas and solicitations."[46]

The detailed description of the pair's first encounter reveals an important aspect of the erotic tensions permeating social relations among young people in Lucca. In the summer, Girolamo frequented the river in order to watch boys swim. On many occasions he asked Paolino to take his mule bathing "and in this way he [Paolino] mounted it nude many times and made it swim, and Girolamo gave him a *barbone* or sometimes a *grosso* [both are coins]."[47] It is highly probable that Nucchelli's presence was not coincidental,

---

[44] "come giovane"; "Interrogato con che animo venne a questi atti con Girolamo rispose che avendo visto che Girolamo instantemente li aveva domandato di vedere inarcato il suo cotale, fu, che se l'havesse richiesto che ne l'havesse fatto, che *come giovane* l'havrebbe compiaciuto"; Onestà 2, 1572, fol. 3ᵛ. Emphasis added.

[45] Pertile, *Storia del diritto penale*, 146–164. On reckless behaviour and juvenile criminality in urban society in the modern age, see Crouzet-Pavan, "A Flower of Evil"; Rossiaud, *Medieval Prostitution*, 11–26. On the relationship between citizenship, age/gender, and dynamics of exclusion/inclusion in urban society, see Canepari, "Civic Identity, 'Juvenile' Status and Gender." On violence and youth formation, see Karras, *From Boys to Men*. On young men and violence against women, see the next chapter.

[46] "item interrogato disse che da quel tempo in qua ne l'ha fatto più et più volte, ad instigazione sua di Girolamo che tanto lo stimulava et li dava denari, *però come giovane* a tante preghiere et instigazione di detto Girolamo più volte l'ha sogdomitato"; Onestà 2, 1572, fol. 6ʳ. I have analyzed the relationship between masculinity, erection, and honour in this case in greater detail in Grassi, "Shame and Boastfulness."

[47] "et egli così nudo più volte ci montò su et lo faceva notare, et Girolamo li dava quando un barbone et quando un grosso"; Onestà 2, 1572, fol. 11ᵛ.

since sources describe the river (as in Florence) as a common meeting place for men seeking same-sex liaisons. Indeed, it had previously been one of the main locations for clandestine encounters in an extended network of sodomitic relations brought to light in a series of trials in the 1550s and 1560s. In this case, however, the sources are very different (less comprehensive, almost totally devoid of details and narrative aspects) from those that allowed us to reconstruct the story of Nucchelli and his young partners.[48] In the earlier series of trials, the notary simply recorded the age of the defendant, his and/ or his father's profession(s), the nature of his crime, the number of partners and the relations consummated with each one, and, finally, the verdict. Confessions were encouraged by the 'settlement of the sentence,' a kind of plea bargain that, as we have seen, guaranteed far less severe punishments than those established by the Statutes.

Some defendants reappear more frequently than others in the records for these years. For example, during trials conducted between 1553 and 1556, Vincenti and Salvestro, sons of a master weaver called Stefano, are often mentioned times in depositions. While the latter was mentioned by only one individual, who admitted to their sexual relations,[49] Vincenti was first mentioned in a 1552 investigation[50] and then in the depositions of four other defendants the following year.[51] After confessing to having at least five partners at the age of fifteen, he was tried and convicted,[52] but the following year he was again accused by four more partners[53] and punished once again (although without aggravating circumstances, despite his recidivism).[54]

Vincenti's partners included Giuseppe, son of Maestro Antonio, a bricklayer from Fagnano, who was tried and found guilty in 1552.[55] Giuseppe's sixteen-year-old brother Vincenzo was also frequently mentioned by those

---

[48] We will investigate the causes of these differences in the way that judicial activities were reported in different periods in Chapter 9.

[49] Onestà 1, 1554, fol. 42[r], deposition of Vincenti di Maestro Antonio da Fagnano.

[50] Onestà 1, 1552, fol. 16[v], deposition of Belgrado di Nicolao Altogradi.

[51] Onestà 1, 1553, fol. 22[v], deposition of Belgrado di Nicolao Altogradi; fol. 24[r], deposition of Jacopo di Antonio Carnucci, called "il Riccio"; fol. 26[r], deposition of Giovanni di Vincenzo Bandoni; fol. 27[v], deposition of Marco di Chimento, barber.

[52] Onestà 1, 1553, fol. 23[v].

[53] Onestà 1, 1554, fol. 41[v], deposition of Cesare di Matteo Granucci; fol. 42[r], Vincenzo di Maestro Antonio da Fagnano; fol. 42[r], depositions of Captain Romano Chiariti and Giovan Battista, son of Alessandro Sensale; fol. 43[v], deposition of Giulio di Alberto de Nobili.

[54] Onestà 1, 1554, fol. 42[v].

[55] Onestà 1, 1552, fol. 14[v].

under investigation in 1553.[56] The following year, Vincenzo was formally summoned to respond to the accusations and confessed to many relations with the two sons of Stefano the weaver, for which he was imprisoned for six months.[57] Similarly, in 1552[58] and 1553[59] Belgrado di Nicolao Altogradi admitted to having relations with the sons of both Maestro Stefano and Maestro Antonio. The list of names grew longer when the magistrates summoned those mentioned in the depositions or when individuals appeared spontaneously — probably driven by the ensuing agitation — in the hope of guaranteeing immunity before they were denounced by others. There are repeated mentions of Alessandro di Orsolino, Paolino di Parigi, Gregorio di Vincenti Berti, Giovan Battista the son of a weaver named Vincenzo, Nicolao and Cesare di Madonna Sarra, "Tognone" son of Andrea the blacksmith, Lorenzo di Francesco Menabbi, his brother Tomeo, and Silvestro the weaver, along with various shop boys, spinners, brokers, and many others besides. All appeared in each other's depositions, the increasing number of which illustrates the promiscuous nature of their network.

The work of the Office of Decency reached one of its peaks in the 1560s, with seventy-nine and seventy-eight defendants in 1560 and 1568 respectively (of whom forty-eight and fifty-four were convicted). In terms of legal procedure, the Officers acted largely as they had in earlier trials. Similar types of relations are also described in the records. The key figures changed, however, whether because the protagonists from the previous decade had been removed through persecution or because the passage of time had led to lifestyle changes that led them to embrace less turbulent and more socially acceptable relationships.[60] The only link with the cases from the previous decade was a tailor who lived in Pescara, Cesare di Matteo Granucci, known as Cesare "di Stella," who in 1554 had denounced one of the sons of Stefano the weaver,[61] was convicted in 1556,[62] and returned to ask for immunity in

---

[56] Onestà 1, 1553, fol. 22^v, deposition of Belgrado di Nicolao Altogradi; fol. 23^v, deposition of Vincenti, the son of Stefano the weaver; fol. 27^v, deposition of Marco di Clemente, barber.

[57] Onestà 1, 1554, fol. 42^r.

[58] Onestà 1, 1552, fol. 15^v. He was sentenced to pay a fine of thirty gold *scudi*.

[59] Onestà 1, 1553, fol. 22^v.

[60] We will return to situational homosexuality in adolescence in Chapter 7.

[61] Onestà 1, 1554, fol. 41^v.

[62] Onestà 1, 1556, fol. 52^r.

1560 regarding relations with a young boy, Giovanni Poli.[63] Accused by four individuals (who were perhaps involved in investigations already underway), Poli confessed and revealed the identity of seven partners, all of whom were summoned. [64] Their testimonies triggered a new wave of trials and denunciations. In 1560, the central figure was Jacopo di Cirigliano Nocchi, convicted of repeated relations with fourteen people both as an 'active' and a 'passive' partner.[65] The men in question were all embroiled in reciprocal relations and several of them confessed in the courtroom that they had had many partners.

Certain common elements — the interchangeable nature of relationships, an indifference towards insertive and receptive roles, and frequent recourse to the river and city walls as meeting places — suggest the existence of a clandestine, but structured, social community featuring a broad social cross-section with predominantly equal sexual exchanges. Although the majority of those tried and convicted belonged to the middle and lower-middle classes (tradesmen such as tailors, barbers, cobblers, bakers, and weavers), there were also individuals who were positioned slightly higher on the social hierarchy such as members of the notarial class, distinguished by the title Ser before their fathers' names (including Tarquinio di Ser Lazzaro Cioni[66] and Curzio di Ser Sforzo del Vigna[67]). Some even came from the most influential Lucchese families, like Jacopo Balbani and Vincenti di Paulo Trenta. While Trenta is mentioned in only one deposition as a sexually receptive partner of Jacopo di Cirigliano Nocchi,[68] appearing no further in official documents, Balbani is named by five defendants, including one of his relatives (Agostino di Bernardo Balbani), and was tried and sentenced to a punishment of his choice: a five *scudi* fine, twenty-five lashes, a month in prison, or a year in exile.[69]

A similar social cross-section is evident in the trials held in 1568, ranging from the (distinctly prevalent) world of tradesmen and the middle classes

[63] Onestà 1, 1560, fol. 2[r].

[64] Onestà 1, 1560, fol. 2[r-v].

[65] Onestà 1, 1560, fol. 8[v].

[66] Onestà 1, 1560, fols. 8[v], 9[r], 10v, 11[r-v].

[67] Onestà 1, 1560, fols. 10[v], 11[r-v],12[v].

[68] Onestà 1, 1560, fol. 8[v].

[69] Onestà 1, 1560, fol. 20[v]. We will return to these individuals in the next chapter for their involvement in heretical unrest in Lucca. See below, Chapter 8.

to members of minor families, like the Sandonninis,[70] the Paulettis[71] and the Chellis,[72] to even more prominent families, like the Spadas[73] or others at the top of the Lucchese elite (like the Serdini family). Here, too, one man stands out in the dizzying interweaving of reciprocal relationships and exchanges, connecting many investigations due to his large number of relations. Baldassare, known as "Berretta", son of a bookseller nicknamed "il Sordo" (the deaf one), was mentioned by nine defendants and eventually confessed to relations with fifteen individuals involved in the investigations.[74]

Despite the sketchy nature of these trial records, it is possible to reconstruct a collective history. The resulting analysis reveals some previously unknown aspects of the experience of homoerotic relations in Italian urban society between the fifteenth and sixteenth centuries. It is a well-established fact that sodomy was the most worrying moral infraction committed by young men in the eyes of political, moral, and religious institutions. However, the idea that it took shape solely and exclusively as a power relationship is not fully substantiated in the context of Lucca. The Lucchese sources depict a partially different situation from the one described by Marina Baldassari in her study of the prosecution of sodomy by ecclesiastical tribunals in sixteenth-century Rome where sex was an instrument of hierarchical affirmation and a corollary of the violence of juvenile gangs against a backdrop dominated by criminality, mendicancy, social exclusion, and poverty.[75] The trials in Lucca in the 1550s and 1560s featured more promiscuity than oppression. Admittedly, there is always some doubt over the reliability of the sources and significant nuances may have been omitted in these brief trial records. However, because

---

[70] Eighteen members of the family held the position of Elder on thirty different occasions. ASL, ATL, 18. Nicolao di Tommaso Sandonnini was tried and convicted by the Office on 6 October 1568; Onestà 1, 1568, fol. 36ʳ.

[71] One of them was an Elder three times: ASL, ATL, 17. Ascanio di Messer Vincenzo Pauletti demonstrated his innocence in the torture-chamber; ASL, ATL, 1568, 17.

[72] In the fifteenth century, Antonio di Filippo was an Elder eight times, ASL, ATL, 11. Antonio Chelli is mentioned in numerous depositions; Onestà 1, 1568, fols. 28ᵛ, 34ʳ, 44ʳ; he was finally tried and convicted between 22 and 25 October; Onestà 1, 1568, fols. 40ᵛ and 43ᵛ.

[73] During the sixteenth century, fifteen members of this family assumed the position of Elder one hundred times, as well as Gonfalonierato on two occasions. ASL, ATL, 19. Tommaso di Giannino Spada was tried and convicted on 5 October 1568 (Onestà 1, 1568, fol. 34ʳ).

[74] Onestà 1, 1568, fol. 24ʳ⁻ᵛ.

[75] Baldassari, *Bande giovanili*.

violence committed in the consummation of a relationship was an aggravating circumstance in criminal prosecution, it seems highly unlikely that notaries would have systematically failed to document such details. Violence does not, therefore, emerge as a constitutive element of the homosexual relationships documented in the Lucchese sources.

The nature of these records should also be taken into consideration, as in all likelihood consensual relations had more chance of evading detection by the justice system than cases of rape, abuse, brutality, or occasional sex — even if consensual — consummated in specific and easily identifiable meeting places. It is probable that the conduct of many of the young men investigated in the 1550s and 1560s was anything but impeccable, with criminal trials (some of which are documented) for violence, bodily harm, fighting, and disorder, but this aggressive energy does not seem to have been channelled into homosexual relationships.

With regard to locations, homosexual acts were associated with other areas of juvenile 'deviance' such as gambling, high spirits, night-time parties, and the frequenting of inns, taverns, and pubs (*osterie*). Regularly spending time in such places was often enough to raise suspicion with the authorities and frequently targeted by judges. When "interrogated on several occasions about his habits and why he frequented *osterie*," fifteen-year-old Silvio di Antonio Pieraccini justified himself by explaining that he had no accommodation in the city because he came from Bagni di Lucca. Nevertheless, he reassured the Officers that he had no "friendship with anyone and it will never be discovered that he committed the sin of sodomy."[76] In 1582, a suspect under investigation said that his sexual relations with two partners were done in order to repay huge gambling losses: "I accommodated their wishes."[77] In another case, in 1599, the Officers of Decency conducted a long series of interrogations with many witnesses in an attempt to understand what had happened one night in an *osteria* near the convent of San Frediano when a group of men had remained after closing time.[78]

In early modern urban societies youths thus constituted a social group with its own distinctive status and with much more porous class boundaries

---

[76] "più volte interrogato della pratica che teneva et perchè frequentava l'hostarie"; "amicizia di nessuno et non si troverà mai che habbi conmisso il vitio sogdomtico"; Onestà 2, 1578, fol. 10ʳ. "Have a friendship" ("tenere amicizia") was a phrase synonymous with sodomitic relations; see below, Chapter 7.

[77] "io mi accomodai alle loro volontà"; Onestà 3, 1582, fols. 7ᵛ and 9ʳ.

[78] Onestà 4, 1599, fols. 93ʳ–110ʳ.

than the rest of the social body. Criminal, aggressive, and nonconforming behaviours were part of the everyday life of young men. However, they were not the only social actors populating the urban scenario. As we will see in the following pages, women and children were also involved in varying capacities in this troubled street life.

CHAPTER 5

WOMEN

Although sodomy was clearly defined as male-male sexual intercourse in the Statutes,[1] the Office of Decency also prosecuted male-female anal sex to a considerable degree. Heterosexual sodomy actually accounted for ninety-four cases in the surviving trial records (see Table 7). Transcribed in rich detail, these sources are of immeasurable value for reconstructing the daily life, social relations, and cultural horizons of the lower-class women who populated the streets of Lucca. In many instances, the wheels of justice were set in motion in response to sexual violence, but, as we shall see, women were often treated without compassion or mercy because the Officers were frequently inclined to protect rapists. The trial records from Office of Decency are an invaluable source for investigating the life conditions of low-born women in an early modern urban society. In these contexts, the boundaries dividing public prostitution and occasional hustling were blurry. This uncertainty was a source of anxiety that pre-Tridentine Catholic society was able to cope with by balancing control and toleration. In the third part of this volume we will analyse the institutional efforts to change this state of affairs after the outbreak of the Reformation and the Church's response to it in the second half of the sixteenth century. But now, we will limit ourselves to observing how women living on the streets, as it were, were able to construct solidarity networks, engage in mutually loving relationships, and live according to a system of moral values that, while differing from those of official Church teachings, was integrated in larger societal dynamics. Moreover, the documents also provide us with meaningful insights into the everyday life of married couples. In cases in which husbands were accused of sodomy, it is highly probable that this accusation, by its own nature hard to prove, could have been used by wives to free themselves from the yoke of an unsatisfactory, and often abusive, relationship, which could not have been legally interrupted otherwise.[2]

---

[1] See below, Chapter 7, 138.

[2] For a general assessment of the world of prostitution in Renaissance Italy, with a particular focus on love, see Ruggiero, "Prostitution."

Violence against women was, unfortunately, a constituent element of early modern Lucchese society, a consequence of the structural societal problems highlighted in the previous two chapters. Premarital social relations featuring violent behaviour on the part of men was a common trait found in other urban settings at that time. Over the last few decades, new historiographical awareness of criminal and judicial sources has led to an increasingly vivid reconstruction of the history and practices of temporary and spontaneous associations of young men — united by their age and consolidated by their profession or friendship — whose members developed social relations with their own form, rules, and customs. Criminal conduct was an integral element of such groups, expressing a shared social feeling of deep frustration.[3] Young men were both excluded from full participation in public life and disadvantaged in the marriage market, with around a third of available women purloined by men in their forties. In this strong conflictual context, as terrible as it may sound, violence against women served as an 'outlet' for intergenerational tensions. While rape was frequently documented in the criminal sources of the time, estimates of the real total are undoubtedly understated; current social and criminological research has shown that the crime is evident only to an extremely limited extent even in societies that offer more 'protection' to women and children than those of the fifteenth and sixteenth centuries. Moreover, it is no coincidence that 80% of the cases are collective assaults. Rape was used as a form of release: insults, degradation, beatings, and humiliation were a means of aggressive self-assertion, a way for males to 'assert' their socially threatened virility. The rape of defenceless victims symbolized the rejection of a social order based on adult men's authority that young rapists perceived as unjust.[4]

In July 1560, Maddalena, a young woman from the countryside, arrived in Lucca after serving at Bonaventura Minutoli's rural residence.[5] The fact that she had been sent away when her master's wife joined him at the house suggests that her domestic duties were actually a form of temporary concubinage. Minutoli, however, was reluctant to abandon her and entrusted her to one of his maidservants, who in turn introduced her to Giovan Battista

---

[3] Crouzet-Pavan, "A Flower of Evil."

[4] Rossiaud, *Medieval Prostitution*, 11–26.

[5] Thirteen members of the Minutoli family were elected seventy-nine times as Elders and four times as Standard-Bearers of Justice (Lucca, ATL, 15), including a Bonaventura, potentially the man in question, who served as an Elder eight times between 1537 and 1561 (Lucca, ATL, 311).

Bedini.[6] Maddalena served Bedini in the city for about a month, living and sleeping with him. During this cohabitation, Bedini sodomized her (apparently with her consent) on several occasions.[7] When Bedini (who always denied the accusations levelled against him) left Lucca (also, in this instance, to rejoin his wife), he took the girl to an innkeeper, Giulio di Berto da Milano, hoping that she could be provided with accommodation and assigned to a new master. She stayed in Giulio's *osteria* in Chiasso Barletti for a little over a week. According to the trial records, the patrons there saw the presence of a defenceless woman as *carte blanche* to repeatedly take advantage of her, perhaps encouraged by Giulio. After falling ill, Maddalena never left her room, but her bed was still visited by a series of men who abused her:

> and at this time many young men whom she does not know came to her, and had sex with her in the right way, and some sodomized her against her will by placing weapons against her throat so that she yielded to them out of fear. They tormented her, tossing her about here and there [...] and they took her by force in such a way that they left her in a sorry state in the bed in the *osteria*, badly battered.[8]

As soon as she regained her strength, Maddalena decided to seek a more permanent dwelling. She met Giovanni, known as "il Magnano," a butcher and friend of Bedini. Although he was reluctant to host her himself, he took her to the house of another acquaintance, "a hunchback who works in Jacopo della Gimignana's bottega" and left her there after having sex with her. He met her again the following Saturday and, this time, took her to a guesthouse.[9] Despite her ill health, once again Maddalena did not stay for long, leaving after an altercation with the landlady. She followed another man, who took her to an *osteria* owned by a friend named Tognetto. Although the cook and

---

[6] Onestà 1, 1560, fol. [14ʳ]. All records for this trial are in an unnumbered folio dossier bound at the end of the 1560 documentation. The folio numbering is mine.

[7] Onestà 1, 1560, fol. [6ʳ].

[8] "et in questo tempo ci sono venuti di molti giovani che non conosce, et hanno usato con lei a buon modo, et di quelli l'hanno sogdomitata contra la voglia sua, che li ponevano le arme alla ghola a tal che per paura li contentava, et la straziarono tirandola hora in qua et hora in la [...] et per forza [lha] abuzzoravano di maniera che l'hanno malridutta nel letto del'hostaria dove si ritrova molto mal concia." Onestà 1, 1560, fol. [3ʳ⁻ᵛ].

[9] "un gobbo che lavora in bottega di Jacopo della Gimignana"; Onestà 1, 1560, fol. [7ʳ⁻ᵛ].

innkeeper showed an interest in her, no one wanted to have sex with her because she appeared to be seriously ill. The only exception was a servant, who gave her a few coins before abandoning her to her fate.[10]

The Officers focused exclusively on the many men she claimed had raped her while staying at Giulio's *osteria*. After obtaining the men's names and identities from Giulio (five were innkeepers, one a soldier), the magistrates summoned them for interrogation. Moderate torture was used in some cases, but no one admitted to sodomizing her; when they confessed to carnal relations, they always specified that they had done it "in the right way." Many also insinuated that Maddalena was not "usable": for example, Leonardo Mattei, a native of Navarre, explained that he had decided to pay her a visit when he could not find Giulio. However, after "he kissed her and touched her breasts [...] he did no more to her because he suspected [she had] the French disease." Similarly, after being invited by the innkeeper to meet Maddalena, Bernardo Giulini, the Caporale di Custodia, "went upstairs and started to talk" to her; she complained, telling him "that she had a temperature. He wanted to have sex with her, but she pressed her legs together, saying that she was ill. Because something stank, he let her be and did not have any kind of sexual relations with her."[11] This was probably why none of the accusations led to convictions. On the one hand, the testimonies tended to discredit the woman, whose morality was easily called into question: "Magdalena is a prostitute with all the men who wanted her."[12] On the other hand, the medical report at the end of the dossier supported the accused men's theory that she was 'unfit for the purpose'. After being encouraged to seek help by the landlady whom she had briefly stayed with, Maddalena was finally admitted to hospital.[13] Two surgeons sent by the Office of Decency oversaw her treatment so that an account could be provided:

> and both of them together judged that this disease was, as it actually was, a form of gangrene both in her nature [vagina] and

---

[10] Onestà 1, 1560, fols. [8ʳ–9ᵛ]. These pages feature, in order, the depositions by the landlady, the intermediary, the innkeeper, and his servant.

[11] "a buon modo"; "adoperabile"; "la baciò et li toccò le puppe [...] non li fece altro dubitando il mal francese"; "andò di sopra et cominciò a ragionare"; "come haveva la febre, et così la volse cominciare a usare et stringendo le gambe, dicendo esser malata, et sentendo puzzare la lassò stare, et non la usò in parte nessuna"; Onestà 1, 1560, fol. [13ᵛ].

[12] "la Magdalena è meretrice con tutt'homo che la voleva"; Onestà 1, 1560, fol. [14ʳ].

[13] Onestà 1, 1560, [fol. 8ʳ].

in her anus.[14] This derives from great heat and could be because of frequent sexual relations, although a similar ailment usually comes and can occur, and actually occurred, on a daily basis in another part of the body. They treated her in the following places: in her mouth, breasts, legs, nature, and all over her body. These are stinking things that itch and give off great and intense inflammation and disagreeable, malicious moods. They cause high temperatures, or rather, in most cases, high temperatures cause the aforementioned similar diseases and this is the truth. It became so malignant because she did not disclose it [at an earlier stage].[15]

Almost twenty years later, in November 1579, a girl from Camaiore, Pasquina di Giovannino, reported that she had been raped at the public baths, the *stufa* at the fish market. A *stufa* was a place of rest where people went to wash, relax, have a haircut, or undergo bloodletting. Over time, the baths in Lucca, predominantly managed by Germans throughout the Middle Ages,[16] became a meeting point and place of amusement that included male social relations that did not always comply with the common moral code. In 1448, when the General Council was called to examine a petition filed by Jacopo di Giovanni della Magna, a bath-keeper (*stufaiolo*) accused of allowing a prostitute to enter the establishment "at dinner time," it decided to allow public women to enter stufe and to permit the *stufaiolo* to welcome them,

---

[14] The original term is *secesso*, meaning a secluded and solitary place; evacuation of faeces, defecation. I suggest that here the term may indicate, by metonymy, the anus. I do so because the medical report contrasts it with *natura* (female genitalia), following a logic that was common in treatises dealing with sexual sins. The *natura* was indeed called so in contrast with the anus, which was the orifice that could be used "against nature" in sexual intercourse.

[15] "et tutti e due insieme hanno giudicato che questo male sia et così è un male domandato, una cancrena tanto nella *natura* quanto per *secesso*, et questo deriva da calidità grande et puole essere per frequentatione dell'usare benché simil male, suole et puole venire et ne venne quotidianamente in altra parte del corpo, et loro ne hanno medicato venute in infrascripti luoghi et in bocca, nelle puppe, nelle gambe, nel membro, et per tutta la parte del corpo, et sono cose puzzolente et prudeno, da calidità grande et infiamatione intensa et malignità d'humori et pestiferi et causano febre grandi, anzi le gran febre causano il più delle volte contrascripti mali simili et questo essere la verità et ha proceduto a gran malignità per non haverlo manifestato." Onestà 1, 1560, fol. [15ʳ].

[16] Bongi, *Bandi lucchesi*, 379.

with eighty-one voting in favour and five against.[17] In the nineteenth century, there were still two public baths in Lucca, one in Via del Corso (the present-day Corso Garibaldi) and the other in Via Buiamonti ("Bagni Buiamonti").[18] *Stufe* were also havens of sexual licentiousness in Florence. In the entry for 13 November 1506 in his *Diario Fiorentino*, Luca Landucci mentioned a statue of the Virgin Mary over the portal of the church of San Michele Bertelde (in present-day Piazza degli Antinori), that was situated directly opposite a *stufa*. It was believed that the statue had closed her eyes so as not to see the sins committed there.

Pasquina, who might have been a servant or a peasant, said that she had been approached by a young man while wandering the city streets, taken to the *stufa*, undressed and washed,

> and there she found around twelve people, whom she does not know by name [...] and one at a time they took her to various small dark rooms in the *stufa* and in this place they had sexual relations with her in the right way and in the wrong way [...] and having been abused she came to the Palace [of the Podestà] to make a complaint on St Martin's Day.[19]

The owner of the *stufa* denied any complicity in the matter, saying that he had been elsewhere that day.[20] Although several defendants stated that they had heard her complain ("and she complained that she had been mistreated"), they all referred to her behaviour in defamatory terms, describing her as "a woman who reeked of filth [...] who danced and jumped about" and "who played jokes by lifting up her garments."[21] The young man who had lured her to the *stufa* said that he wanted to have her wash, "seeing that she

---

[17] "all'ora del desinare"; Bongi, *Bandi lucchesi*, 387.

[18] Manlio, *Lucca*, 202–204.

[19] "et vi trovò circa il numero di xij persone le quali non conosce per nome [...] et di mano in mano la conducevano in certi stambugi della stufa et in tal luogo la usorno in buon modo et a mal modo [...] et essendo stata mal trattata venne il giorno di San Martino a palazzo per lamentarsi." Onestà 2, 1579, fol. 41ʳ.

[20] Onestà 2, 1579, fol. 42ʳ.

[21] "et lei si lamentava che era stata maltrattata"; "una donna che puzzava di lezzo [...] che ballava et saltava"; "che faceva alcune baie alzandosi li panni"; Onestà 2, 1579, fols. 43ᵛ, 45ʳ.

was grimy."[22] Some of the defendants denied abusing her, stressing that she had given her full consent to their sexual relations, while others stated that they had paid her, and others still that "she was there with her dress raised, showing her private parts and complaining that she had not been paid."[23] Some of those present corroborated Pasquina's claim that she had been raped by saying that they had heard "the woman complaining and that it was true that [...] she lifted up her dress and showed her nature, saying that she had been hurt,"[24] still, in the end, all defendants were acquitted. Even the man who admitted to sodomizing her, Marsilio di Maestro Pietro *barbiere*, was granted immunity in return for denouncing other men with whom he had previously had homosexual relations.[25]

It cannot be excluded that the frequent references to Pasquina showing her vagina were invented by defendants and witnesses to refute the accusations of anal sex. Throughout the judicial proceedings, the Officers were more interested — in keeping with their mandate — in ascertaining whether the 'vessel' used had been appropriate (*debito*) or not (*indebito*) than in establishing a clear separation between rape and consensual sex. Indeed, none of the defendants were questioned about an aspect of the case that is documented only on a loose note written two days before the start of the trial (probably as part of the preparatory stage), that states that Pasquina had also been beaten up in the *stufa* and had suffered injuries to an arm.[26]

Not all cases of rape reported to the Office due to the aggravating factor of sodomy involved collective abuse; in many instances, maidservants were violated by only one man, their masters. However, none of the maids in our sources brave enough to lodge a complaint were successful in court. This might have been because their accusations were false, but it is more probable that the court adopted a biased view that favoured their alleged tormentors.

One of these cases was brought to light by a surgeon, Mastro Francesco di Biagio dal Casentino, who stated that he had treated a woman "who had two or three rhagades in her anus as a result of being forced [...] and that he believes that she was taken by force in that place by men and will therefore

---

[22] "vedendo che era lercia"; Onestà 2, 1579, fol. 46ʳ.

[23] Onestà 2, 1579, fol. 45ʳ, 42ᵛ; "stava con i panni alzati mostrando la natura dolendosi che non era stata pagata"; Onestà 2, 1579, fol. 44ᵛ.

[24] "lamentare tal donna et che fu vero che [...] si alzò i panni et mostrava la natura dicendo che l'havea fatto male"; Onestà 2, 1579, fol. 42ʳ.

[25] Onestà 2, 1579, fol. 47ʳ⁻ᵛ.

[26] Onestà 2, 1579, unnumbered folio.

need another surgical procedure."[27] A subsequent appraisal, however, suggested that the young woman had not been injured by violence and that her lesions were instead caused by the "French disease."[28] At this point, she admitted that she had feigned abuse, hoping that her alleged rapist would give her something. This confession, however, did not lead to the acquittal of the man because in the end he admitted that he had committed acts of sodomy with her; the fact that they were apparently consensual acts was irrelevant.[29]

When a fifteen-year-old named Bettina was sent "to serve as a maid to Francesco Magrini's wife," and even though her mother reminded Magrini of the importance of "her honour", the girl was molested almost from the start, seemingly with the complicity of her master's wife: "and although she complained to her mistress, she could do nothing about it." Bettina told the magistrates that shortly after taking up her duties "she had to start pleasing him and was threatened and beaten." Their relations led to the birth of a baby girl.[30] Magrini denied using violence and sodomizing her, adding that the girl's pregnancy was not the accidental result of an act of violence, but that "he had a baby from her" because "he wanted to have children and he did not have any from his wife."[31] After a counter interrogation in which Bettina repeated her accusations "countless times," the Office decided to imprison the man in solitary confinement, threatening that the next step would be "rigorous examination."[32] His resistance to this torture later led to his release and acquittal.

In more than one case men incriminated themselves in order to obtain immunity, accusing women who were then tried and convicted even when they claimed to have been raped.[33] The Lucchese Statutes clearly reveal how little importance was given to a woman's consent in rape cases. With regard to non-marital sexual relations, the violation of a woman's will played an

---

[27] "che aveva due o tre setole di sforzamento drieto [...] et che tiene che sia stata usata per forza in detto luogo da homini et così sarà tenuto da ugn'altro pratico cerusico"; Onestà 1, 1568, fol. 44ᵛ.

[28] "mal francese"; Onestà 1, 1568, fol. 45ᵛ.

[29] Onestà 1, 1568, fol. 46r.

[30] "a stare come fanciulla con la moglie di Francesco Magrini"; "l'honor suo"; "et non ostante che si lamentasse con la padrona, mai ci poté rimediare"; "bisognò cominciasse a contentarli et per minaccie et per botte"; Onestà 3, 1581, fol. 12ʳ⁻ᵛ.

[31] "ne ha hauta una bambina [...] desiderava avere figliuoli perché non ne haveva dalla moglie"; Onestà 3, 1581, fol. 14ᵛ.

[32] "infinite volte"; "rigoroso examine"; Onestà 3, 1581, fols. 15ʳ–16ᵛ.

[33] Onestà 1, 1553, fol. 30ʳ; 1554, fol. 37ᵛ; 1556, fols. 62ᵛ–63r.

important, but not central role in assessing the seriousness of the crime; the rights of fathers, husbands, and brothers in matters of honour were always given greater consideration than the marital status of the rape victim. The initial term used was "kidnapping" (*ratto*), establishing that the abduction of a woman who was a virgin "or was reputed to be a virgin," acting "against her will" and "with the intention of obtaining carnal knowledge," was punishable by death regardless of whether she had been raped. However, the culprit did not incur any penalty if he offered a reparatory marriage along with an appropriate dowry "in consideration of his faculties and the woman's circumstances."[34]

In cases in which the woman or girl had consented, the penalty was instead a substantial fine of five hundred *lire* followed by three years of exile, with significantly reduced sentences for destitute victims.[35] A female citizen of Lucca who "is raped or abducted against her will" did not suffer any legal consequences but was, in any case, punished and forced to submit to the will of the men who held authority over her (her father, 'paternal-line ancestors,' or brothers), who could lawfully "chastise her, correct her, beat her, and keep her imprisoned at their will in any place, provided that they do not kill her." If the victim was a single woman who was not a virgin (therefore, a widow), "in good circumstances and a good citizen," she received a fine of three hundred *lire* even if she had not consented, while her abuser was sentenced to death.[36]

The legislators adopted a more humane stance towards married women, who also had to submit to the will of their husbands if they had consented to the adultery but who were legally protected against the abuse they suffered, at least when they were subjected to violence against their will.[37] Adultery, rape, and incest were the only cases that could proceed by accusation alone without *inquisition*, illustrating the delicate nature of the matter and the difficulty that judges faced in intervening between male authority and women. Indeed, in cases of adultery proceedings could proceed only if the husband

---

[34] "o che per vergine riputata fusse"; "contra la voglia sua [...] con animo de carnalmente conoscere"; "considerate le facultà sue, et la conditione della donna"; *Gli Statuti della città di Lucca*, Book IV, Chap. 102

[35] Varying between two hundred *lire*, if the victim had not consented, and one hundred, in the absence of violence.

[36] "contra sua voluntà stuprata o rapita sia"; "castigarla, correggerla, batterla, et in carcere ritenerla a loro arbitrio in ogni luogo, pur che non l'uccidino"; "di buona conditione e cittadina"; *Gli Statuti della città di Lucca*, Book IV, Chap. 102.

[37] *Gli Statuti della città di Lucca*, Book IV, Chap. 99.

wanted to lodge a complaint. It is here that the exceptional nature of the crime of sodomy is revealed once again because in cases of adulterous relations consummated outside the "proper vessel" (*vaso debito*), it was possible to proceed in any case "by *inquisition*, and also *per officio* and by accusation." This was because "everyone should be considered, and actually is, a potential accuser for the vice of sodomy."[38] Thus, the rejection of the 'law of nature' was the only circumstance that could limit the categorical imperative that placed the protection of male honour above all else.

It cannot be excluded that accusations of sodomy were sometimes levelled by women in an attempt to reverse the unbearable power hierarchy in their favour. For married women, such cases could be seen as resistance to the conjugal obligation. Tellingly, trial records frequently uncover family solidarity networks protecting the most oppressed women. One denunciation, made with the intention of being granted immunity (*animo conseguendi impunitatem*), was made by a father who noticed that shortly after his daughter married Giovanni, a baker from Castiglione, she was in pain. The girl had gone crying to her mother, "saying that she did not want to stay with her husband, and they pushed her so much that they understood certain things that they did not like, namely that he sodomized her." The family were so concerned about the girl that they spied on her in the privacy of her conjugal bed in search of evidence of the abuse.[39]

Even those outside the immediate family sometimes intervened to support oppressed women. When a seventeen-year-old complained about her abusive husband to a friend and in-law in church, a support network was created forthwith, leading the girl's father to denounce the matter to the Standard-Bearer of Justice (*Gonfaloniere di Giustizia*).[40] The abused wife was known to everyone as "extremely respectable" and a "good and honest

---

[38] "vaso debito"; "per inquisitione, et anchora per officio, et per accusa"; "di tal vitio di sodomia ciascheduno s'intendi, et sia idoneo accusatore"; *Gli Statuti della città di Lucca*, Book IV, Chap. 1.

[39] "dicendo che non voleva stare col marito, et tanto li furno attorno che inteseno certe cose che non li piacquero cioè che la sogdomitava"; Onestà 1, 1551, fol. 5^v. Unfortunately, these fragments are all that we have from the trial. A few months later, in November 1551, another woman who came forward in person took advantage of the benefits of immunity to denounce her husband, telling the Officers that in about eight months of marriage he had sodomized her on four occasions, the first two of which had been on their wedding night. Onestà 1, 1551, fol. 7^r.

[40] Onestà 2, 1572, fols. 18^r–27^r.

girl"[41] "No stain [on her character] has ever been heard," and it was common knowledge and "heard from many people" that "she is always maltreated and beaten by her husband."[42] It is possible that the accusation of sodomy was the only option available to her in her effort to regain freedom from a man whom the sources described as a tyrant. Indeed, it was not the first time that she had expressed the desire to separate from him: "I want to put my shame behind me and go to the vicar to spurn him."[43] While offering comfort, her mother-in-law reminded her that "because there is a marriage between you, this cannot be done." It seems to have been at this point that she started to explore the option of denouncing him for the 'nefarious crime': "I know a case that I can bring against him that will be my ruin and the ruin of all the family." According to the testimonies, her mother-in-law reacted to this with a mixture of horror and sympathy for the girl's plight.[44] When the case concluded, her husband was sentenced to pay a fine of twelve and a half *scudi*.[45] The fate of their relationship after the trial is, however, unknown.

On other occasions, accused husbands were acquitted. One of these, Tomeo, known as "il Pontino," clearly hinted to the Officers that he had been wrongfully denounced by his wife. He explained that because "she wished to act as she wanted, to his dishonour," he had decided to report her to the Podestà for adultery: "she can say this out of revenge" but "it will never be found that he mistreated her."[46] A little over ten years later, an accused husband defended himself by saying that his wife and mother-in-law had started the proceedings "because they want to have my dowry and what I possess."[47] He added that the two women also hated him because he refused to tolerate their behaviour, most notably, their thefts of his things. In the end, after long interrogations, the man was cleared of the accusations because of his ability

---

[41] "molto da bene"; "buona et honesta figliola"; Onestà 2, 1572, fols. 20ʳ, 21ʳ.

[42] "non si è mai saputa una minima macchia"; "dire da più persone [...] è sempre mal trattata et battuta da detto suo marito"; Onestà 2, 1572, fol. 20ʳ.

[43] "io voglio mettere la vergogna sotto i piedi et andare al vicario per rifiutare costui"; Onestà 2, 1572, fol. 20ʳ.

[44] "siandoci matrimonio tra voi questo non si può fare"; "io so una causa di lui che io posso fare, che questo è la ruina mia et di tutta la casa"; Onestà 2, 1572, fol. 20ᵛ.

[45] Onestà 2, 1572, fol. 27ʳ.

[46] "volendo lei fare quello le pareva con dishonor suo"; "costei può dire questo per vendetta [...] non si troverà mai che l'abbi usata a mal modo"; Onestà 3, 1581, fol. 29ᵛ.

[47] "perché voleno la mia dote et quello che ho d'havere"; Onestà 3, 1592, fol. 5ʳ⁻ᵛ.

to withstand torture. However, his release was conditional on pledging to pay a fine if he abused his wife after walking free.[48]

As we have seen, not all the women who testified before the Officers were married. The sources offer many portraits of single women who were exposed to the violence and brutality of street life, but who also managed to survive by creating solidarity networks, finding casual work, and, in some cases, building loving relationships. It is not always possible to distinguish those who regularly worked as prostitutes from those who did so only on an occasional basis. However, the fluidity that sometimes existed between the two options was a source of anxiety for the community, and so efforts to regulate prostitution were partly made in order to provide some necessary clarity on the matter.[49] Many different life paths could lead to selling sex. For girls, employment as a servant was seen as an opportunity to put aside enough money to self-finance a dowry and get married. If, however, the plan did not succeed for any reason (damage to honour as a result of rape or an unwanted pregnancy could be determining factors), these young women entered adult life in a state of utter precarity. Some remained in service on a permanent basis, while others survived on occasional jobs, sometimes returning to work as servants when their age prevented them from doing other manual work.[50] Prostitution was always at the door, so institutions sought in many ways to contain the risk or at least to provide an alternative option to the large number of young women struggling on a daily basis to make ends meet. However, these institutional responses did not always provide an enticing alternative; in some cases, they required what was essentially forced labour, while in others cases the unsafe living and working conditions led to premature death, sometimes for reasons that are not easy to fathom.[51]

In these circumstances, prostitution could be experienced by women in different ways. It could be suffered as a form of brutal exploitation by pimps and other intermediaries or transformed into an expression of entrepreneurship and self-support. The lowest rung of the social hierarchy was occupied by women selling sex occasionally for extra earnings. They were ill-regarded by 'professional' prostitutes working regularly in authorized brothels not only because they were seen as competition, but also because they did not pay the required fees and taxes and so were, strictly speaking, working illegally. They

---

[48] "dando pagaria"; Onestà 3, 1592, fols. 8ᵛ–9ʳ.

[49] This was a common trait in European society. See Karras, *Common Women*, 3–12.

[50] Terpstra, *Lost Girls*, 15.

[51] See Terpstra, *Lost Girls*.

were also a public order problem because they often caused discontent in the neighbourhood and so were brought to the attention of the justice system by accusations from the community.[52]

Other prostitutes, instead, worked legally either independently or under the control of a male or female procurer (*ruffiano* or *ruffiana*). Although in the early sixteenth century the vast majority of procurers were men, as the century progressed many women — often mothers or former prostitutes — established themselves in the business. In these cases, the level of exploitation seems to have been less violent.[53] *Ruffiane* were irreverently celebrated in literature but acknowledged for their 'useful' role in society. In a sketch contained in an anonymous volume entitled *The Playing Cards for Forty Whores of the City of Florence* (*I Germini sopra quaranta meretrice della Città di Firenze*), a prostitute representing the tarot number nineteen states:

I'm #19 and I was a whore
Much honoured in the flower of my youth.
Till thirty-eight years I kept my health
Then like an old plucked magpie lost my hair.
To keep myself, I turned to be a pimp
For this girl I wetnursed as a child,
And lest she come to harm, I lend her around
To those who want her, and she lives with me.[54]

In Lucca, Caterina, a young prostitute whose work was coordinated by her mother, confessed to a client that her father was a sergeant. When asked how it was possible that "she had ended up in that brothel" if her father "was a gentleman," she replied laconically that "ill fortune had wanted it thus."[55]

---

[52] Ruggiero, "Prostitution," 160–161.

[53] Ruggiero, "Prostitution," 162.

[54] "Io sono il Dicianove e fui puttana / nella mia gioventù molto onorata. / Per fino in trentotto anni stetti sana, / poi venni come gazzera pelata. / Per sostentarmi mi feci ruffiana / d'una figliuola che m'ero allevata / e perché male ella non capitassi / la presto a chi la vuole e meco stassi." Anonymous, *I germini*, 30; translation from Terpstra, *Lost Girls*, 12. The "Germini" was a Florentine card game based on the tarots.

[55] "lei si era condutta in quel bordello"; "era un galanth'uomo"; "la cattiva sorte haveva voluto cosi"; Onestà 3, 1595, fol. 135ʳ. A young woman tried in 1592 stated that her father had guided her into prostitution; Onestà 3, 1592, fol. 36ᵛ.

The young woman and her mother were the keepers of a private brothel. The legal case was probably launched after resident prostitutes had levelled defamatory accusations at each other following disagreements caused by cohabitation and competitiveness in the workplace.[56] Here, too, allegations of sodomy may have been used as a pretext to solve interpersonal conflicts of an entirely different nature. As well as being relevant to our topic, the trial reveals interesting and significant details about the daily experience of relationships between men and women outside the framework of marriage. For example, it is surprising that, at least in these documents, prostitutes were anxious to learn about the respectability of their potential clients before deciding whether to accept them:

> on a feast day, immediately after dinner, Paulino turned up at Maria's house where I was sitting down [...] he came up beside me and put his hands on my breasts, saying: "This is good stuff, do you want me to do it to you for a bit?" I told him that I did not know him, although I knew him by sight. When I asked [the brothel keeper] who he was and if I could offer him service, I was told that he seemed like a nice young man and that I should provide service, and that if I did not do it to someone like him, whom did I want to do it to, a baron? And I was told to get paid, so I went back to him and said that I would offer him service if he paid me, to which he replied that he would not pay in advance.[57]

Such narratives confirm that the sex market was regulated by unwritten rules that placed it in a liminal, but not marginal position compared to society as a whole. It shared the same value systems that guided everyday life in the city streets and quarters. Both criminal and literary sources show that respectability was important among prostitutes. Just like the elite group of

---

[56] Onestà 3, 1592, fol. 142^r.

[57] "un giorno di festa il doppo desinare subbito capitò detto Paulino in casa di detta Maria dove io ero a sedere [...] mi si mise a lato mettendomi le mani in seno mi disse: 'questa è una buona robba vuoi ch'io te lo faccj un poco?' Io li dissi che non lo conoscevo, se bene lo conoscevo di vista, et domandato [alla tenutaria, ndr] se io li potevo fare servizio et chi era, mi disse che li pareva un buon giovane et da farli servizio, et se non ne facevo a un par suo a chi ne volevo fare, a qualche baronaccio? Et che io mi facessi pagare et io ritornato da lui li dissi che li farei servizio se mi pagava il qual mi rispuose che non pagava avanti." Onestà 4, 1595, fol. 13^v.

high-class courtesans, working-class sex workers strove to make a name for themselves and often sold much more than just sex: the lexicon of love had a role in their business. Furthermore, working as a prostitute and having a stable long-term relationship were not mutually exclusive.[58]

There are similarities between the everyday life of ordinary people as described in the trial records and depictions of the working classes in literature. Like many of his peers, Ludovico Ariosto portrayed the life of a prostitute in his well-known play *La Lena*. The eponymous character, whose name was closely associated with procurers, is first encouraged to sell sex by her husband, Pacifico. Then, at a more advanced age, she begins acting as an intermediary, also working as a servant to Fazio, an elderly lover, for extra earnings. Although Pacifico accepts this relationship, he sees red when he believes that Lena is having an affair with Flavio, a young man she is helping in his efforts to seduce Fazio's daughter. Lena reacts furiously to her husband's jealous rage, reminding him that it was only because of his spending sprees and debts that she was obliged to start working as a prostitute. Once again, sodomy is used to mark the boundary between honesty and ignominy, which she makes a point of underlining:

> If I had accepted all those whom you had recommended me, I know of no prostitute at the Gambaro who would be more public than me; this front door hardly seemed wide enough for you to receive them all, and you even advised me to make use of the back door.[59]

In 1595 in Lucca, a mother and her two daughters who practised the profession together appeared in court. In this case, it seems that their fall from grace was triggered by a sudden reversal of fortune. In her first deposition the mother explained that her eldest daughter, Angiorina, had been married to

---

[58] Ruggiero, "Prostitution."

[59] "S'io avessi a tutti quelli, che propostomi / Ogn'ora hai tu, voluto dar ricapito, / Io non so meretrice in mezzo al Gambero, / Che fosse questo dì' di me più pubblica. / Né questo uscio dinnanzi per riceverli / Tutti bastar pareati, e consigliavimi / Che quel di dietro anco ponessi in opera." Ariosto, *Commedie e satire*, 258; translation from Ariosto, *Comedies*, 197. The Gambaro, where the play is set, was located near the church of San Cristoforo and was the only known public brothel in Ferrara; see Ghirardo, "The Topography of Prostitution in Renaissance Ferrara," 404.

a man "who went off and never came back."[60] Despite the mercenary nature of their interaction with sex and the body, their depositions reveal that there was also a more compassionate dimension to their relations. Indeed, the same men who used them for pleasure often invited them to their homes (in broad daylight), gave them something to eat, and enjoyed their company before asking for another appointment, even at a later date: "come to my house because no one else is there and we will dine together."[61] On another occasion, the women were in the courtyard of their building when a soldier invited them to breakfast in the rooms occupied by the army. According to the depositions, it was on this occasion that, after one of the daughters had had sex with a soldier "in the right way," she was sodomized by another serviceman.[62] Rushing to the scene when she heard the screaming, her mother despaired at the sight of blood: "I started crying and, turning towards the soldier in question, I told him 'A nice young man like you does not do that.'"[63]

Maria was a prostitute from the mountains of Genoa who had previously worked as a servant. One day, while on her way to wash clothes at Porta San Donato, she met "some soldiers of the watch, including a certain Tofano who implored her at length" and, in the end, persuaded her to surrender her virginity. The following day, he took her to Messer Lodovico, a soldier in the courtyard of the Palace of the Podestà, who, in turn, handed her over to another comrade in arms, Muzio da Ascoli.[64] This was the beginning of a fairly long relationship between Maria and Muzio that was characterized, as far as can be ascertained from the sources, by mutual affection and solidarity. Indeed, she stayed in the courtyard for four months until Muzio was forced to send her away by the "Most Illustrious Lords" who ruled that public women could no longer be kept on Palace premises.[65] Even though Maria moved to "behind the church of San Girolamo to the house of Pasquina the prostitute,"[66] Muzio continued to take care of her. When she fell ill, she asked

---

[60] "che se ne andò et non è mai più tornato"; Onestà 4, 1597, fol. 57ᵛ.

[61] "venite a casa mia che io non ci ho nessuno et desineremo insieme"; Onestà 4, 1597, fol. 57ᵛ.

[62] "a buon modo"; Onestà 4, 1597, fol. 58ʳ.

[63] "mi attaccai a piangere et voltatami verso detto soldato li dissi non si fa così un garbato giovane come voi"; Onestà 4, 1597, fols. 59ᵛ–60ʳ.

[64] "dei soldati di guardia tra i quali vi era un Tofano dal quale fu tanto pregata"; Onestà 3, 1595, fols. 98ʳ.

[65] "Illustrissimi Signori"; Onestà 3, 1595, fol. 120ᵛ.

[66] "dietro a San Girolamo in casa di Pasquina meretrice"; Onestà 3, 1595, fol. 98ᵛ.

him to act as guarantor for payments to a barber who was providing her with treatment. Later, when she required further assistance, he promised to help her find accommodation. Finally, however, he flew into a rage when she refused to follow his advice to seek hospital treatment for the "French disease" that was by now consuming her.[67]

We will return to the connections between the regulation of sodomy and the spread of the French disease later in the chapter, but first let us explore the relationship between the practice of anal sex and contraception in cases of heterosexual sodomy. Anal intercourse was only one of a wide range of alternative options available to early modern couples for the prevention of conception. Often, different-sex partners practised *coitus interruptus* or used other forms of contraception, such as condoms made from animal intestines, in order to avoid pregnancy.[68] Why were these practices not denounced and anal intercourse was? It is difficult to understand the reasons for this prevalent concern with anal sex, or 'sodomy'. Was it really the most widespread form of non-reproductive heterosexual intercourse? Or was it simply the one that most concerned authorities?

The sense of disquietude caused by anal sex was the result of triggering ancestral fears. On the one hand, there was trepidation about violating the 'laws of nature' established by God the Creator (who, according to Church teachings, wanted sex to be for the sole purpose of procreation). On the other hand, there was profound unease with anal sex due to the 'shamelessness' of the act, as well as repugnance at faecal matter. Women making denunciations — and, indeed, men attempting to defend themselves — frequently said that they were horrified by such practices because "they seemed like things that Turks or beasts would do." One defendant stated: "I'd rather eat wild grass like beasts than do that, and although I'm a whore, I don't want to be buggered."[69] Such attitudes were the result of centuries of anti-sodomitic and anti-Islamic rhetoric. Anal sex contradicted the natural dignity of human beings and God's natural law; it was believed Turks, beasts, and sodomites

---

[67] Onestà 3, 1595, fols. 121ʳ–123ʳ.

[68] On premodern contraception, see McLaren, *History of Contraception*; Himes, *Medical History of Contraception*.

[69] "parevan cose da turchi o bestie"; "Prima che fare questo terrei a patto di mangiare herbe salvatiche come le bestie et se bene faccio la puttana non mi voglio far buggiorare"; Onestà 4, 1597, fol. 66ʳ.

practiced it.[70] The prostitute cited above was striving to lay claim to her humanity; her use of the word "although" (*sebbene*) shows that she was aware of her liminal position between inclusion in and exclusion from the community. Even if this was an artfully constructed defence strategy, it was based on the same underlying logic: that she would never have practised sodomy because she was a human being, not a beast or an 'infidel.'

This is not the only time when defendants answered accusations of sodomy by claiming that they did not indulge in practices that were deemed worthy of animals. In 1595 a cobbler was tried for having had anal sex with the prostitute Maria da Pariana. Possibly to defend himself, he defined sodomy as a degrading inhuman behaviour: "when I used this woman, I did it as human beings do."[71] In the Middle Ages and the Early Modern Period sodomy was constructed in an ambivalent way. Though socially tolerated in certain circumstances, in the rhetoric of preachers it was depicted as the embodiment of evil and the subversion of both the divine and the human order. Its animalistic nature was the most negative aspect of this contradictory construct. Its borderline status as barely human had extremely profound philosophical and theological implications. The 'popular' perceptions that have emerged in these Lucchese cases reflect a centuries-long theological debate that aimed to establish the boundaries between what was believed to be human and what was not. In order to understand the construction of this bestial and feral stereotype, we ought to analyze its rhetorical counterpart, marriage, in its ambiguous relation with 'human nature.' Canon law asserted that the 'natural' union between the sexes was perfected by establishing marriage as a sacred rite. Shifting the 'natural' coupling of the sexes onto the semantic and ceremonial level of marriage was interpreted in continuity with the essence of natural law.[72]

This was but one aspect of a much broader cultural phenomenon. In the Western Christian tradition, the process of integration between natural law and divine revelation came to full fruition in the philosophical and theological work of Thomas Aquinas (1225–1274). His systematic organization of Christian doctrine in the *Summa theologiae* became the cornerstone of

---

[70] On the dehumanization of the sodomite in theology and late-medieval rhetoric, see Todeschini, "Soddoma e Caorsa." We will further expand on this in Chapter 12.

[71] "quando ho usato questa donna l'ho fatto come fanno li huomini"; Onestà 3, 1595, fol. 127ᵛ. Similar opinions were allegedly held by a prostitute in 1597; see below, Chapter 7, 147–148.

[72] Todeschini, "Soddoma e Caorsa," 65.

subsequent Church teachings.[73] All reasoning in this work stems from principles that Thomas believed were "known naturally."[74] Natural law, instilled in human minds by God, was simply the way that rational creatures participated in eternal divine law.[75] Sin was thus an unnatural deviation that removed man's resemblance to God his creator and downgraded him to a status similar to that of the animal kingdom. This strengthened the view that everything in nature was designed for a fruitful purpose and that unproductive and sterile behaviour totally frustrated the goal of nature.[76] Previously, in his *Summa contra Gentiles*, Thomas had emphasized the 'natural objective' of the emission of male seed: "every emission of semen is contrary to the good of man, which takes place in a way whereby generation is impossible; and if this is done on purpose, it must be a sin [...] wherefore such sins are called sins against nature."[77] In *Summa theologiae*, Thomas qualified sexual intemperance as an

---

[73] Jordan, *Invention of Sodomy*, 136. Thomas also made important reflections in his commentary on Aristotle's *Etica nicomachea*, featuring an approach to the subject of male homosexual desire that was more neutral and observational than judgemental: *Sententia libri ethicorum*, Book 7, Lect. 5.

[74] Aquinas, *Summa theologiae*, I/2, q. 91, a. 2, *ad secundum* (reply to objection 2): "Every act of reason and will in us is based on that which is according to nature, as stated above (Question [10], Article [1]): for every act of reasoning is based on principles that are known naturally, and every act of appetite in respect of the means is derived from the natural appetite in respect of the last end. Accordingly the first direction of our acts to their end must needs be in virtue of the natural law." I refer here to the Benziger Bros. edition (1947), trans. by the Fathers of the English Dominican Province. Available online at: https://aquinas101.thomisticinstitute.org/st-iaiiae-q-91#FSQ91A2THEP1

[75] Aquinas, *Summa theologiae*, I/2, q. 90, a. 4, *ad primum*: "The natural law is promulgated by the very fact that God instilled it into man's mind so as to be known by him naturally" (https://aquinas101.thomisticinstitute.org/st-iaiiae-q-90#FSQ90A4THEP1). These passages are discussed in Todeschini, "Soddoma e Caorsa," 67.

[76] "totaliter intentio naturae frustratur"; *Sent.* IV, d. 31, q. 2, a.3, *expositio textus*. I refer to the edition printed in Parma in 1858, available online at: https://www.corpusthom-isticum.org/snp4027.html#19818. See Todeschini, "Soddoma e Caorsa," 68–69, 71. My translation.

[77] "Ex quo patet quod contra bonum hominis est omnis emissio seminis tali modo quod generatio sequi non possit. Et si ex proposito hoc agatur, opportet esse peccatum [...] propter quod huismodi peccata contra *natura* dicuntur." Aquinas, *Summa contra Gentiles*, III.122.5. I refer to the 1961 Marietti's print edition, available online at: https://www.corpusthomisticum.org/scg3111.html#26752. My translation. The passage is discussed in Faggioni, "L'atteggiamento e la prassi della Chiesa," 494.

immoral evil because it dimmed "the light of reason from which all the clarity and beauty of virtue arises."[78]

Sin is therefore the animalization of man, leading him to deviate from the sphere of nature and his rationality. Incomprehension or abandonment of Christian law is akin to straying from the path of nature, giving man the "appearance of a mare" (*formam iumentitiam*) to use Thomas of Chobham's vivid image.[79] The loss of a 'natural state' turns animalized men into caricatures of beasts: "some become pigs [...] others lions [...] others donkeys."[80] This does not mean, however, a lower creatural condition — which would not be a departure from the natural realm — but rather a total loss of identity, annihilation following the forfeiture of the resemblance to God triggered by the sin: "Man is not only transformed into a beast; in addition to this, he becomes perverted, deteriorating into nothingness. Indeed, because sin is nothingness, it transforms men into nothingness."[81]

---

[78] Aquinas, *Summa theologiae*, II/2, q. 142, a. 4 "I answer that." https://aquinas101. thomisticinstitute.org/st-iiaiiae-q-142#SSQ142A4THEP1. The passage is discussed in Faggioni, "L'atteggiamento e la prassi della Chiesa," 495. Sins against nature were extensively addressed in the section on lust in articles 11 and 12 of Quaestio 54 of the Secunda Secundae.

[79] Thomas de Chobham, *Summa*, VI.1, 145–146: "Est iterum alia causa quare debemus vitia vitare et virtutes diligere: vitia sunt quasi contra naturam, et virtutes sunt a natura. Turpissimum autem homini est naturam suam relinquere et quasi contra naturam vivere. Factus est autem homo ad ymaginem et similitudinem Dei [...] Et sicut dicit Dionisius: homines facti sunt deiformes. Hanc autem formam duxit homo per peccatum et induit formam iumentitiam." The page numbers refer to the 1988 Brepols edition. The passage is commented in Todeschini, "Soddoma e Caorsa," 69. Chobham quotes Psalm 48:13 (from the numbering of the Vulgate edition).

[80] Thomas de Chobham, *Summa*, VI.1, 146: "Quidam enim se faciunt porcos per inmunditiam; quidam leones per crudelitatem; quidam vulpes per dolositatem; quidam serpentes per invidiam; quidam asinos per stoliditatem, et ita de ceteris animalibus, sicut in pluribus locis sacre Scripture legitur." See Todeschini, "Soddoma e Caorsa," 68.

[81] Thomas de Chobham, *Summa*, VI.1, 147: "Aliud vilissimum est: quod homo non solum se commutat in bestiam, sed etiam se pervertit in nichilum. Peccatum enim sicut nichilum est, ita homines commutat in nichilum. [Aug. In Ioann. 1, 13; De civit. D., XII, 1–2; Petrus Lomb. Sententiae, III d. 37 c. 2, II d. 37 c. 1] Sicut dicit Iob quod pravi homines factis sunt *socii eius qui non est* [18, 15] Sicut probat Boetius [De consol. Philosoph. IV 3] quod mali homines non sunt quia recedunt a vero esse. Unde dixit Dominus ad Adam cum peccasset in Genesi III: *Adam ubi es?* Quasi diceret: numquam es; si enim alicubi esses ego te viderem, quia ubique sum." In the edition consulted, the sources cited in brackets are reported in the footnotes. The passage is discussed in Todeschini, "Soddoma e Caorsa," 68.

Going back to the 1559 trial, in response to the judges' suspicions about the state of health of Maria da Parriana, the cobbler claimed that he had had sex with her in the "right way." When describing his relations with her, he showed that both he and she were aware of the need to prevent venereal disease. When he suspected that she had a sexually transmittable disease, he asked her to be honest, reassuring her that he would still give her money even if they did not have sex. His reference to venereal disease was interpreted by the judges as a sign of guilt; the cobbler was asked whether the suspected disease in the woman's vagina led him to have intercourse with her "in the wrong way."[82] As we have seen, the presence of syphilis was a recurring consideration in the trials of the Office of Decency. The transmission of the disease was often used as proof of consummated intercourse or, conversely, to substantiate someone's claims of innocence. In cases of homosexual sodomy, especially when abused minors were involved, the spread of syphilis was crucial in determining the policing of prostitution in early modern Europe.

Known at the time as 'the French disease' ('mal francese') or 'the pox', syphilis had become a serious scourge in sixteenth-century Italy. The foundation of the oratories and confraternities of Divine Love in the early sixteenth century — key players in the Church reform movement that paved the way to the Tridentine watershed — stemmed partly from the strong commitment to managing the crisis of the spread of venereal disease. Many of the various hospitals that were established to help deal with the disease were dedicated to St. Job, the celebrated Old Testament icon of human suffering who became the patron saint of syphilitics. Although these institutions were known as Hospitals of the Incurables, the mortality rate inside them was extremely low. It seems that patients benefitted considerably from guaiacum wood imported from Spanish colonies in South America: as a decoction, it could be drunk or used for baths and compresses. Many devout upper-class women raised funds for the purchase of this expensive commodity. In the climate of violent clashes between Protestants and Catholics, syphilis and necessary preventive care soon became part of confessional polemics.[83] In 1529, Paracelsus (Philippus Aureolus Theophrastus, 1498–1541), a physician, philosopher, alchemist, and radical spiritualist, denounced guaiacum as ineffective and accused the Fuggers — a dynasty of Augsburg bankers — of speculating on a product for which they had acquired a marketing monopoly. The family had paid homage

---

[82] "a cattivo modo"; Onestà 3, 1595, fol. 127ʳ.
[83] MacCulloch, *Reformation*, 609–610.

to their 'fortunate' circumstances by founding the largest hospital in the Holy Roman Empire for the treatment of the French pox. As Paracelsus noted, the Fuggers had also been involved in Albert of Brandenburg's scandalous sale of indulgences. Denying the benefits that the medication seemed to have brought to the sick, Paracelsus claimed that the monopoly was further demonstration of the corrupt interests linking the Fuggers to Rome.[84]

It is clear that the Lucchese government associated female prostitution and the practice of sodomy with the spread of the French pox, which it attempted to limit by mobilizing officers and medical staff. The number of cases in which, as we have seen, surgeons were called to testify during trials at the Office of Decency proves that the regulation of sexual morality at this dramatic juncture was also partly dictated by public health concerns.[85]

---

[84] On Paracelsus's opinion about the French pox see Cunningham, Grell, *Four Horsemen*, 308–309.

[85] See Hewlett, "French Connection."

CHAPTER 6

CHILDHOOD AND ADOLESCENCE

The fine line that separated a life of borderline survival from occasional pros-titution touched not only women, but adolescents as well. Disadvantaged young boys were frequently led to satisfy the sexual desires of older males in exchange for small gifts or the offer of some bread, a few sausages, a piece of cheese, or a glass of wine. Sometimes older males used the pretence of asking for a small service; other times they offered temporary relief from the hardship of life on the street, a place where children and teenagers shared experiences such as gambling and nocturnal wanderings in search of amuse-ment with adults.[1]

This situation was an endemic problem in early modern Italian urban societies. It has been calculated that in this period around half of the popu-lation of cities was under the age of fifteen, with the under-eights probably accounting for about a third. The presence of so many children of varying ages free to roam the streets led to rising concerns and a search for solutions by both private individuals and civil and religious institutions.[2] Their major complaint was that the younger generation was undisciplined, devoid of moral principles, badly educated, and prone to early exposure to violence and abuse. Historians have interpreted the fact that children entered the adult world at a tender age as symptomatic of a lack of care, a consequence of the more general absence of feelings of affection within families.[3] This, however, is a completely inaccurate reconstruction.[4] If parents encouraged their children to leave home

---

[1] On the early integration of children into the adult social world, see Niccoli, *Il seme della violenza*, and Klapisch-Zuber, "Il bambino, la memoria e la morte."

[2] Terpstra, *Abandoned Children*, 1.

[3] This theory was supported by Ariès, *Centuries of Childhood*. Lawrence Stone sug-gested that the emotional sphere was largely absent from premodern households, a hy-pothesis long accepted by social historians of the family. Conjugal and filial love were seen as the result of a revolution that started in the aristocracy and spread into the middle classes between the eighteenth and nineteenth century; see, Stone, *Family, Sex and Mar-riage*.

[4] Direct critiques of Ariès and Stone were developed by Haas, *The Renaissance Man and His Children*, and Ozment, *Ancestors*. See below, Chapter 7, 141–143.

early, it was to offer them opportunities that they were unable to provide on their own. Children thus found themselves living in other people's houses for periods ranging from a few days to years, serving as apprentices in workshops (*botteghe*) or working temporarily in houses and their kitchens. This separation, which could happen as early as when the child was around eight, was a necessary and rational choice because reliance on a broader support network guaranteed the survival and wellbeing of offspring. This extended concept of kinship helped families cope with frequently precarious economic and material conditions; support networks could centre on a workplace, a neighbourhood, a guild, a confraternity, or another form of associative life.[5]

The city of Lucca was staunchly dedicated to *educating* its children, including those who were poor, and so it fostered a system of public primary schooling that was rare for its time. Although the Republic was not a centre of studies and never had a university, it achieved distinction through its commitment to *education*. Illustrious teachers from across the peninsula — above all, grammarians and humanists — were invited to teach in the city for handsome salaries.[6] Even more modest primary school teachers were paid by the Council in order to guarantee a minimum level of *education* for those who could not afford it. Municipal schools were first established in the fourteenth century when the plague left a significant number of children without teachers or guardians; it was decided to pay a master so that at least some of the children would be dissuaded from loitering in the city streets.[7]

In 1545, three primary schools were opened, each with a tutor, and a fourth was added in 1556. This trend continued, albeit with fewer schools opening, until the nineteenth century. These 'little schools' (*scolette*) were under the supervision of the Office of Schools (*Offizio sopra le Scole*). Teachers had to display a wooden board above the door throughout the day bearing the message "School of the Magnificent Commune where teaching is without any payment."[8] The many schools in Lucca run by private tutors were also supervised by the Republic; in addition to passing an exam, their teachers had

---

[5] Terpstra, *Abandoned Children*, 1–2.

[6] Barsanti, *Pubblico insegnamento*, 3. This circumstance favoured the spread of heretical ideas, which happened at length with the approval and support of the government, as we will see in the third part of this book. For a general overview of the teaching system in Italy, see Grendler, *Schooling in Renaissance Italy*.

[7] Barsanti, *Pubblico insegnamento*, 50–51.

[8] "Scuola del Magnifico Comune dove s'insegna senza pagamento alcuno"; Barsanti, *Pubblico insegnamento*, 51.

to demonstrate that their moral behaviour was irreproachable.[9] Steps were taken to ensure that even the poorest children, those who could not afford books or, sometimes, shoes and basic clothes, were given the opportunity to receive an *education*. Half of the fines imposed by the Office of Schools on non-compliant teachers was used to subsidise destitute pupils.[10] In 1620, the General Council resolved to provide a more structured service, noting that:

> many poor children do not attend the district schools, or they abandon them for lack of many necessary items, above all books, sometimes appearing there without a hat, shoes, and other things. They are thus forced by the rain and the cold to renounce their benefit [of free *education*] with the evident danger of falling foul of a sin that will lead them to ruin. Therefore, some assignation is required to partially remedy the aforementioned needs. In this way, learning to read will pave the way for these poor children to apply themselves to a profession for their profit and support.[11]

However, in other respects, the Lucchese government had a less developed approach to managing the problem of poverty than other contemporary political bodies on the peninsula. While elsewhere charitable institutions were state-run, in Lucca most were still managed by private individuals or the Church. The state managed public order issues and economic crises on the basis of an obsolete procedure with debatable results. This lack of involvement might also partly explain the dearth of sensitivity shown by the Office of Decency (which, as we know, was a direct expression of the government) towards weaker subjects called to defend themselves against accusations of sodomy. It seems that children were given no special consideration by the Officers and their word was often questioned. Even when suspicions and

---

[9] Barsanti, *Pubblico insegnamento*, 52.

[10] Barsanti, *Pubblico insegnamento*, 53–54.

[11] "molti poverelli non frequentano le scole delli tersieri, overo le abandonano per mancamento di molte cose necessarie et in particolar di libri, comparendo in esse alle volte così sprovveduti di cappello, scarpe, e altre cose, che sono forzati dalle pioggie et dal freddo ritirarsi dal benefizio proprio con manifesto pericolo di incorrere in qualche vitio che li conduca alla rovina; onde si chiede qualche piccolo assegnamento per rimediare qualche poco alli bisogni suddetti, ché, così, imparando questi poverelli a leggere li viene aperta strada facilissima di applicarsi a qualche esercizio per utile et sostegno loro." CG 100, 1621 (12 January) cited in Barsanti, *Pubblico insegnamento*, 54.

accusations against abusive adults were given credence, minors were occasionally saddled with some of the moral responsibility for such actions.

At the end of the sixteenth century, fifteen-year-old Giovannino di Guasparo Bonturelli was invited by an older boy, the butcher Giuseppe del Sarto, to join him in some gambling in the square. [12] Although Giovannino refused to bet any money, he and Giuseppe spent more than three hours together. When they met up again the following week, Giuseppe arranged a trip for the coming Sunday. After obtaining permission from his parents, Giovannino accompanied Giuseppe to the house of some Germans in the near-by village of Guamo, about 6 km south of Lucca. They stopped off along the way, first to eat at a farmer's house and then to gamble with acquaintances. When it started to get late, Giovannino (according to his statements) insisted that they should return to Lucca, hoping to get back before the city gates closed. Giuseppe denied his request and, when Giovannino burst into tears, threatened him with a belting (*cintonate*). One hour after sundown, the pair stopped for dinner before returning to dance and gamble until three hours into the night. After their last drink, a butcher from San Lazzaro, half-way between Lucca and Guamo, provided them with makeshift accommodation in a hut.

It was here that Giuseppe, perhaps prompted by the alcohol he had consumed, attempted to take advantage of the boy. When the latter resisted, Giuseppe immediately abandoned his intentions. The next day, on their return to Lucca, Giovannino asked Giuseppe for a loan, which the latter granted without requesting anything in return. At this point in the story, the Officers started to question Giovannino's testimony, highlighting some of the contradictions in his narrative. Giovannino then continued and told the Officers how the pair had met up again the following night in an area of Lucca called Pescaria, where Giovannino had gone to buy some cheese, how Giuseppe started to touch his arse and kiss him and press himself againt him. Giuseppe promised him money, which Giovannino refused. Once again Giuseppe let him go without resorting to violence, but he persuaded the youth to agree to meet the following day. Giovannino did not attempt to back out of this promise and duly arrived on time at his butcher's shop to buy some meat, offered at a vastly reduced price.

After rigorously interrogating Giuseppe, the magistrates decided to torture Giovannino, too, on account of his contradictory behaviour. While

---

[12] The following narrative is drawn from "Onestà 4, 1599, fols. 113^r–123^v.

the latter's fate is not indicated in the records, Giuseppe was found guilty of attempted rape and punished with two years' exile from the city of Lucca, effective from when he earned the right to leave prison by making a security payment so that he would not attack Giovannino or his father Guasparo.

In other cases, the most brutal violence against children and adolescents was part and parcel of masters exercising power over their subordinates. At times, the professional relationship itself seems to have been merely a pretext implemented by adults to access coveted prey. When Girolamo dalla Spezia appeared before the Officers, he obtained immunity through self-incrimination by revealing the abuse he had suffered at the hands of two goldsmiths, Nicolao Fiorentino and Lorenzo di Francesco Baldini, who had enticed him with a job offer.[13] On other occasions, young apprentices in workshops were subjected to heavy advances and physical threats not only from their masters, but also from customers, who took advantage of their ready availability with a sometimes obsessive level of persistence.[14] Giovanni Battista di Piero da Nocchi had been sent by his father to Ippolito Simuccori, a cobbler, to learn the trade. On 3 April 1560, he went before the Officers to report abuse that had started two years previously, approximately three or four months into his apprenticeship. Giovanni Battista claimed that, after dining with some soldiers, the cobbler — who also served as a corporal at the main door of the district gate — forced him into bed, raped him brutally and infected him with scabies.

In order to understand the context of this abuse, it is important to know that the apprentice-master relationship was strictly regulated, with work undertaken by children from poverty-stricken families or orphans in workshops set forth in agreements reached with the master artisan. In Lucca, servants and apprentices were totally subordinate to the authority of their masters, regardless of the craft or trade in question. This was most apparent in the desire to bind them to the contract until its expiry date; young adolescent apprentices signed restrictive agreements to which they were committed for at least four, if not six or even eight years. Masters did everything possible to prevent apprentices who had learnt their profession from breaking their agreements in order to seek higher remuneration elsewhere. There was an established corporate principle among workshop owners that no one would employ apprentices who were still contractually bound to others.

---

[13] Onestà 2, 1551, fol. 4ᵛ.
[14] Onestà 1, 1552, fol. 13ʳ.

Employment contracts also included many penalty clauses that justified the heavy financial repercussions for servants who failed to comply with the agreement, often reducing them to a state of semi-slavery. Apprentices were provided with board, lodging, and clothing, but not monetary remuneration, except in exceptional cases in which part of the payment in services was replaced by wages. It was only after the third or fourth year that an apprentice started to earn a salary, but it was generally too small to allow him to save enough to establish a small business.[15] Therefore, while sexual violence was sometimes one of the consequences of these power relations, an accusation of sodomy, whether legitimate or not, may also have been the only means available to an apprentice wishing to leave a contractual position and seek better remuneration elsewhere.

As well as apprentices, young domestic staff of both sexes — a sizeable category of workers in Lucca — were also subjected to violence from adults in position of power over them. We have already seen that servants from the Versilia and Garfagnana regions worked in the houses of the most important families in the city. However, their rights were rarely safeguarded by contracts. Their precarious situation and their almost total subjugation to the will of their masters are illustrated by the fact that they frequently cited testaments in which the wealthiest Lucchese citizens reminded their heirs to settle unpaid wages.[16]

In 1578, Guglielmo, a twelve-year-old boy originally from Sicily, charged his master, Ruberto Guinigi, with abuse. The master began his defence by specifying that Guglielmo was not his apprentice, but his slave, and that he was not surprised by "such an allegation" because the lad had previously accused him of killing his mother and stealing family property. Guinigi had forgiven both this and Guglielmo's latest accusation "because he [Guinigi] was a saint." The relationship of servitude had begun seven years previously when Guglielmo was no more than five or six years old and his master lived in Messina. The boy occasionally slept with him at the foot of his bed, but most other nights he slept with the maidservant, on a crate, on a sack of potatoes, or on the floor. On several occasions Guglielmo had run away because of the beatings he had received from Ruberto, but the latter defended himself claiming that the boy had deserved them "for his bad behaviour," thereby suggesting that the boy's denunciation was a result of his churlishness rather than

---

[15] Berengo, *Nobili e mercanti*, 76–81.
[16] Berengo, *Nobili e mercanti*, 81–82.

any actual abuse. Ruberto always maintained his innocence with regard to the accusations of rape and earned his acquittal through resistance to torture and stubborn denials. His release was conditional on a security payment to protect the accuser from being attacked by the acquitted defendant. The trial record ends with a note stating that this clause would be declared null and void if Ruberto could demonstrate that Guglielmo was his slave.[17] We do not know whether he was able to provide such proof and, if he was, what fate awaited the boy.

As we have seen in the analysis of the aggregate data, the Officers of Decency tended not to absolve minors — even if they had clearly been subjected to violence — unless they appeared of their own accord to incriminate themselves. Adolescents and children were more frequently seen as consensual subjects than as victims of manipulation. In statements by defendant they were often accused of behaving provocatively, seductively, vulgarly, or violently and this was also the prevalent attitude among the Officers. A complicated trial from 1572 provides a clear account of how an adolescent suffered from bullying, disdain, and blame. The proceedings opened with a statement by Simone di Michelangelo da Sesto, who appeared before the Office to obtain immunity by denouncing his repeated sexual relations with fourteen-year-old Giovanni Battista di Lanzi Facchino, the servant of a bath-keeper named Mastro Achille.[18] The deposition Giovan Battista gave the following day began with a long list — featuring forty-two names — of the men that had had sexual relations with him. This launched one of the most challenging judicial procedures undertaken by the Office, leading to more than thirty people being summoned and interrogated, many of whom were convicted and sentenced.

When questioned about his duties, Giovanni Battista replied that he was paid to wash people. In the depositions and interrogations that followed, the presence of a callow boy in such a place was, in itself, acknowledged as a source of temptation. Many customers took advantage of him, and when he lamented about it to his master, he was told "that it was his fault." When he sometimes cried out for help, Mastro Achille beat him, "telling him that he should think only about working."[19] One of the accused, who was later acquitted, mocked him with the nickname "budellaccio bardassone," an extremely

---

[17] "tal imputatione"; "per essere uno santo"; "per mali portamenti suoi"; Onestà 2, 1578, fols. 7ʳ–11ᵛ.

[18] "preso et condotto in prigione"; Onestà 2, 1572, fols. 31ʳ–67ᵛ.

[19] "che ne aveva colpa lui"; "dicendoli che attendesse a lavorare"; Onestà 2, 1572, fol. 32ʳ.

pejorative, and almost untranslatable Tuscan epithet that can be rendered as "a slutty sausage casing [i.e. a rectum] ready to be filled with some good meat."[20] Another defendant mitigated his confession by saying in his defence that Mastro Achille was responsible for what had happened "because he puts the boy in the baths just to wash people [...] and it is clear that he kept this both as bait."[21] After admitting that he had 'only' spanked him, a third defendant, Andrea di Niccolo Pieraccini, confessed that he had sodomized him on one occasion, again blaming the bath-keeper simply for having "a boy like that" on the premises.[22]

It seems that many of these relations were mercenary in nature because Giovanni Battista received money or food. In one of many counter interrogations, Giovanni Battista recounted an occasion when Fedele di Arrigo "gave him half a loaf of bread and a glass of Trebbiano in his inn (*osteria*) and did not charge him."[23] When questioned about how he used this money, Giovanni Battista replied that "he gave it to his mother, who set it aside to buy him shirts and clothes."[24] The woman appeared in a subsequent deposition, stating that "one day she noticed a stain of blood on her son's shirt." In light of this, Giovanni Battista was forced to visit a barber to seek treatment for his damaged backside.[25]

When Mastro Achille was asked "if he knew that so many filthy people go to the baths and that a boy could easily end up in a bad way," he replied that he was perfectly aware of it and (contradicting his employee) that he had frequently rushed over to help him. When pressed on the point that "it is improbable that he did not know about it because this roguery had occurred many times," he replied with an almost flamboyant confidence: "let them search and observe, and if they discover that he [Mastro Achille] in any way knew about it, may he be hanged," adding that "if he had known such things, he would never have kept him [Giovanni Battista] in the baths, and that if he

---

[20] Onestà 2, 1572, fol. 33ʳ.

[21] "perché mette dentro la stufa detto ragazzo solo a lavare le persone [...] et si vede che teneva questo ragazzo per adeschare"; Onestà 2, 1572, fol. 33ᵛ.

[22] "un simile ragazzo"; Onestà 2, 1572, fol. 41ʳ.

[23] "li de un mezzo pane et un bicchiere di trebbiano alla sua hostaria et non lo fece pagare"; Onestà 2, 1572, fol. 39ʳ.

[24] "li dava a sua madre che ne li serbasse per comprarli delle camicie et panni da vestire"; Onestà 2, 1572, fol. 42ʳ.

[25] "vidde un giorno la camicia del detto suo figlio un pogo brutta di sangue"; Onestà 2, 1572, fol. 50ʳ.

had known, he would not have tolerated it and sent him away immediately." If he allowed Giovanni Battista to "move around freely," it was because he thought "he was good."[26] Mastro Achille thus suggested that as soon as the truth of the accusations was discovered, the boy was *ipso facto* deemed morally responsible for the violence he had suffered.

We have seen that youth was considered an extenuating circumstance in cases of heterosexual rape and sodomy, in keeping with the idea that 'boys will be boys.' However, while aggressive (penetrative) lust was treated with benevolent compassion by the judges, the moral weakness of the penetrated seems to have been viewed with contempt and mistrust. Duplicity, unreliability, and a tendency to lie are all characteristics that in the trial records were attributed to sexually-receptive adolescents. It appears that young, receptive sodomites faced the same prejudices that, for centuries in Christian moral treatises, were expressed against women. An age-old textual tradition attributed immoderate levels of licentiousness to women; the receptive sodomite was believed to possess the same intense sexual voracity.

In Peter Damian's *Liber Gomorrhianus*, the first treatise on sodomy in Western Europe,[27] sodomitic behaviour was explicitly associated with effeminacy. Damian believed that the desire governing the union between a man and a woman was the only 'natural' form of desire, in a vision in which attraction was generated precisely by the 'difference' between the sexes. In his eyes, any deviation from this schema was an aberration:

> Unmanned man, speak! Respond, *effeminate* man! What do you seek in a male which you cannot find in yourself? What sexual difference? What different physical lineaments? What softness? What tender, carnal attraction? What pleasant, smooth face? [...]

---

[26] "se sapeva che alla stufa ci va di più sozze persone et facilmente poteva, un ragasso capitare male"; "non è verisimile che costui avendo tante volte fatto di queste furfanterie che lui non l'habbi saputo"; "che cerchino et ritrovino bene, et se trovano che per via nessuna l'habbi saputo lo impicchino"; "se havesse saputo punto simil cose mai l'harebbe tenuto nella stufa, et se l'havesse saputo, non l'harebbe sopportato, et mandato via subbito"; "alla libera"; "fusse buono"; Onestà 2, 1572, fol. 64r-v.

[27] The *Liber Gomorrhianus* is a well-known letter from Peter Damian to Pope Leo IX. Written in the second half of 1049, it was first given its current title in the fourteenth century. Criticizing the spread of sodomy among the clergy, Damian put himself forward as a reformer of the Church. The pope's response was somewhat lukewarm, however, encouraging an attitude of temperance. On this matter see Jordan, *Invention of Sodomy*, 45–66, and Cantarella, "Pier Damiani."

In fact, it is *the rule of natural appetite* that each seek beyond himself what he cannot find within the cloister of his own faculty.[28]

According to Damian, a man finds his self-completion in the softness of the female body, not in the hardness of another man's body. The receptive sodomite is thus fundamentally an effeminate man who embarks on an illusory quest for the masculine partner who will complete him by providing him with the vigour that he should have already possessed himself.[29]

Although not always so directly related to the normative link between sexual difference and erotic desire, the association between sodomy and effeminacy was a recurring theme in medieval theological and medical literature. Joan Cadden has analyzed the Latin commentaries on the passage in the pseudo-Aristotelian *Problemata* 4.26, which explores the reasons for male homosexual desire and, in particular, the causes of the pleasure felt by some men in being penetrated.[30] The author of the *Problemata* believed that either a congenital deformity or a blockage in the semen canals led to an accumulation of sperm in the rectum, triggering a desire that could be vented only through anal sex. This inclination could either be innate or acquired by habit and become a common practice (Ps. Arist. *Pr.* 4.26), meaning that the 'unnatural' desires in such cases were not morally imputable. The manuscripts of the *Problemata* were translated into Latin by Bartholomew of Messina in the thirteenth century, and many different versions, now held in libraries across Europe, were in circulation during the Middle Ages, supplemented by commentaries, abridgements, and indices.[31]

Focusing in particular on the *Expositio Problematum Aristotelis* by Peter of Abano (circa 1250–1318), Cadden has highlighted the main theoretical

---

[28] Peter Damian, *Book of Gomorrah*, 68. Emphasis added. "Dic, vir evirate, responde, homo effeminate, quid in viro quaeris, quod in temetipso invenire non possis? Quam diversitatem sexuum, quae varia liniamenta membrorum, quam mollitiem, quam carnalis illecebrae teneritudinem, quam lubrici vultus iocunditatem? Terreat te, quaeso, vigor masculini aspectus, abhorreat mens tua viriles artus. Naturalis quippe appetitus officium est, ut hoc unusquisque extrinsecus quaerat, quod intra suae facultatis claustra reperire non valeat." Peter Damian, *Die Briefe*, 1:313, 13–22.

[29] Olsen, *Of Sodomites*, 389–390.

[30] Despite being relatively neglected by contemporary critics, the work was hugely successful in the Middle Ages and the Renaissance. Although it cannot be attributed to the Greek philosopher, its Aristotelian inspiration is indisputable; see Centrone, *Studi sui Problemata*.

[31] Cadden, *Nothing Natural*, 9–10.

dilemmas raised by the analysis of this passage, which was laboriously harmonized with Christian morality. Male homosexual behaviours were also associated with gender nonconformity in this body of texts. While the pseudo-Aristotelian work equated receptive men to various forms of 'imperfection' and sexual 'incompleteness' (eunuchs, sterile and impotent men, adolescents), the main issue in medieval commentaries on the *Problemata* — albeit to a varying degree depending on the text and the author — was the association between the receptive sodomite and the female sex.[32] The description of men who enjoyed being penetrated thus reflected the cultural stereotypes generally used at the time to label women. As a result of their supposedly flawed nature, they were considered to be both weak passive subjects and, in a somewhat contradictory manner, creatures driven by uncontrollable sexual appetites in their thirst to fill the void.[33]

Examples of the association between sodomy, passivity, and effeminacy can also be found in the Early Modern Period not only in theological treatises and moral works, but also in the voices heard during judicial proceedings. The Florentine documents sometimes indicate sodomitic relations through the concept of 'knowing' a lover "like a woman" (*ut feminam*). In the same way, informers often reported that "such-and-such a person" kept a boy "for use as a woman," "as a woman," or "as a female" ("a uso di donna," "come donna," "come una femmina").[34] Such testimonies do not seem to suggest that the individuals in question were knowingly subverting gender norms; their young age, subordinate status, and sexual passivity were enough for them to be identified as symbolic women (by others). There are, however, other examples in which subjects made conscious use of their gender identity, such as the fourteenth-century cross-dresser Rolandina, a prostitute tried by the Venetian Inquisition who decided to embrace a female identity after having been socialized as a man by her family.[35]

Spanish sources provide rich resources for exploring the link between sodomitic practices and effeminacy.[36] During a 1572 trial by the Inquisition of Valencia, a witness told the inquisitor that a friar, Pedro Pizzarro, was

---

[32] Cadden, *Nothing Natural*, 107–108.

[33] Cadden, *Nothing Natural*, 110.

[34] Rocke, *Forbidden Friendships*, 108.

[35] Ruggiero, *Boundaries of Eros*, 136. Cases of cross-dressing and intersexuality were often confused; see Soyer, *Ambiguous Gender*.

[36] The short summary that follows is taken from Grassi, *Sodoma*, 100–101. See also Grassi, "Emotions and Sexuality."

"ordinarily in the habit of speaking in a highly effeminate manner and imitating women's things," thereby earning the feminine nickname "Pizzarra."[37] Homoerotic relations were frequently described in heterosexual terms. One man under investigation was accused of showering his lover with "lots of caresses and playfulness as if he were a damsel," while the locution "make use of a man as a woman" (a synonym of sodomy) was sometimes adopted. Alternatively, it was said that two men slept together "like husband and wife."[38] Pedro de León, a Jesuit who served in the prison in Seville to comfort those condemned to death, wrote extensively in one of his works about local sodomites sentenced to burn at the stake, providing an edifying and apologetic account of his duties. His notes underlined that feminine posturing was one of their most distinctive signs.[39] Domingo Palacio, who was burnt alive in 1593 "for the nefarious sin" had previously been driven out of a house of Jesuits in Seville where he worked as a cook because "he looked like a faggot."[40] The term *maricón*, which the twenty-first century Spanish-speaking gay world has reappropriated in a creative and humorous manner,[41] is still in use as a derogatory way of referring to a homosexual man. In the 1611 dictionary by Sebastián de Covarrubias y Orozco it was defined as an "effeminate man, with an inclination for female activities," in an entry that associated this gender anomaly with the equivalent *marimacho*, namely, a woman who liked to assume "male mannerisms."[42]

The records of the Office of Decency in Lucca do not feature any such poignant or explicit accounts of the association between receptive sodomy and effeminacy. Nevertheless, the few testimonies in which the receptive partner in a homosexual relationship was equated to a woman refer to young

---

[37] "tiene ordinaria costumbre de hablar muy afeminadamente e imitar las cosas de mujeres"; AHN, Inquisicion, legajo 844, no. 3 (1572), cited in Carrasco, *Inquisición y represión sexual*, 135.

[38] "tantas caricias i puterías como si el fuera una doncella"; "usar de hombre como mujer"; "como marido y mujer"; AHN, Inq. leg. 840, no. 50 (1625); leg. 844, no. 3 (1572) and leg. 550, no. 17, cited in Carrasco, *Inquisición y represión sexual*, 107–108.

[39] León, *Grandeza y miseria*, 435–437.

[40] "por el pecado nefando"; "parecía maricón"; León, *Grandeza y miseria*, 489.

[41] On the role of insults in the construction of gay identity, see Eribon, *Insult and the Making of the Gay Self*.

[42] "hombre afeminado, que se inclina a hazer cosas de mujer, que llaman por otro nombre Marimaticas; como al contrario decimos Marimacho la mujer que tiene desembolturas de hombre"; Covarrubias y Orozco, *Tesoro de la lengua castellana*, fol. 540r. See also Garza Carvajal, *Butterflies will Burn*, 68–71.

men in the youngest age bracket and present them as prostitutes, especially if they behaved unscrupulously. In 1573, a fifteen-year-old boy was accused of selling sex to many different partners. However, "it is said for certain" that one of these partners was a regular customer, a twenty-four-year-old weaver who was convicted shortly thereafter: "he acts like a prostitute, and particularly with [...] Mancino da More."[43] A small unnumbered sheet among the documents for 1574 records a direct exchange between a boy and a young man attempting to win his favours:

> on Thursday evening [...] an hour and a half after sunset, on the road to Marlia [...] there were four people, and one of them stopped a boy named Bernardo di Michelino [...], who was dressed in a Moorish fashion. This person told him that he wanted to do him, but he did not want to, so the young man added: "you give it to others, I've got a small one." The young boy replied: "I'll give it to whoever I like, and I don't want to give it to you." At this point, the young man said; "you could also give it to me, I've got a small one and I won't hurt you," but, since he really did not want to satisfy him, he let him go, calling after him: "dirty bugger."[44]

It seems, therefore, that the feminization of the receptive partner was related to a tender age and a lack of inhibitions. Victimized and derided, sexually-receptive young men were equated with prostitutes (*bardassa* usually referred to a young male whore), and, just like the latter, were held responsible for their subjection to male violence, which was believed to be uncontrollable and, therefore, pardonable.

As we have seen, there were well-structured relations between the cultures of sexual nonconformity and society in general. Margins of tolerance

---

[43] "si dice per certo"; "fa come una meretrice, et particolarmente con [...] Mancino da More"; Onestà 2, 1573, fol. 7^r.

[44] "giovedì sera [...] a hora 1 ½ di contra alla voltaccia del Marlia [...] erano 4 persone, et uno di loro prese un ragazzo che ha nome bernardo di michelino [...], che è vestito da morello, et quel tale li disse che li voleva fare, et lui non volendo et allora questo giovane soggiunse dicendo: 'né dai ad altri, io l'ho piccolo,' et il fanciullo rispuose: 'ne voglio dare a chi mi pare et non ne voglio dare a te,' et lui soggiunse: 'ne potresti dare anchora a me, l'ho piccolo non ti farò male,' et non volendo per forza lo lassò andare dicendoli: 'bardassaccia.'" Onestà 2, 1574, unnumbered folio.

towards sodomitic behaviour emerged to the extent that homosexual relations worked in liaison with the patriarchal hierarchical structure of society at the time, in which pederasty seems to have played an important role. It was practised not only through recourse to violence or payment, but sometimes also with more subtle (though no less dangerous) weapons of persuasion. In his depositions, fourteen-year-old Jacopo di Battista da Diecimo, a workshop apprentice, described how he was obsessively courted by a man, Belgrado di Nicolao Altogradi, who was later sentenced to pay a fine of thirty gold *scudi*:

> Belgrado [...] asked him to come with him because he wanted to do him [...] and when he refused, he took the key to the workshop from him, and when he went crying after him, he gave it back and kissed him [...] he said that Belgrado had been to his workshop many times to see him because he wanted to go with him for money, showing him money and asking him to do it [...] When asked to state whether there was anything else to confess, he said that [...] one evening at the Merchants' Lodge [...] Belgrado forced him to masturbate him. He then said that on another occasion he was forced to masturbate him in [the church of] San Piero Cigoli.[45]

The courting of young Riccardo, son of Ser Girolamo Gerini, by the older Ser Biagio Pauli was less aggressive but more complex and psychologically subtle. Their first encounter took place at the home of the boy, whose mother Pauli had gone to visit. The attraction must have been instant, given that there was an immediate invitation to go for a walk. While they were strolling along by the walls, the seducer started his advances: "Ser Biagio began to ask him about what he did for a living, telling him: 'You go around dressed so badly, have you ever done anything with anyone?'" Pauli boasted about his financial status and offered money and clothes, along with an invitation to his house: "You won't want for money, and you'll be able to get a cloak made

---

45 "Belgrado [...] lo richiese che andasse seco di volerli fare [...] et lui ricusando li levò la chiave di bottega, et andandoli piangendo drieto, ne la rese et in questo lo baciò [...] item dixe che detto Belgrado più volte è stato a bottega sua, a ricercarlo che voleva andasse seco al soldo monstrandoli denari et richiedendolo [...] Interrogato che dichi che se sa che cie altro dixe che [...] quella sera alla loggia de mercanti [...] ditto belgrado lo constrinse che lo masturbasse. Item dipoi dixe che un'altra volta lo costrinse a masturbare drento S. Piero Cigoli." Onestà 1, 1552, fol. 15ᵛ.

and you'll have money at your disposal." Clearly aware of the suspicions that might be raised if they were seen walking the city streets together, Pauli told the boy that he would go first. He asked him to follow and wait a little before knocking. The boy must have panicked, though, and fled. Pauli subsequently sought him out at his workplace, Giovanni Guinigi's loan desk, extending another invitation to visit him at home. Terrified of seeing him again, the boy stopped going to work for a few days. When called to account by his superior, he confessed the reason for his absence, telling Guinigi openly "that Ser Biagio was harassing him," adding that he had heard from other sources that Pauli had molested others and infected them with the French disease.[46]

On learning this, the Officers called in the other youngsters who had been seduced, concluding their investigations by summoning Pauli and sentencing him to pay a fine of fifty gold *scudi*.[47] Pauli employed a similar approach with all ten of the adolescents with whom he admitted having relations. Although the invitation to his house often led to out-and-out carnal violence, in the case of Paulino, son of Michele Fondora, Pauli's courting was so steadfast and patient that it came across more as a romantic attachment. Pauli was a friend of Jacopo Burlamacchi, a young man who lived in a ground-floor room in the house of the Fondora family. Bedridden due to a chronic illness, Burlamacchi was often visited by Pauli, and young Paulino soon joined in their conversations:

> Paulo [i.e., Paulino] sometimes went there to play the lute and Ser Biagio [Pauli] would be there and started to get to know him. Ser Biagio caressed him a lot and showed that he was fond of him, telling him that he was the son of a gentleman. Ser Biagio demonstrated this friendship and kindness for over a month, continuing to go and spend time with Jacopo in his room.[48]

---

[46] "detto Ser Biagio cominciò a domandarli quello che faceva, dicendoli: 'tu vai si mal vestito, hai avuto mai a fare con alcuno?'"; "non ti mancherà denari, et ti potrai fare una cappa et haverai denari a tua posta"; "come ser Biagio lo molestava"; Onestà 2, 1573, fols. 14^r–15^r.

[47] Onestà 2, fols. 28^r–29^r.

[48] "esso Paulo ci andava alle volte sonacchiando il liuto dove ci praticava detto ser Biagio, et li lo cominciò a conoscere, il qual Ser Biagio lo carezzava molto et monstrava volerli bene, et li diceva sete figliuolo di un galantuomo, la quale amicizia et benevolenzia li dimostrò detto Ser Biagio per più di un mese, il quale continuava andare a stare con detto Jacopo nella detta camera." Onestà 2, fol. 22^r.

These demonstrations of affection soon turned into heavy-handed wooing, and the young object of desire stated that Pauli started to follow him everywhere:

> he followed him constantly and went to see him at the loan desk and at school, under the pretext that he wanted to talk, and he went to see his father and mother. Among other things, he once told him that he was happy just to go up to his house, promising him that if he ever needed hunting dogs or money, he would not want for them.[49]

Pauli's expectations also developed into outbursts of candid jealousy:

> and when he [Paulino] left the loan desk, he was always accompanied by the cashier, Ipolito di Vincenti Landucci. When Ser Biagio saw them together, he wrote to Ipolito that it would please him if he did not accompany him. [50]

Ippolito discussed the matter with his friend, complaining that he had been followed and threatened. Pauli's persistence must, however, have produced the desired effect since Paulino eventually yielded to him, according to the statements he made in court:

> And to speak quite freely, Ser Biagio flattered me so much that his kind words made me go to his house. He led me onto the loggia of his house and with his kind words and persuasion he sodomized me on one occasion.[51]

---

[49] "lo seguitava di continuo et lo andava a trovare et al banco et a squola sotto pretesto che volea parlare et a suo padre et a sua madre, et fra le altre una volta li disse che si contentasse andare fino a casa sua promettendoli che sempre che se li occorresse cani da caccia o, denari, che non li mancherà." Onestà 2, fol. 22ʳ.

[50] "et quando si partiva dal banco era sempre accompagnato dal cassiere Ipolito di Vincenti Landucci a tal che Ser Biagio vedendolo accompagnare scrisse al detto Ipolito che li haveria fatto piacere che non lo accompagnasse." Onestà 2, fol. 22ᵛ.

[51] "Et per dirla *liberamente* questo Ser Biagio tanto mi lusinghò et per tanto che con buone parole mi fece andare a casa sua dove condutto il detto Ser Biagio andato in loggia di essa sua casa con tante buone parole et persuasioni mi sogdomitò una volta." Onestà 2, fol. 22v.

The situation became almost paradoxical when the youngster confided in the Officers that he no longer knew how to rid himself of Pauli because he had become close to his parents. He then accused Jacopo Burlamacchi of being an accomplice, pointing out quite rightly that the attention he received must have been noticed because of its explicitness, and that when he had spoken about the advances, he was warned sternly not to confess everything to his father as he wanted to.[52] When interrogated, Jacopo initially denied having any complicity in the matter ("it will never be found that the party in question was pushed to subjugate Paulo to Ser Biagio"), but ended up confessing that he himself had been Pauli's lover, receiving a fine of twelve and a half *scudi*.[53]

Despite these examples, it would be counter-productive both for historical understanding and political repercussions to identify pederasty and pedophilia with homosexual behaviours. It is not a matter of adapting research to agendas dictated by present-day LGBTQI activism, which would equate to falsifying history; there are no grounds for considering significant age gaps as a distinguishing feature of only homosexual behaviour in the Early Modern Period. The violence that young apprentices suffered from their masters was no different from that dished out to barely adolescent female servants working in upper-class households. The fact that more cases of rape against young children and boys were documented in the trial records of the Office of Decency is due to the nature of the sources. The court investigated cases of anal sex rather than violence against minors. It would be necessary to analyze other sources in order to conduct an adequate study of pedophilia (homo- and heterosexual), and it is hoped that new research in the fields of social history and the history of sexuality will lead to more rounded conclusions on the matter by working on aggregate data.[54]

When working on the Early Modern Period, it is also necessary to adopt a conceptual distinction between pedophilia and love for adolescents. However disgusting it may seem through the lens of present-day value systems, it should not be forgotten that girls could enter the marriage market after their twelfth birthday. Although the average age at first marriage rose during the sixteenth century, the studies conducted by David Herlihy and

---

[52] Onestà 2, fol. 23^r.

[53] "mai si troverà che esso constituto sia stato mosso a sottomettere Paulo a Ser Biagio"; Onestà 2, fols. 23^v–25^r.

[54] On violence against women, see Feci, Schettini, *La violenza contro le donne*; Corbin, *Violences sexuelles*.

Christiane Klapisch-Zuber on the Florentine cadastre reveal that at the end of the fifteenth century the average age at first marriage was around sixteen for girls, with husbands who were, on average, between ten and fifteen years older.[55] Because equivalent data for Lucca in the fifteenth and sixteenth centuries is not available, little more can be done than to raise the issue in the hope that new research will provide answers. If the pattern of age at first marriage in Lucca corresponded with that in Florence, then the age difference in homosexual relations documented by the Office of Decency would appear to be far less pronounced overall.

One particularly wretched case can be used to compare the abuses against male and female adolescents. In 1582, an eleven-year-old girl was lured into a barn by her peer Apollonia, who had run off with "a headcloth and a neckerchief" so that she would give chase:

> and as soon as she was in the said place Apollonia made as if to shut the door and then picked up some straw and threw it at the party in question; in the meantime, a man entered the stable and covered her with a cloak that he had and the straw so that she could barely breathe. Scared stiff, she started to cry, and Apollonia put a hand over her mouth [...] so that she could not scream; meanwhile, the man that entered the stable threw her into the straw and did what he wanted to her, both in front and behind. When he had done what he wanted, [and] when a haycart passed in front of the barn she was sent out.[56]

Apollonia, the young accomplice, admitted that she had acted on commission and then revealed that she and two other girls named Oliva and Laurina were part of a gang of occasional underage prostitutes. These

---

[55] Herlihy, Klapisch-Zuber, *Tuscans and their Families*, 203–211.

[56] "una pezza di capo e un tovagliuolino da collo"; "et come fu in detto luogo detta Apollonia fece atto di serrare l'uscio, et poi prese della paglia et la tirava addosso a ditta constituta; intanto entrò uno in detta stalla et con il ferraiuolo che havea et con la paglia la coperse di modo che non poteva a pena fiatare et tutta spaurita cominciò a gridare, et detta Apollonia li misse la mano alla bocca [...] acciò non potesse gridare; intanto quell'huomo entro in detta stalla, la buttò in detta paglia et fece quel che vuolse con lei per divanti et per dietro, et fatto quanto volse, passando un carro di fieno davanti detta stalla fu mandata fuora." Onestà 3, 1588, unnumbered folio (9 June, deposition of Alessandrina di Betto da Terranuova).

twelve- and thirteen-year-old girls roamed the city, alone and together, going "to various men's houses for carnal knowledge."[57] Whether they were raped or paid, forced or consenting, the girls appeared before the Officers on several occasions to answer the same question: had they had relations against nature? The judges showed little interest in their extremely young age or their suffering. Many men were summoned, imprisoned, and tortured as a result of their depositions; some were convicted and sentenced to ten years in exile, while the girls were released on condition that for four months they would be supervised by their mothers whenever they went out. The girls were later called back to testify and were tortured because there were doubts about the truthfulness of their accusations. Because there is a gap in the sources, the conclusion to their story remains unknown. Nonetheless, we can see that no respect was shown to young teenagers and children, be they male or female, when the spectre of sodomy haunted their reputation.

---

[57] "a casa di questo e di quello per farsi conoscere"; Onestà 3, 1582, unnumbered folio.

CHAPTER 7

SEXUAL ACTS, HOMOEROTIC FEELINGS

While the first part of this book attempted to explain the reasons for the institutional regulation of sodomy, the second explored the sociability and everyday life of those caught up in the judicial prosecution of the 'nefarious crime.'
This elusive phenomenon involving complex areas of human experience
such as urges, affections, and emotions cannot be reduced to a mechanistic
explanation. As I have already stated in the Introduction, studies on male
homoeroticism based on criminal sources often tended to reflect the perspective of the judicial institutions. In fact, we need to keep in mind that it was the
sexual act itself, and not the motivation behind it, that was prosecuted and
punished. Superficial use of the sources will provide only an extremely reductive picture of male homoerotic desire and its forms of expression. However,
the reduction of early modern homosexual practices to mere mechanical
acts was one of the main conceptual frameworks that dominated the social
history of male homosexuality in studies conducted in the 1980s and 1990s.
This approach quite rightly provoked reactions, with Alan Bray's research on
homoerotic friendships marking the watershed. Bray was not concerned with
demonstrating whether, and if so to what extent, sex played a role in these
relations, and criticized previous historians for their obsession with seeking
evidence of the consummated act.[1]

Effective solutions to these methodological problems were first outlined
in studies on female homosexuality. There are significantly fewer trial sources
relevant to historians of lesbianism than those available to their counterparts
studying male homosexuality.[2] A reason for this is to be found in the fact that
legislation identified sex with penetration — a reflection of the mentality of
the time —, so female sexual acts did not fall under the jurisdiction of the
criminal courts unless a dildo was used or one of the partners had (or rather

---

[1] Bray, *The Friend*, 6. Some of the theoretical reflections in this chapter draw on my
recent chapter, "Emotions and Sexuality."

[2] Trial records, however, are not completely lacking, as evidenced in: Puff, "Female
Sodomy"; Velasco, *Lesbians in Early Modern Spain*; Vainfas, "The Nefarious and the Colony," 357–363. For an overview of female sodomy in criminal law, see Crompton, "Myth
of Lesbian Impunity."

was believed to have) a sufficiently developed clitoris to allow penetration (which had to be attested by a medical report).[3] It was this difficulty in collecting concrete evidence that prompted new methodological solutions. Lilian Faderman and Adrienne Rich focused on the importance of friendship in establishing female homoerotic bonds.[4] Judith M. Bennett wondered to what extent the exclusive legislative focus on penetration might have increased the scope of freedom for same-sex attracted women, providing useful methodological suggestions for working with the elusive evidence of this 'covert' history.[5] Some critics have claimed, however, that this historiography runs the risk of excessively 'desexualizing' lesbian desire by inadvertently reinforcing certain heteronormative stereotypes about the supposedly 'ethereal' and 'sublimated' character of female sexuality.[6]

As we discussed in the introduction, Queer theories had an extremely productive impact on the history of homosexuality, broadening the horizons of research and using new theoretical tools to shift attention onto new sources, from the literal to the figurative.[7] However, in the context of the early modern period these developments led to the abandonment of the bottom-up approach to social history, with researchers focusing instead on members of society who were able to document their experiences in forms other than defence statements in criminal courts.

Recent studies in the field of the history of emotions — an increasingly consolidated discipline — have generated a set of interpretative tools that are now enabling historians to return to criminal sources, integrating the critical insights from queer history into their analysis.[8] As Zeb Tortorici's *Sins against Nature* has recently and convincingly proven,[9] these new methodologies can now provide a rich array of previously inaccessible meanings, moving beyond the institutional desire to reduce moral infractions to episodes of sexual contact devoid of any significance and showing instead their various impacts on the subjectivity of those subjected to prosecution, those who exerted control above them, society as a whole, and, last but not least, the historian who uncovers their stories.

---

[3] Traub, "The (In)Significance of 'Lesbian' Desire"; Simons, "Lesbian (In)Visibility"; Alfieri, "Impossibili unioni di uguali."

[4] Faderman, *Surpassing the Love of Men*; Rich, "Compulsory Heterosexuality."

[5] Bennett, *History Matters*, 108–127.

[6] Donoghue, *Passions Between Women*.

[7] See above, "Introduction," 15–16.

[8] See above, "Introduction," 20.

[9] See above, "Introduction," 17.

This chapter will apply these new interpretative tools to three areas of historical research on premodern male homosexual desire. It will start by deconstructing the functionalist 'hydraulic' template that sometimes influenced historians who used criminal archives when they attempted to 'explain the reasons' for the spread of sodomitic practices. Following Monique Scheer's interpretation of emotions as social practices, it will then examine the meaning of 'hook-up' rituals in semi-clandestine sodomitic sociability, analyzing the performative power of collective practices and their value in the construction of social identities. Finally, it will explore the complex emotional lexicon occasionally reported by notaries in their trial records in an attempt to understand the implications of the interpersonal dynamics characteristic of same-sex interaction in early modern societies, in relation to normative models and expressions of love in the heterosexual family.

When investigating past homoeroticism, bottom-up studies reconstructing the history of homosexuality in the early modern age have sometimes been affected by mechanical models. Although often extremely refined in their analysis, historians sometimes manifested implicit assumptions regarding the nature of sexual urges and emotional life; these assumptions can now be identified and thus overcome. The definition of a 'hydraulic model' draws on psychological theories and common-sense views that depict emotions using the metaphor of a 'fluid' filling the mind and body. The pressure exerted by this fluid is said to explain many aspects of psychological life, such as feeling an urgent need to express certain emotions, frustration at the inability to do so, conflict created by the need to contain them, and uncontrolled emotional outbursts. The hydraulic metaphor may be valid in some instances, but it cannot be applied to all aspects of emotional life. Our conceptual horizons have been broadened by the new scientific acquisitions. One of the most significant changes is the understanding that emotions contribute to cognitive processes. Emotional phenomena are no longer interpreted as independent from the intellect that keeps their 'disruptive' flow in check. Instead, the focus is on discovering the complex relationship of interdependency between cognition, volition, desires, and feelings. Emotions do not exist independently from the controlling self; they can also be nurtured, refined, even desired, as well as controlled.[10]

---

[10] Solomon, *True to our Feelings*, 142–149.

A dualistic interpretation of emotional life based on the rationality-irrationality dichotomy was used as a subtext in early twentieth-century studies, such as *The Autumn of the Middle Ages* by Johan Huizinga (1919) and *Civilizing Process* by Norbert Elias (1939), that paved the way for the history of emotions.[11] Since these pioneering works were published, new discoveries in the fields of the neurosciences and social sciences, and especially in anthropology and ethnography, have helped to transform our understanding of emotional phenomena and influence historical research.[12] As with any implicit assumption, the dualism between 'reason' and 'feelings' operates like a subconscious 'plot' that cannot be used knowingly, revisited, or modified unless it is first understood.[13] In this respect, the materialistic explanation of the spread of sodomitic behaviours among young men in premodern urban contexts reflects a reductive interpretation of a complex phenomenon, and not simply a consequence of an absence of 'legitimate' partners (namely, women). We have seen that the defendants in trials conducted by the Office of Decency were mostly young. While belated access to marriage and full social maturity was the reason for their unruliness, as well as the relative institutional tolerance of their non-normative behaviour, this cannot fully explain the spread of homosexual practices in this age group. As we have seen in previous chapters, society was not rigidly divided by sex and gender. The idea of requiring an outlet for urges (valid in segregated places such as prisons, the army, the navy, and monasteries) is thus only partially pertinent to an Italian urban context in the fifteenth and sixteenth centuries; as we have seen, the presence (and relative acceptance) of prostitution, along with many female figures expressing their sexuality quite openly, made women widely accessible objects of desire.

---

[11] The effects of the 'hydraulic model' can nevertheless still be found, in my opinion, in Reddy's *Navigation of Feelings*, though the author is well aware of the new theories on emotions developed by the neurosciences. In Reddy's view, revolutions are caused by an accumulation of tensions resulting from the adoption of overly restrictive 'emotional regimes,' leading to the construction of 'emotional refuges' and eventually the collapse of political authority under the impetus of subversive forces.

[12] There is an excellent summary in Plamper, *History of Emotions*, 75–146 (on social sciences); 206–250 (on neurosciences). A controversial attempt to use the neurosciences in historical research was made by Boddice in his *History of Emotions*.

[13] Although significantly predating the development of the field of the history of emotions, and not actually related to it, Hayden White's *Metahistory* is fundamental for an understanding of the influence of subconscious 'plots' on the writing of history.

Material and practical factors contributed to the formation of value systems that included time- and place-specific concepts of morality and sexual behaviour. Homosexual desire was not only a prohibited drive or an originally a heterosexual urge re-oriented towards more accessible outlets. Indeed, it occupied a place in a unique economy of desire where same-sex relations within a certain age group were deemed to be a possible pleasure-seeking option. This held true both for equal relations between peers, who were relatively free to experiment, and those with a wider age difference.

The Officers' habit of 'negotiating' sentences for young offenders and of handing out far softer penalties than those imposed by the Statutes shows that, in practice, controlled freedom of experimentation was allowed in this area. It might have been precisely for this reason that the rhetoric of laws was so harsh, using written reprimands to counterbalance the mildness of the actual court proceedings. While a certain amount of laissez-faire was accepted, it was important for the Statutes to highlight the danger of a habit that was in any case considered anti-social and sinful; it could not be allowed to spread beyond the boundaries of human, civil, and spiritual maturity imposed by the transition into adulthood. As Michael J. Rocke pointed out in a study on Bernardino da Siena, even the famous fifteenth-century preacher, who was one of the most hardened fifteenth-century critics of the 'nefarious sin,' thought that it was still possible, within certain time limits, to convert one's practices to the socially and morally acceptable heterosexual pattern, tacitly admitting that sexual desire was not fully defined before the age of thirty. It was only when a sodomite's sexual practices continued beyond this threshold that his fate became dangerously irreversible.[14] Therefore, young men did not turn to same-sex intercourse in order to 'compensate' for the absence of women; they lived in a climate where homosexual desire could be nurtured and expressed in concrete acts, albeit under constant surveillance. In these contexts, desires and emotions that were (and still are) subjected to more radical prohibition in other emotional regimes could flourish and be explored.

---

[14] As Michael J. Rocke writes: "Bernardino's curious insistence that thirty-two or thirty-three was a crucial turning point in a young man's sexual life can only be understood in light of two further considerations. Florentine demographic studies have shown that precisely during the years Bernardino was preaching in Florence, men married at an average age of around thirty or thirty-one. This might not necessarily have much bearing on Bernardino's argument were it not for a second point: the preacher insisted equally strongly that men who failed to marry were or became sodomites." Rocke, "Sodomites in Fifteenth-Century Tuscany," 17–18.

The leeway that was deliberately given to express this desire led to the construction of a culture that, although semi-clandestine, did not exist in isolation, but was determined by relations with other social agents. In the case of Lucca, the richest sources for reconstructing semi-clandestine sodomitic sociability are the trials in the 1550s and 1560s that we examined in the second part of Chapter 4. The documents revealed a material culture of homosexual relations not unlike what historical studies uncovered in other European urban contexts in the Middle Ages and the Early Modern Period. Apart from certain distinctive features, the trial records from Lucca, Venice, Florence, cities in England, Germany, Switzerland, France, Spain, Portugal, and colonies in the great Iberian empires all share many common traits.[15] In each city there were designated places for encounters (some more specific, like the city walls or river in Lucca and Florence, others more common, such as public baths and pubs) and precise hook-up rituals, with sometimes ambiguous sexual allusions between adults, and offers of gifts, food, and small sums of money for the youths. There seems to have been a general prevalence of anal sex and masturbation, with only very incidental accounts of oral sex

Although occasional sex is the distinctive feature of this semi-clandestine sociability, it cannot be inferred that this was a neutral act, a simple outlet for urges with no impact on self-perception or the place occupied by the self in society. First and foremost, despite the relatively laissez-faire attitude sometimes adopted by society as a whole, same-sex intercourse could in any case lead to a criminal charge and, in the worst-case scenario, the death penalty. A verbal and physical communication code was thus required to convey intentions in a clear but implicit way. We have already seen various examples of how hook-ups often started with allusive references to something (not directly named) that the interlocutor was supposed to grasp. Studies on the Spanish Inquisition have revealed interesting details about body language

---

[15] For Venice, Ruggiero, *Boundaries of Eros* and Martini, *Vitio nefando*; for Florence, see Rocke, *Forbidden Friendships*. For England, see Bray, *Homosexuality in Renaissance England*; Norton, *Mother Clap's Molly House*. For Germany and Switzerland, see Hergemöller, *Sodom and Gomorrah*; Puff, *Sodomy in Reformation Germany and Switzerland*; Naphy, "Sodomy in Early Modern Geneva." For France, see Merrick, Sibalis, *Homosexuality in French History and Culture*. For Spain, see Carrasco, *Inquisición y represión sexual*; Berco, *Sexual Hierarchies*. For Portugal, see Johnson and Dutra, *Pelo Vaso Traseiro*. For the Iberian empires, see Tortorici, *Sins Against Nature*; Sigal, *Infamous Desire*; Trexler, *Sex and Conquest*; Vainfas, Ronaldo. *Trópico dos pecados.*

and the signs used by defendants to negotiate their sexual relations.[16] Moral theology works and educational handbooks warned about clothes that were overly refined or other external signs that feminized boys.[17] Clothing was indeed a crucially important element in the normative definition of gender in early modern societies. Sixteenth-century sartorial conventions gradually strengthened the distinctions between men and women, and treatises made an association between the sense of appropriateness and gender performance, encouraging a clear separation of the male and female spheres. Clothes were seen as a 'second skin' that helped to decipher the underlying biological structure.[18] Erasmus applied this concept when he wrote that "clothing is in a way the body's body."[19] The analogy between skin and clothing was a powerful metaphor of Renaissance culture, one that sodomites were accused of exploiting for their sexual purposes. In order to navigate the waters of sexual transgression safely without becoming entangled in the nets of criminal justice (civil or secular), the repertoire of all these communication codes had to be learnt through experience.

Monique Scheer has suggested that Pierre Bourdieu's theoretical considerations on social practices should be adopted to study the history of emotions. The repetition of certain social rituals involves a process of internalizing and incorporating rituals and collective practices that, by becoming automatic, come to be part of a semi-conscious mental universe and are thus far more powerful in determining an individual's behaviours and cognitive processes. In the case of homoerotic sociability, we have no reason to believe that, while the act of entering this semi-clandestine world did not necessarily mean knowingly subscribing to a counter-cultural model, it did not also alter the sense of self of those involved. This is even more plausible given the extent to which identity construction in early modern societies was largely dominated by membership in variously structured social groups in the form of communes, guilds, classes, confraternities, military companies, courts, and local neighbourhoods among others. Although there is no evidence for this

---

[16] Body language emerged most notably in the study of Spanish Inquisition sources by Carrasco, *Inquisición y represión sexual*, 135. There is an extremely vivid description of the effeminate gestures of sodomites in a seventeenth-century text by the Jesuit Pedro de León, *Grandeza y miseria*, 437–438.

[17] Rocke, "Sodomites in Fifteenth-Century Tuscany," 12–13.

[18] Talvacchia, "Introduction," 12–17.

[19] Erasmus, *On Good Manners for Boys*, 278. The passage is discussed in Talvacchia, "Introduction," 17.

in Lucca, it should be remembered that in contemporary Florence, which as we know used strong measures to control sodomy, a well-known painter such as Giovanni Antonio Bazzi (1477–1549) could provocatively assume the name "Sodoma," irreverently affirming his sexual preferences in a climate where some of the most influential voices in the community used the story of heavenly fire descending on Sodom and Gomorrah to justify burning sodomites at the stake.

Sodomy was not a fixed category. Legal and legislative sources in Lucca seem to corroborate the idea of an association between sodomy and male-male sexual intercourse. The 1539 Statutes clearly defined the crime as a form of "detestable rape that is done against nature with a male and is called sodomy."[20] This definition needs to be unpacked. First, there are some issues with translating the word *stupro* from ancient Italian. Although in modern Italian it means "rape", in medieval and early modern Italian legal language, or indeed common usage, the term was not necessarily used to label non-consensual and violent sexual intercourse. The term could, for example, describe consensual sex with a virgin woman. Regardless of violence, which along with consent is crucial to our definition of a sexual offence, *stupro* was considered a serious wrongdoing to the extent that it damaged the honour of the aggrieved party and compromised her future ability to marry.[21] The term, however, was also used to label any use of sexuality that was deemed improper or inordinate in the eyes of Christian morality. Therefore, in this context the term *stupro* should not be interpreted as a synonym of homosexual rape. Furthermore, sodomy was defined as the type of sex against nature that was committed among men. This is reminiscent of a long tradition influenced by Aquinas that used to qualify sodomy as a subcategory within the broader framework of 'unnatural' sexual sins. Crimes against nature and sodomy are not synonyms and, at least in theological terms, the two definitions cannot be conflated. From the second half of the sixteenth century onwards, Aquinas's definition equating sodomy to homogenitality (male-male and female-female sex) was often repeated in the context of moral theology and casuistry. Unreproductive sex between women and men, conversely, was not catalogued as sodomy but as an 'improper mode of intercourse.'[22] It is worth

---

[20] "stupro detestabile, il quale si dice contra *natura* farsi nel maschio, lo quale chiamano sodomia"; *Statuti della Città di Lucca*, Book IV, Chap. 108, fols. 216ᵛ–221ᵛ.

[21] See above, Chapter 5, 96–98.

[22] Hurteau, "Catholic Moral Discourse on Male Sodomy," 8–12.

noting, however, that the Lucchese legislators mentioned only male-male sex, disregarding female homosexual relations. This is further proof of the idea of the 'invisibility' of female homoeroticism outlined at the beginning of this chapter. The clarity of the legal definition of sodomy as male homosexual intercourse is, however, contradicted by actual judicial procedure. The confused nature of the taxonomies that preceded Aquinas's systematization appears to survive in the popular understanding, seemingly confirmed by the fact that the Office of Decency also tried men and women charged with anal intercourse. Due to the abundant presence of such cases, sodomy and homosexuality cannot be seen, in practice, as two overlapping categories. It looks therefore as if there was a discrepancy between written laws and judicial practice and, as we will see at the end of the chapter, between different understandings of homoerotic attraction in popular culture.

A complex picture of sexual behaviours emerges from the documentation, one that features cases in which defendants clearly stated that they had sex with both men and women. On 3 April 1554 an eighteen-year-old Lucchese haberdasher was imprisoned for three months for sodomitic relations with two men and four women. In 1560, a prostitute from Camaiore confessed that she had committed the crime with two men, one of whom, Stefano di Francesco Bella Barba, still eighteen at the time, was convicted of sodomizing a boy a few days later. Bella Barba reappeared in the Office records the following year, although it is unclear whether in reference to fresh allegations or another trial, and again in 1579, when he was thirty-seven, as one of the men present at the *stufa* when Pasquina was raped (see Chapter 5). Although there were no charges against him on that occasion, the fact that he frequented public baths might suggest that he was a repeat offender, along with three of his brothers whose names crop up several times in the 1550s and 1560s.

There were also married men, although the documentation on this matter is somewhat scant; little was stated about the marital status of defendants and relations with women were mentioned only in the limited number of cases involving anal sex. It is thus probable that many men who were tried for homosexual encounters also had undocumented relations with women, but these heterosexual relations had no criminal relevance because they did not involve moral infractions. It is equally likely, although impossible to document, that many hid their homosexual desire behind cover-up marriages.

In 1592, a thirty-five-year-old man from Lucca with a wife and children was charged for his long-standing relations with a younger boy named

Bartolomeo. The two were arrested and tried after being caught in flagrante during a nocturnal raid by one of the *targetti* from Gattaiola and the Bargello. As the older man explained, their relationship began when, "after leaving prison this youngster became my friend and often came round [to my house] to eat but did not sleep there." After meeting up regularly for a year, the man decided to give Bartolomeo his daughter in marriage and welcomed into the family home on an almost permanent basis, as well as gave him financial support. Given the uncertainty of the defendant's finances, who claimed to "be a poor man", the Officers found it less than "plausible" that he would maintain the youth for two years without "any certainty or promise of marriage [to the daughter]." They thus urged him to "tell the real reason for his intimacy with Bartolomeo, since it is known that he ate and conversed with him not as a future son-in-law but as an equal and with great familiarity."[23] The man's wife was also questioned several times. Despite her claims that she had been involved in her husband's decisions and was happy to have Bartolomeo as a future son-in-law because he was "a good and honest lad," her many inconsistencies were highlighted and she was found to have made false statements in an attempt to protect the two men.[24] Even Bartolomeo said that the man "never openly said that he would give me his daughter, but he told me: 'if you're a good boy, we could become in-laws.'"[25]

In the end, a confession was extracted through agonising torture. While Bartolomeo corroborated the man's offer of his daughter's hand in marriage, he also admitted having carnal relations with him for the previous two years: "I was passive and was never anything else [...] he never sought to be passive himself [...] he never caused me any ruptures or made me bleed."[26] After his

---

[23] "et uscito di prigione questo giovane prese mia amicizia et veniva spesso a mangiare ma non ci dormiva"; "sendo pover'homo"; "verisimile"; "certezza né promessa alcuna del matrimonio"; "dire la vera causa della intrinsichezza con detto Bartolomeo, poiché si sa che mangiava et conversava seco non come futuro genero ma come equale et molto familiarmente"; Onestà 3, 1592, fols. 21ʳ–23ᵛ.

[24] "buon figliuolo et honesto"; Onestà 3, fol. 29ʳ⁻ᵛ: "And when told that both things cannot be true as they are contradictory, she did not know what else to say" ("Et dettoli che non può stare che sia vero l'uno et l'altro sendo contrarii, non seppe dire altro"), fol. 29ᵛ.

[25] "non mi ha mai scoperto alla libera di darmi sua figliuola, ma mi diceva bene: 'se sarai buon figliolo ci potremmo apparentare insieme'"; Onestà 3, unnumbered folio and fol. 30ᵛ.

[26] "io ero paziente et non sono mai stato altrimente [...] esso non mi ha mai ricerco di essere lui paziente [...] non mi ha mai fatto rottura alcuna né fatto uscire sangue"; Onestà 3, fols. 31ʳ–33ʳ.

admission of guilt, his man also crumbled before the Officers after lengthy torture, confirming: "I was always active and never passive." He justified himself by saying that he was "of a mind to give him my daughter in marriage and overcome this mistake."[27] Both men were exiled, the youth for four years and the adult for twenty. The latter was also deprived of all privileges of citizenship in perpetuity.[28]

This case shows that premodern homosexual desire does not necessarily have to be studied within the theoretical framework of counter- or subcultures. The attempt the wife made to cover up her husband's infractions gives the impression that among common people there was a high degree of flexibility in adapting the established Christian moral codes to the everyday life. This resulted in nuanced and porous boundaries dividing normative and non-normative behaviours. It could be suggested that focusing on homoerotic desire *within* the boundaries of the family would lead to a better understanding of some features not only of past homoeroticism but also of premodern conjugal life. As already mentioned in the introduction, for a long time the history of the family devalued the intensity and quality of emotional and affective bonds in early modern households. The hierarchical nature of spousal relationships, the autocratic power exercised by paterfamilias over his subjects (women and minors), the strategical considerations that customarily oriented the choice of partner in upper-class families, the mostly economical nature of the family unit in lower class environments, as well as other factors such as the high rates of (especially child) mortality have led scholars of the family to believe that feelings of affection and deep emotional connections were not allowed to flourish within the boundaries of the premodern family.[29] This well-established interpretation has long been under challenge. Scholarship on the history of emotions has recently contributed to shaping a much more nuanced picture of the emotional depth of familial relationships in medieval and early modern times.[30] Looking at the intensity of homoerotic feelings within the family unit might help to take further steps in this direction, shedding light on the complexity of past emotional lives. As the case analyzed above shows, shifting the focus from parental and spousal

---

[27] "io sono stato sempre agente e non mai paziente"; "di animo di darli mia figliuola per moglie e di uscire di questo errore"; Onestà 3, fols. 33^r–34^v.

[28] Onestà 3, fol. 35^{r-v}.

[29] Ariès, *Centuries of Childhood*; Stone, *Family, Sex and Marriage*; Shorter, *Making of the Modern Family*; Trumbach, *Rise of the Egalitarian Family*.

[30] Ozment, *Ancestors*; Barclay, *Love, Intimacy, Power*.

relationships to the household as a whole might contribute to widening our horizons.[31] While a liberal tradition in studies on the family has tended to associate the growth of feelings of affection among family members with the development and progressive affirmation (in the West) of the nuclear family based on the free choice of partners, the extended networks that character-ized the premodern household (which included labourers and servants) may be read as the site of differentiated sets of emotional bonds that deserve to be understood. Moreover, what has been interpreted as an absence of privacy within these contexts could instead be viewed as a chance to multiply layers of intimacy and solidarity, as well as opportunities for diversified forms of sexual gratification.

In other social and historical contexts, scholars have proven that the lexicon of homoerotic affection was often modelled on the vocabulary of heterosexual spousal love. The most significant documents to this end are probably letters confiscated by the Portuguese Inquisition in the seventeenth century, rediscovered by Luiz Mott and Aroldo Assunção.[32] There are, how-ever, also lots of other less poetic and moving accounts in sixteenth- and seventeenth-century trial records, especially with regard to the Iberian Pen-insula and colonies. Homosexual relations were often described using the lexicon of conjugal love. When alluding to sodomy, it was said that two men had slept together "like husband and wife."[33] Amorous vocabulary included expressions such as "falling in love," "speaking in loving terms," "requesting love," and "making merry and love" ("enamorarse," "decir amores," "requerir amores," "haciéndose fiestas y amores").[34] This association between spousal love and homoerotic relations is a significant element not only for under-standing homoaffectivity but also for providing a broader perspective on the concept of family relations both in the elites and the popular classes. These el-ements seem to further prove that the binary opposition between interest and feeling in the social history of the family and the claim that affective ties were missing in contexts where material needs and survival were of the essence

---

[31] Historical studies now show that strategic decisions were often made in households (units of affection and production cells) to conserve the unity and cohesion of the group even at the expense of more immediate economic benefits: Barclay, "The Emotions of Household Economics."

[32] Mott, Assunção, "Love's Labors Lost." There is another equally touching epistolary in Mott, "My Pretty Boy."

[33] Carrasco, *Inquisición y represión sexual*, 108.

[34] Carrasco, *Inquisición y represión sexual*,102.

are products of contemporary Western dualism. The fact that people from the lower classes at the time used the lexicon of spousal love to describe the emotional and passionate aspect of homosexual relations seems to confirm that in certain contexts the quality of love in a conjugal relationship offered a universally applicable reference model in their mental universe. This love was therefore not limited to the simple necessity to guarantee material security to the parties in a marriage contract and all those living under their roof.[35]

In his study on Florence Michael Rocke hypothesized that sometimes upper-class families were involved in the liaisons of their male children with mature homosexual partners and that these relations could play a strategical role comparable to that of the marriage alliances of their young daughters. We cannot exclude a priori that this was the case in the story of the relationship between Ser Biagio Pauli and Paulino di Michele Fondora, described in the previous chapter. The interactions between Pauli and Fondora's parents may hide something more than what is explicitly reported in the sources. Whatever the case may be, Ser Biagio's free circulation in the home of his younger object of desire seems to suggest that the boundaries between familial life and the practice of sodomy where much more porous than previous historical analysis might suggest. What is more, the highly emotional description of the older man's attachment to his young beloved seems to prove the intensity of the emotional life that could accompany homosexual interactions in the early modern world.

In contrast with many other examples elsewhere, the few cases where the Lucchese notaries recorded details that bear witness to emotional involvement between two men use a vocabulary that predominantly referred to friendship rather than familial affection. The occasional sexual encounters documented in trials in the 1550s and 1560s include relations of varying lengths. When "accusing himself," Girolamo di Paulino dalla Cuna confessed that he had had many partners, including one with whom he had had sex "many times last winter at Tommaso Spada's house, during the day and at night, and likewise during the summer of this year at night."[36] After three weeks in prison following his confession that he "had been sodomized" by seventeen individuals, Baldassarre *del sordo* (son of the deaf man), who as we

---

[35] For a fuller discussion, see Grassi, "Emotions and Sexuality."

[36] "se accusando"; "più volte la invernata passata, in casa di Tommaso Spada, di dì e di notte, et questa estate parimenti di questo anno di notte"; Onestà 1, 1568, fol. 38ʳ. Girolamo di Paolino's lover was Rocco Boccella, a spinner.

have seen was one of the main figures in the 1568 trials, added other names to his long list. Only in one of these cases were the relations ongoing (a dozen times), and the youth described their bond by saying that he "had become friends" with him "since Lent."[37] It is possible that the delay in making a statement was an attempt to protect his lover.

They "had become friends." As already mentioned, historical research has revealed the connections in the Early Modern Period between the lexicon of friendship and homoerotic ties. While historians of homosexuality have contrasted the model of conjugal love to that of same-sex friendship in the shaping of homoerotic desire (at least up to the eighteenth century), I suggest that these paradigms might have played a concurrent role at a much earlier time already. According to previous interpretations, many of the elements that are now considered constituent parts of the ideal of romantic conjugal love were established features characterizing same-sex friendships. The family was the basic constituent of society, a production unit that also transmitted the core values of the social order. Friendships between well-educated cultured people were credited with intellectual fecundity and shared values that rarely featured in the more functional and pragmatic accounts of conjugal love. This interpretation, however, suffers from an excessive devaluation of the emotional depth of premodern familial bonds.

If we go beyond this binary, however, and analyse the cultural construction of same-sex friendship, we can shed more light on some important aspects of late medieval and early modern homoeroticism. These ties often took shape as preferential relations that were socially accepted and respected.[38] In *The Friend*, Alan Bray analyzes forms of ritual kinship by examining indirect sources, above all funerary monuments that depicted pairs of 'sworn brothers,' suggesting that they could be remnants of "practices and experiences that have simply no modern equivalents."[39] Bray rejects the idea that emotional life in premodern societies was somehow less profound than today and questions the liberal concept that intimacy is the result of the middle-class nuclear family in modern Western societies. Although Bray was a gay activist, in this work he bucks the militant historiographical trend of outing

---

[37] "essere stato sogdomitato"; "aver preso amicizia"; "da quaresima in qua"; Onestà 1, fol. 24ᵛ.

[38] In addition to Bray, *The Friend*, see the pioneering work by Gaetano Cozzi, *Una vicenda della Venezia barocca* (I thank Stefano Villani for this recommendation); Gowing, Hunter, Rubin, *Love, Friendship and Faith*; Puff, "Early Modern Europe."

[39] Bray, *The Friend*, 40.

historical figures retrospectively by using these friendships as evidence of the transhistoricity of modern homosexuality.[40] As David Halperin notes in *How to Do the History of Homosexuality*, a seminal methodological work, these interpretations suffer from an inability to read texts through the filter of the rhetoric of the time in question. It should not be forgotten how much the lexicon of friendship was deeply indebted to literary models that were part of the self-fashioning process used by educated men in the sixteenth century.[41]

The Middle Ages saw a resurgence of interest in friendship, a subject rooted in classical antiquity. The most celebrated example of this was Aelred of Rievaulx's *Spiritual Friendship* (twelfth century), which celebrated the importance of friendship for inner growth and the practice of 'agape' in monastic communities. His treatise offered a Christian reworking of the issues addressed by Cicero in *Laelius de Amicitia*, which provided the rhetoric of feelings of friendship.[42] Such sentiments strengthened relations between scholars of the humanities in the fifteenth and sixteenth centuries, helping to create an international community of correspondence that shaped the cultural life of Europe at the time. Erasmus had affectionate friendships with Thomas More, the Valencian humanist Juan Luis Vives, the German humanist Beatus Rhenanus, and the Antwerpian printer Pieter Gillis. Pietro Bembo's correspondents included Raphael, Baldassare Castiglione, and the humanist bishop Jacopo Sadoleto. In the Low Countries, Justus Lipsius was in contact with the geographer Abraham Ortelius, the poet Janus Dousa, the printer Cristopher Plantin, and the painter Peter Paul Rubens. The epithets used by these men of letters to address each other included expressions such as "sweetest" (*dulcissime*), "incomparable friend" (*amice incomparabilis*) and "sweetest and dear to my eyes" (*dulcissime mihique oculis charios*).[43]

The revival of the theme of Platonic love was also of great importance. Unlike the Ciceronian model, however, a more explicit context was created from Ficino onwards for the celebration of homoerotic attraction, albeit in chaste form, that survived until it was stamped out by the Counter-Reformation.[44] While the rhetoric of friendship developed on the basis of classical models, new social practices documented in source material helped to

---

[40] The most significant example in this respect is Crompton, *Homosexuality & Civilization*.

[41] Halperin, *How to Do the History of Homosexuality*, 117–121.

[42] Pezzini, "Aelred's Doctrine of Charity and Friendship."

[43] Burke, "Humanism and Friendship," 94.

[44] Dall'Orto, "'Socratic Love' as a Disguise for Same-Sex Love,"

strengthen friendships between intellectuals: inscriptions in books, portraits (such as the famous case of Erasmus and Pieter Gillis, painted by Quentin Massys) or the convention variously known as *Album amicorum*, *Liber amicorum* or *Hortus amicorum*, notebooks in which travellers collected the signatures of those encountered on their wanderings. Hundreds of examples of these can be found today in libraries throughout Europe.[45]

While historians must be aware of these cultural tropes when dealing with past homoeroticism, it would nevertheless be equally risky for them to exclude a priori that this rhetoric might have been used to legitimize homosexual love. Rather than studying past 'ancestors', it is more important to understand how a past cultural climate could offer the opportunity for the expression of same-sex attractions. It is no coincidence that the subject of virile friendship inspired by classical models was a constant in the construction of homoerotic discourse even when the first forms of homosexual self-awareness started to emerge more explicitly.[46] A more complete overview can be obtained by cross-checking different types of sources. Prescriptive sources such as moral treatises and behavioural handbooks, for example, recommended monitoring friendships on a constant basis for fear that they could be hiding homosexual relations. In her influential book on early modern female homoerotic desire, Valerie Traub claimed, for example, that from the early modern period onwards the unsettling spectre of Sapphic and tribadic love became part of the literary topos of female friendship, inspired by the model of Platonic love.[47] In *De Ratione Studii* (1511), a treatise on teaching the classics, Erasmus of Rotterdam wondered whether the passage from Vigil's second *Eclogue* about the love of the shepherd Corydon for young Alexis ("Formosus pastor Corydon ardebat Alexim") should be studied by altering the original text (an option not even considered) or risking the corruption of youngsters. To solve the problem, he invited teachers to use the passage to introduce a moral reflection on the differences between good (and appropriate) and bad friendships.[48] In his analysis of the passage, Helmut Puff shrewdly highlighted the risks of Erasmus's reasoning, namely that incorporating homoerotic desire within the model of virile friendship could lead to

---

[45] Burke, "Humanism and Friendship," 97–98.
[46] Norton, *Myth of the Modern Homosexual*, 127–130.
[47] Traub, *Renaissance of Lesbianism*, 276–325.
[48] Erasmus, *De ratione studii*, 83.

an association of the figures of friend and sodomite.[49] These risks seem to have been justified, given that the concept of "to become friends" (*prendere amicizia*) was used in Italy to refer to homosexual relations not just among the learned elite but also among the common people.

Given the scarcity of references to the emotional life of the defendants prosecuted by the Office of Decency, we do not, unfortunately, know what values were attached to homoerotic friendship in the juvenile environments that constitute the core of this research. Conversely, we have been able to observe the extent to which homoerotic relationships were shaped in a variety of cases depending on the life stage and social position of the individuals involved. We have seen the abuse of children but also strong emotional bonds between adults and younger partners. We have observed that homosexual relationships could be lived out within the intimate sphere of the household but also in public spaces such as streets, city walls, inns, and bathhouses. Along the river Serchio that flowed past Lucca this all took the form of a juvenile semi-clandestine culture. Homoerotic desire could express itself through the rhetoric of friendship, but was also integrated into the everyday life of extended households. The two models, friendship and familial love, were thus far from being mutually exclusive.

A brief fragment from a trial deposition provides an interesting final insight on the common perception of the relationship between sodomy and homoerotic attraction at the time. A young prostitute stated that a soldier had asked her for some unconventional sexual services, explaining that "he's not aroused by the front" because "he doesn't like women."[50] Regardless of whether this was a slanderous accusation against the accused, what counts for the purposes of this study is the fact that the woman was able to formulate such an allegation. The meaning of this extremely succinct phrase might have been seen as self-evident: the man had certain preferences. He may have been known for his misogyny, in line with the widespread feelings against women explored above.[51] Nevertheless, his reason for not liking women seems to be linked to the performance of an act — anal sex — rather than a preference for one gender (male, or in any case 'non-female'). At the same time, he saw one gender as significantly less attractive than the other ("non le piace le donne").

---

[49] Puff, *Sodomy in Reformation Germany and Switzerland*, 70–71. See also Grafton, *Defenders of the Text*, 38.

[50] "non ci tira davanti"; "non le piace le donne"; Onestà 4, 1597, fol. 58ᵛ.

[51] See above, Chapter 6, 119.

This connection is clearly contradictory; if his preference was for anal intercourse, it could have been satisfied with partners of either sex (which his choice of a female prostitute seems to suggest). However, if he did not like women, why did he decide to seek out a female prostitute for anal sex? From what we have seen, there seems to have been no shortage of available male partners at the time. The point is that the phrase combined two contrasting concepts of sodomy, irreconcilable opposites that typify its semantic instability. The first of these, which was always attributed to the category of 'sodomy' in the past by 'constructionist' historians, views it as a simple act carried out indifferently with men or women from the penetrator's perspective, while the second is a 'minoritizing' model that perceives sodomy as a preference despite its polymorphic aspect. When it took shape in this form, judging by the words of this uneducated prostitute it still seemed to gravitate hazardously, for men, towards the homosexual option.[52] Sodomy and homosexuality do not overlap, but they were, and still are, dangerously close friends.

---

[52] On 'minoritizing' versus 'universalizing' interpretations of homosexuality, see Sedgwick, *Epistemology of the Closet*, 9.

The Regulation of Sexual Behaviours in the Religious Crisis of the Sixteenth Century

CHAPTER 8

SODOMITES AND HERETICS

Although the Protestant Reformation never triggered any significant political upheaval on the Italian peninsula, the complex system of small states was a hotbed of religious ideas and experimentation. Support for Reformed doctrines was found, for the most part, in urban centres, assuming different characteristics according to the specific local context. Cities such as Venice, Ferrara, Modena, Cremona, Florence, and Naples had their own heterodox 'conventicles' that practiced a simpler faith, free from the superstitious beliefs and rituals, deeply critical of ecclesiastical corruption and skeptical about the calculations of merits and demerits underlying Church teachings. It is not easy to fit the plurality of religious experiences in sixteenth-century Italy into precise confessional frameworks, especially since most of the sources available for reconstructing episodes of dissent were drafted by the inquisitors fighting against them. Calvinism had a healthy following, as did more radical movements such as Anabaptistism and Antitrinitarianism, and one should also not forget the influence of more subtle reformers such as the Spanish Juan de Valdés.[1]

Along with Venice, which the historian Massimo Firpo described as the "gateway of the Reformation" in Italy,[2] Lucca was one of the cities that raised the most concern regarding the spread of heresy. The Republic was divided between followers of Catholic orthodoxy centred on the Dominican convent of San Romano and members of the new pro-Reformation movements centred at the Augustinian convent of San Frediano. By preaching the doctrine of justification *ex sola fide* (by faith alone) from the pulpits of the latter, the canons built up a following of proselytes that included important members of the mercantile and governing elite as well as members of middle- and working-class families.

---

[1] For an introduction to the Reformation in Italy, see especially Caponetto, *The Protestant Reformation in Sixteenth-Century Italy*, Seidel Menchi, "Italy," and Firpo, *Juan de Valdés and the Italian Reformation*. On Calvinism in Italy, see Felici, *Giovanni Calvino e l'Italia* and Barton, *Calvin and the Duchess*. On the radical reformation, see Biagioni, *Radical Reformation*.

[2] Firpo, *Riforma protestante ed eresie*, 11.

The year 1542 marked a turning point in the Roman Curia's effort to impose orthodoxy on the Italian peninsula with the institution of the Tribunal of the Holy Office of Rome (*Sant'Uffizio Romano*).[3] For over thirty years, Lucca resisted the Curia's constant attempts to establish an office of the Inquisition in the city, defending its jurisdictional and political autonomy at the cost of a draining diplomatic battle.[4] Although officially Lucca's institutions were always loyal to the Church of Rome, in practice they protected heretics by holding their own trials at their own secular magistracy — the Office of Religion (*Offizio sopra la religione*) — and by helping suspected citizens flee the peninsula.

The creation of this special court was a direct response to pressure from Rome. On 9 December 1543, a message arrived from Rome that read remarkably like a threat: if the city did not take prompt and definitive measures to wipe out heresy, "a doctor might well come there from outside, and God knows what medicine he may bring,"[5] a clear allusion to the Inquisition. On 12 May 1545, fearing that the situation might degenerate, the General Council established a graduated system of penalties for heresy meant to refine those already contained in the Statutes (exile and confiscation of property).[6] A fine of fifty gold ducats was now imposed for the first conviction, with confiscation of property for the second, while those who were "persistent and irredeemable [...] after the first and second punishment" and lapsed back "into the aforementioned errors" were sentenced to burn at the stake. Compliance with these measures was guaranteed by an Office of Three Respectable Citizens (*Offizio di tre spettabili cittadini*) operating in conjunction with the Standard-Bearer of Justice (*Gonfaloniere di Giustizia*). Elected annually, the purpose of this Office was to "find and prosecute delinquents, and deliver them to the Podestà of Lucca so that they can be sentenced in the manner of the Office of Decency according to the form of the Statutes."[7]

---

[3] On the Roman Inquisition, see Prosperi, *Tribunali della coscienza*; Romeo, *L'Inquisizione nell'Italia moderna*; Wickersham, *Rituals of Prosecution*; Black, *Italian Inquisition*.

[4] The seminal work on the religious crisis in Lucca is Adorni-Braccesi, «*Una città infetta*». See also Berengo, *Nobili e mercanti*, 357–454 and Ragagli, "La Repubblica e il Sant'Uffizio."

[5] "sarà facile che di fuori li venghi un medico, il quale Dio sa quale medicina li possi portare"; Berengo, *Nobili e mercanti*, 420.

[6] ASL, Statuti, 17, Book IV, Chap. 97, fol. 213r, *Della pena di eretici et scismatici*.

[7] "ostinato e immendabile [...] doppo il primo et segondo castigo"; "ne' sopraddetti errori"; "Offizio di tre spettabili cittadini"; "proceder et ritrovare i delinquenti, et

The resolution, which concluded with an index of prohibited books, thereby established a direct link between the court created to police sodomy and the instrument used by the government of Lucca to drive away the looming threat of heterodoxy, with the former providing the operational model for the latter. This was no coincidence because the association of crimes against nature with religious heterodoxy had been widespread since the Middle Ages. The Statutes of Siena, for example, grouped together the persecution of sodomites, heretics, and Patarines. According to a law of 1329, the extermination of sodomites was needed to honour God, guarantee peace, maintain good morals, and sustain a praiseworthy life.[8] Just as the offender's crimes exposed the community to the danger of God's vengeance, the community itself had to firmly refuse and prosecute sodomy in order to avoid being co-responsible through tacit approval of the immoral conduct of a few citizens. In Siena, institutions and individuals alike had to take responsibility for the elimination of impurity from the social body.[9]

The 1308 Statutes of Lucca, the first to have survived in their entirety, also did not treat sodomy as an offence in its own right, but as a crime associated with heresy. In the Statutes we read that the personal oath the Podestà was required to take obliged him to "purge" (*purgare*) the city of Lucca of heretics, Patarines, sodomites, and other "wicked sects" (*inique sette*).[10] In so doing, the legal code echoed the theoretical assimilation of religious heterodoxy and sexual non-conformity that was found in the work of moralists, preachers, and men of law from the first half of the thirteenth century onwards. The terms identifying deviant sexual behaviours in common use in the Middle Ages and the Early Modern Period show how deeply rooted this pairing was in the collective imaginary. The Germanic world made indifferent use of the noun *Ketzerie* to refer to both sodomy and heresy, while the associated verb *ketzern* described unconventional sexual relations.[11] While in German-speaking countries this etymological root of the term 'Cathar' reverberated in terms indicating deviance, in England, France, Spain, and, subsequently, also Italy, it was the Latin word *bulgarus* (referring to the originally Bulgarian

---

quelli consegnar al sig. Podestà di Lucca, per condannarli quale lo spettabile Offizio sopra l'Onestà per la forma delli statuti"; ASL, Riformagioni, armario 45, no. 18, fol. 39, cited in Tommasi, *Sommario della storia di Lucca*, 165–168.

[8] Goodich, *Unmentionable Vice*, 84–85.

[9] Davidson, "Sex, Religion, and the Law," 100–102.

[10] Bongi, *Statuto*, 230.

[11] Puff, *Sodomy in Reformation Germany and Switzerland*, 13–14.

heresy of Bogomilism) that left its mark on the vocabulary of sexual non-conformity, variously distorted into *bugger, bougre* or *bouggeron, bujarron,* and *buggeratore.*[12]

The chapter in the Statutes ends with instructions to the Podestà to intervene personally to help the bishop, the Cathedral Chapter, and any-one granted the power of prosecution by the Roman Catholic Church and to swear to apply Pope Clement's constitutions against heretics.[13] This was clearly a reference to the bulls issued by Pope Clement V on 15 April, 4 July, and 11 August 1307 that were followed by measures against Jews, Saracens, and heretics approved at the Council of Vienne (October 1311–May 1312) and subsequently incorporated into the *Corpus Iuris Canonici* together with the other *Constitutiones Clementinae.*[14] The provisions contained in Clement's text that were mentioned in the 1308 Lucchese Statutes were discussed during the troubled Council of Vienne, albeit superficially because of the urgency of other questions of broader political concern. The first of these was the posthumous trial of Pope Boniface VIII, called for by the French king, Philip IV the Fair, to discredit the memory of his political opponent who had questioned the sovereign's power to exact taxes from the French clergy by promulgating first the bull *Clericis laicos* (1296) (which preserved traditional ecclesiastical privileges) and then the famous *Unam sanctam* (1302, which peremptorily reaffirmed the authority of the Holy See over Christian princi-ples). The French statesman Guillaume de Nogaret had stormed the town of Anagni to arrest the pope, who died shortly afterwards. Boniface was accused of being a heretic, a wizard, a protector of sorcerers, and a sodomite.[15] The ac-cusations of sexual 'deviance' were then repeated by Nogaret against the pow-erful Order of the Knights Templar, whose presence in France was ill tolerated by King Philip IV because of their enormous military strength (with around fifteen thousand knights). Overwhelmed by the political instability rocking the Papal States and closely bound to the French monarch, Pope Clement V (himself a Frenchman)[16] gave in to the king's urgent requests to delegitimize

---

[12] Hergemöller, *Sodom and Gomorrah,* 11–12; Goodich, *The Unmentionable Vice,* 9.

[13] Bongi, *Statuto,* 230.

[14] Guglielmi, *Medioevo degli ultimi,* 146. *Corpus Iuris Canonici,* V.2, *Decretalium col-lectiones, Clementis Papae Constitutiones,* Book V, Tit. 2 ("De iudaeis et sarracenis") and Tit. 3 ("De Haereticis"), cols. 1180–1184.

[15] Goodich quotes the specific reference to sodomy, *Unmentionable Vice,* 10.

[16] Bertrand de Got, formerly archbishop of Bordeaux, was elected pope on 22 Octo-ber 1303.

the Order. To do so, the king assembled a framework of accusations focusing on the immorality, infidelity, and offences committed by the Order against Jesus Christ and the sacraments in order to obtain papal authorization to seize their extensive assets through a religious and criminal ruling. This led to many summary trials and confessions extorted under torture that confirmed the image of the 'wicked sect' devoted to demonic worship; the confessions referred to rites in which defendants supposedly trampled and spat on a crucifix, kissed immorally, encouraged sodomy, and worshipped an idol during their initiation ceremonies. The Order was abolished on 22 March 1312.[17]

From the fifteenth century onwards, the association between sodomy and heresy diminished in Lucca, possibly because there were no major episodes of heresy in the Republic.[18] As a result, judicial authorities started to deal with the 'nefarious sin' as a social issue in its own right. In the different editions of the Statutes, although the chapter titles continued to associate religious heterodoxy with sexual non-conformity, the focus in the chapters shifted markedly from persecuting the heterodoxy to regulating non-conformity. As we have seen, an increasingly complex system of penalties was introduced to regulate punishment. The two categories of offence were definitively separated in the 1446 Statutes, which, for the first time, included a chapter entitled "On the punishment of sodomites" ("De pena sodomitarum"),[19] marking the beginning of the escalation of legislative measures outlined in the first part of this book.

The outbreak of religious conflict in the sixteenth century refuelled old fears — which had never been completely alleviated — throughout Europe about the connection between sodomy and heresy. Sodomy was a frequent accusation directed both at 'heretics' by Catholics and at the corruption of the Catholic clergy by Lutheran preachers.[20] With the Italian peninsula traumatized by the wars between France, Spain, and then the Holy Roman Empire — from Charles VII's invasion of the peninsula in 1494 to the trauma of the Sack of Rome in 1572 —, Italians found catharsis in prophetic preaching that interpreted every extraordinary event as a divine sign. The resulting

---

[17] Gilmour-Bryson, "Sodomy and the Knights Templars."

[18] Manselli, *Repubblica di Lucca*, 702–703. The presence of Cathars seems to have been documented in the area of Padule di Fucecchio, but very few names of Lucchese citizens emerge from the inquisitorial documents.

[19] ASL, Statuti 10, Book IV, Chap. 91.

[20] There are many references in Niccoli, *Prophecy and People*; Puff, *Sodomy in Reformation Germany and Switzerland*, 107–166.

message was both threatening and redemptive: if the meaning was grasped, it could lead to conversion, penitence, and reconciliation with God, but if it was ignored or misunderstood, it would become a harbinger of fresh misfortune. Prophets and preachers were called upon to interpret signs ranging from earthquakes, famines, pestilences, and floods to births of deformed animals and babies. Indeed, in the Renaissance prophetic interpretations of deformity gave rise to a literary sub-genre of prophecy.[21]

The Roman diarist Sebastiano di Branca Tedallini describes the birth of one such deformed birth in Ravenna in 1512, the alleged offspring of a nun and a friar, as follows:

> It had a big head, with a horn on its forehead and a large mouth; on its chest, three letters, as you see here: YXV, with three [tufts of] hair on its chest; one leg hairy with a devil's hoof, the other a man's leg with an eye in the middle of the leg; never in the memory of man has there been anything like this.[22]

A description of the Ravenna 'monster' was included in the 1512 Paris edition and extension of Eusebius of Caesarea's *Chronicon* by the Frenchman Johannes Multivallis of Tournai who provided an allegorical interpretation of the creature's deformities: the horn symbolized pride, the wings inconstancy and instability of mind, the absence of arms a lack of good works, and the hoof rapacity, usury, and avarice, while the eye in the leg represented exclusive interest in base and worldly things. In his description, Multivallis also added some details missing from the earlier description, one of which — the presence of genitalia from both sexes, which he interpreted as a symbol of sodomy — became a regular feature of subsequent iconographic depictions of the creature.[23]

---

[21] Niccoli, *Prophecy and People*, 30–60.

[22] "Haveva la testa grossa, con un corno nella fronte et una bocca grande; nello petto tre lettere come vedi qua: YXV, con tre peli allo petto; una gamba pelosa con una zampa de diavolo, l'altra gamba de homo con un occhio in mezzo alla gamba; mai homo se recorda simile cosa." Tedallini, *Diario Romano*, 327, cited in Niccoli, *Prophecy and People*, 35.

[23] "Aliqui interpretati sunt: cornu superbiam; allas levitatem mentis incostantiam; carentiam brachiorum defectum bonorum operum; pedem rapacem rapinam, usuram et omnimodam avaritiam; oculum in genu solum ad res terrenas mentis deflectionem; utrunque sexum sodomiam. Et propter haec vicia Italiam sic bellicis contritionibus quati."

With the outbreak of religious conflicts across Western Europe, pamphlets on monsters became an instrument of confessional propaganda. On 8 December 1522, in Waltersdorf, near Freiberg in Saxony, a deformed foetus was found in a cow's uterus. While some Catholics felt that it represented Luther, Luther himself saw it was a symbolic embodiment of the corruption of Catholic monks.[24] The figure of Luther was also seen in a "deformed and monstrous" baby born in 1526 in Castelbaldo, near Padua. Once again, the symbolic and prophetic meaning of the creature's limbs — a crooked foot and "imperfect arm," — was supplemented by its "male member, which is turned backward," signifying "the very great and putrid sin against nature that reigns in the world today, for which God will promise this false prophet that he will come to scourge Christianity."[25]

The anxieties of prophets and soothsayers were not unfounded — the scourge of war soon followed the outbreak of religious conflict. After Imperial troops ravaged Rome in 1527 to punish the pope's alliance with the French king, many saw the massacre that ensued as divine punishment for the sins of the Church. In a room in Villa Farnesina, a German Landsknecht used the tip of his pike to engrave the word 'Babilonia' (Babylon) on a fresco depicting Rome, leaving a crude testament to the Reformed iconographic cliché of the seven-headed dragon on which the biblical city was built and which foreshadowed the seven hills of Rome.[26] Following the Sack, a Spanish priest described the many *atroci*ties that had stained the world to which he had long belonged, adopting a tone that was sometimes more melancholic than accusatory. Rome was a "triumph of the rich, paradise of whores, purgatory of youth, hell of everyone, toil of beasts, illusion of the poor, den of scoundrels"; "Rome Babylon," "Rome the prostitute," "centre of all sins," and "concubine of all those who arrive there." According to him, Rome was home to "thirty thousand whores and nine thousand pimps" and "the most effective remedies

---

Eusebius, *Chronicon*, fol. 175ʳ, cited with some variations in Niccoli, *Prophecy and People*, 51.

[24] Niccoli, *Prophecy and People*, 122–129.

[25] "difforme et monstruoso"; "brazo imperfecto"; "membro masculino, qual è di dreto via"; "il grandissimo et spuzzolentissimo peccato contro *natura* che ogidì regna al mondo, per il qual Dio prometterà questo falso profeta che'l vegni a flagelar la christianitade"; The anonymous text was distributed in Venice and included in the manuscript of Marin Sanudo's *Diarii*, now reproduced in a printed version, Sanudo, *Diarii*, vol. 40, cols. 652–653. Niccoli, *Prophecy and People*, 129–131.

[26] Niccoli, *Vita religiosa*, 102–103.

against female sterility" were the "nails of a sexton in heat," a "friar's sheet," and a "male cleric's cassock."[27]

Sodomy was a cliché in anti-curial texts and in irreverent satirical verses that targeted the popes. In a sonnet against Pope Julius II, *Soneto fato contra papa Julio Secondo*, composed by a citizen of Cesena to mark the pope's stay in his city during the military expedition against Perugia and Bologna, we read:

> So be content with
> Corso, Trebbiano, and Malvasia wine,
> and with very nice sodomitic manners;
> > you will be less blamed
> with Squarzia and Curzio in your holy palace
> keeping the bottle in your mouth, and the cock in your arse.[28]

Pope Paul III (Alessandro Farnese) and his progeny were targeted by many pasquinades, satirical compositions that brutally denigrated the corrupt customs of the Church. An epistle by a certain P. Aesquillus (that is, the fictive character Pasquillo, who, together with equally fictive Marforio, was the usual alleged author of these scathing poetic compositions) written to mark Paul's death in November 1549 describes his rapturous journey and welcome into the kingdom of demons, along with a reunion with his son Pier Luigi Farnese (1503–1547) who had preceded him into the afterlife. Pier Luigi runs towards his father with a phallus hanging from his neck, surrounded

---

[27] "trionfo dei ricchi, paradiso delle puttane, purgatorio dei giovani, inferno di tutti, fatica delle bestie, illusione dei poveri, covo dei furfanti"; "Roma Babilonia"; "Roma meretrice"; "cappa di tutti i vizi"; "concubina di tuti quelli che vi arrivano"; "trentamila puttane e novemila rufiani"; "i rimedi più efficaci contro la sterilità femminile"; "unghie di sacrestano in calore"; "lenzuolo di frate"; "sottana di chierico maschio"; Firpo, *Dal Sacco di Roma all'Inquisizione*, 32–33. With reference to Delicado, *La Lozana andalusa*, 62, 112, 225, 259–260.

[28] "Bastiti esser provisto / de Corso, de Tribiam, de Malvasia, / e de' bei modi assai de sodomia; / menor biasmo te fia / col Squarzia e Curzio nel sacro palazo / tenir a bocha il fiasco e in cullo el cazo." The sonnet, found in the manuscript copy of Marin Sanudo's *Diarii*, fol. 211ᵛ, is quoted by Niccoli, *Rinascimento anticlericale*, 83. The current printed edition of Sanudo's diaries censures the last verse of the poem; Sanudo, *Diarii*, vol. 6, col. 463. The English translation is from Aldrich and Wotherspoon, *Who's Who*, 277, who translate the verse "bei modi assai de sodomia" as "very nice acts of sodomy," but I believe the phrase has a more aristocratic undertone.

by a group of bare-bottomed young men holding flags bearing the male member, while the pope's clothing closely resembles that of a prostitute. The procession is welcomed into the City of Dis, where triumphal arches depict the brutal rape with which the pope's son was alleged to have killed Cosimo Gheri, the young bishop of Fano.[29] A poem by the writer and pamphleteer Niccolò Franco (1515–1570) describes Pier Luigi Farnese as "that cunning cock and scoundrel / who wanted all the arses for himself."[30] Franco did not spare Pope Paul IV Carafa (r. 1555–59), either; he celebrated Carafa's ascent to the papal throne with the following scathing verses:

> Oh, may you be welcome Messer Chieti,
> are you perhaps coming to my garden for broad beans?
> If this is true, I have some of the best,
> the kind that you priests like.[31]

In referring to the newly elected pope as Messer Chieti, Franco is recalling Carafa's first senior ecclesiastical elevation, that is, as bishop of Chieti, a post he received from his mentor and relative Cardinal Oliviero Carafa, who resigned it in his favour. In so doing, Franco is alluding to the overt patronage appointment and the relatively minor significance of the posting. The reference to the broad beans, instead, is a vulgar Tuscan way to refer to the penis (*fava*).

In Lucca, when Reformed ideas started to spread among sections of the ruling class, thereby opening a rift within the community, the reciprocal accusations between critics and defenders of orthodoxy also often contained allusions to sexual conduct with varying levels of explicitness. However, while these allegations might have reflected the hostility of one section of public opinion against the other, the institutions of Lucca never, in actual procedural practice, made an explicit connection between sodomy and heresy.

---

[29] *Epistola de morte Paulii Tertij Pont. Max.*, 9–16; cited in Niccoli, *Rinascimento anticlericale*, 119–120.

[30] "quel cazzo furbo e mariuolo / che volea tutti i culi per lui solo"; Franco, *Rime*, n. 297, 145, cited in Niccoli, *Rinascimento anticlericale*, 167.

[31] "O sia tu il benvenuto, messer Chieti, / vieni al mio giardino forse per fave? / Se questo è vero, n'ho delle più brave, / e di quelle che piacciono a voi preti." Franco, *La priapea*, n. 145, 103–104.

The names of many religious dissidents appeared in the records of the Office of Decency.[32] The son of Lorenzo da Vorno, whose father was commonly known in Lucca as "Capitano Perugino" (Captain from Perugia), Bernardino di Agostino Balbani, the brothers Jacopo and Bastiano di Matteo Gigli, Tommaso di Lazzaro Fondora, and Vincenti di Alessandro Diodati (individuals who will be introduced shortly) were all mentioned in 1539,[33] three years before the turning point in the institutional repression of religious dissent in Lucca.[34]

Capitano Perugino was in charge of a military garrison of a hundred men at the service of the government of Lucca. He was a prominent (and ambiguous) figure in sixteenth-century Lucchese politics. Involved in all the main political events in the mid-century, he was dismissed from his post as captain under suspicioin of treason and for his Protestant leanings, which he apparently shared with a number of his subordinates. He does not, however, seem to have lost the respect of his fellow citizens for these reasons. In 1551, he was accused of hatching a plot against the city, attempting to hand it over to the Farnese with the help of French galleys. In this case, it seems that he had been seeking fame and honour for his sons, who were described as tearaways devoid of all skills and morals. There seems to have been some basis of truth behind the episode, and the informer was probably initially involved in the project.[35] Capitano Perugino was also an active member of the Reform movement in Lucca. The trial depositions of one of his subordinates, Rinaldino, a

---

[32] Many were included in the indexes of names (Onestà 6, unnumbered folio). The paucity of information contained in this source makes it impossible to ascertain whether the dissidents appeared as defendants or simply suspects. As we have already seen, in most cases in which it was possible to cross-check the data in these lists with the actual trial records, the names correspond to those put on trial. However, as the overlap is not always perfect, for the sake of prudence it cannot be said with certainty that they were formally charged with sodomy unless the report of the trial is preserved.

[33] Onestà 6, 1539, unnumbered folio.

[34] The summer of that year was a watershed moment: after the institution of the Roman Holy Office, the prior of the Augustinian convent of San Frediano, Pietro Martire Vermigli, was informed about suspicions that had been fuelled by his propaganda work and the many conversions inspired by his passionate preaching. He was then helped to escape with some of his fellow brothers, leaving his post and the peninsula to support the Calvinist creed, of which he became a fervent promoter. Berengo, *Nobili e mercanti*, 413–414; Adorni-Braccesi, «*Una città infetta*», 109–143.

[35] Adorni-Braccesi, «*Una città infetta*», 236–239. On Capitano Perugino, see also Sardi, *I capitani lucchesi*, 109–118.

soldier from Verona, are one of the main sources that allow a reconstruction, albeit fragmentary, of the dynamics of heretical dissent originating from the Augustinian convent of San Frediano and the profile of the informal group (conventicle) of Calvinists that had leading members of the ruling class in key roles, referred to in judicial sources as *Ecclesia lucensis* ("Lucchese Church").[36]

Agostino Balbani (father of Bernardino, whose name appeared on the lists of the Office of Decency) was one of the founders of the Lucchese Reform movement. Similarly, Matteo Gigli (whose sons also appeared on the lists) was a leading figure in the *Ecclesia lucensis*.[37] As well as appearing in the Office of Decency's records, Tommaso di Lazzaro Fondora appears on three slips of paper anonymously denouncing many suspected heretics. The slips, probably written by zealous people close to the convent of San Romano and the lay confraternity of the Colombini, were sent to the Office of Religion between 1567 and 1568.[38] Finally, Vincenti di Alessandro Diodati was the brother of Michele Diodati, who, together with Matteo Gigli, was the only Lucchese patrician to be jailed in the Roman prisons of the Inquisition.[39] The 1548 lists also mentioned Matteo Gigli's son Marcantonio, brother of the aforementioned Jacopo and Bastiano, and Ippolito Balbani whose name later appeared among the twenty-two members of the Balbani family suspected of Reformed sympathies during the sixteenth century.[40] Because the trial records have not survived, we have no further information about these cases.

In 1547 the Office of Decency lists also mention Michele, son of the Francesco Burlamacchi, then Standard-Bearer of Justice and conspirator in the famous, but doomed, plot to free Tuscany from the power of the Medici.[41] Michele (1531–1590) was the second-born of seven siblings. After a brilliant career in commerce that took him to France and the Netherlands, in 1566 he married Chiara Calandrini. The following year he fled to France with her family in the hope of being able to freely profess the Reformed faith he had

---

[36] Adorni-Braccesi, «*Una città infetta*», 243–317.

[37] Adorni-Braccesi, «*Una città infetta*», 124–126, 269, 271–273.

[38] Ragagli, "La Repubblica e il Sant'Uffizio," 120–122.

[39] Michele was eventually absolved and released in 1560 and allowed to return to Lucca. Some previously unknown records of the Diodati trial were recently found by Simonetta Adorni-Braccesi: Adorni-Braccesi, "Le carte lucchesi." In 1562, Vincenti was also accused of eating meat and serving it to peasants on a day when it was forbidden by the liturgical calendar; Ragagli, "La Repubblica e il Sant'Uffizio," 121.

[40] Adorni-Braccesi, «*Una città infetta*», 356 n.

[41] Onestà 6, 1547, 1558, unnumbered folios.

espoused. In 1570, when he failed to present himself for examination in Lucca he was declared a heretic and insurgent. He eventually settled in Switzerland, living in Basel and Geneva. He died in 1590 in Saint Denis, France, while travelling.[42]

In 1547, when Michele appeared in the Office of Decency lists, his father Francesco was Standard-Bearer of Justice, but under arrest for his sensational plot against the Medici. Francesco had been betrayed shortly before implementing his plan to travel under arms to Pisa in the hope of instigating an uprising and then proceeding to Florence with the Pisans, overthrowing the Medici, and establishing a confederation of free republics under the aegis of the Holy Roman Empire in a Tuscany now free of Medici rule.[43] In the political and diplomatic crisis triggered by the plot, the government of Lucca defended itself by placing the blame on Francesco's mental instability. However, although rash, his plan was not actually as far removed from the heterodox religious sensibilities of a significant number of families in the government as they wanted others to believe; his plan was fuelled by the rhetoric of the Classical models that inspired the civic humanism of the ruling class.[44]

After the plot had been exposed and become a highly delicate matter of foreign politics, a Lucchese commoner sent a letter accusing the ruling class of conniving with the disgraced Standard-Bearer of Justice Francesco and identifying the Reformed sympathies of this "rebel of God."[45] At the end of difficult diplomatic manoeuvres aimed at avoiding to hand Burlamacchi over to Duke Cosimo de' Medici for a trial, Lucca handed him over to the Imperial Governor of Milan, who had him imprisoned and eventually beheaded two years later.[46] His suspected accomplice was il Capitano Perugino whom we have already met, along with two brothers, Bastiano and Giovambattista Carletti.[47]

Nine years later, in 1556, Giovambattista Carletti fell afoul of episcopal justice when he was arrested, together with the broker Girolamo Santucci and the cheesemonger (*caciaiuolo*) Giuliano da Dezza, under suspicion of being a heretic. Their trial took place at one of the most heated moments of the jurisdictional conflict between the government of Lucca and the Holy See over

---

[42] Luzzati, "Michele Burlamacchi."

[43] Berengo, *Nobili e mercanti*, 191.

[44] On the Influence of humanism on Francesco Burlamacchi see Hewlett, "Fortune's Fool.

[45] "rubelle di Dio"; Adorni-Braccesi, «*Una città infetta*», 183–184.

[46] Berengo, *Nobili e mercanti*, 218.

[47] Adorni-Braccesi, «*Una città infetta*», 175.

control of orthodoxy. Pope Paul IV Carafa had issued a papal brief requesting assistance from the secular arm in Lucca in the Church's fight against heretics. The government decided that the three citizens under indictment — all of whom had reasonable financial means, but were far from belonging to the city's elite — should be handed over to the ecclesiastical court.[48] On 29 January 1559, Carletti, Santucci, and Giuliano da Dezza solemnly abjured their heterodox beliefs in the cathedral, together with four other penitent heretics. In the meantime, the Podestà arranged for the burning in effigy, "as if executing living criminals," of six illustrious citizens who had, in the meantime, become exiles in Geneva."[49]

The sons of Giuliano da Dezza — eighteen-year-old Giovan Paulo and sixteen-year-old Matteo — are also mentioned in the Office of Decency records at the height of the trials against their father, much as Michele Burlamacchi had been during his father's arrest in 1547.[50] It is thus extremely probable that these cases were actually defamatory accusations against members of the two men's families. Regardless of the respect and support that they enjoyed among some members of the ruling class, Giuliano da Dezza had overstepped every acceptable limit, while Francesco Burlamacchi became an unfortunate scapegoat for the tensions between Lucca and Florence. These extreme cases are, nevertheless, the only ones in which the institutions of Lucca seem to have resorted to this strategy.

Marco da Rimini, who in the 1560s would be subjected to concerted judicial persecution by the Office of Religion, was previously formally tried by the Office of Decency.[51] He is first mentioned in the records of the Office of Decency in 1550, in an isolated entry in a list of names;[52] he then reappeared in 1553, a year for which the documentation is, fortunately, complete so we know that two defendants[53] accused him of being part of a group of men, then under prosecution by the Office, who met on the riverbanks or by the

---

[48] Adorni-Braccesi, "Giuliano da Dezza," 108–109.

[49] "come se facesse executione di qualche reo vivo"; Berengo, *Nobili e Mercanti*, 446.

[50] Onestà 6, 1547, 1558, unnumbered folios.

[51] He nevertheless managed to evade justice through the complicity of his relatives and, above all, some influential protectors (Adorni-Braccesi, "Giuliano da Dezza," 131). His name appeared again in 1570 in relation to heresy in denunciations made by councillor Gherardo Compagni, documenting his frequent movements between Pisa and Venice; Ragagli, "Esami per inosservanza," 249–252.

[52] Onestà 6, 1550, unnumbered folio.

[53] Onestà 1, 1553, fol. 23^v and fols. 26^v–27^r.

city walls to consummate their forbidden encounters. Tried on 14 October, Marco was sentenced to two and a half months in prison.[54] The following year, Marco was denounced again, this time by Vincenzo del maestro Antonio da Fagnano, another leading figure in the network of homoerotic social relations identified at the time by the Officers,[55] but this citation was never followed up.

In 1560, Bernardino di Agostino Balbani (the namesake of his aforementioned infamous grandfather) received a light sentence after he confessed to having had sexual relations with his relative, Jacopo di Jacopo Balbani, when he was just fourteen years old.[56] A few days before, Jacopo had been given the same light penalty for various sexual relations with different partners.[57]

In these two cases, the sources did not draw an explicit connection between illicit sexual behaviours and heterodoxy. If the charge of sodomy had been an attempt to damage the position of suspected heretics, the connection(s) between religious heterodoxy and sodomy would have certainly emerged during the trials. What appears to be clear is that, except perhaps in the cases involving Burlamacchi and Giuliano da Dezza's sons, the legal processes in Lucca never used allegations of sodomy for defamatory purposes against religious dissidents. While it is probable that accusations against alleged Protestants and their closest relatives stemmed from denunciations made by the zealous defenders of Catholic orthodoxy, the lack of a clear connection between sodomy and heresy in the trial records seems to demonstrate the desire of government institutions to tone down the smear campaign.

It remains to be seen, however, whether the acceptance of heterodoxy effectively coincided with non-normative sexual behaviours. Statistics certainly do not show any greater tendency among Reformed Lucchesi to indulge in non-conventional sexual behaviours and acts than the general population of Lucca, nor, indeed, that they were subjected to any significant judicial harassment. It is important to underline that a sizeable part of the Reformed movement in Lucca chose to endorse Calvinism, a denomination that rigidly monitored sexual morality.[58] Elsewhere on the Italian peninsula,

---

[54] Onestà 1, 1553, fol. 27ᵛ.

[55] Onestà 1, 1554, fol. 42ʳ.

[56] Onestà 1, 1560, fol. 21ᵛ.

[57] Onestà 1, 1560, fol. 20ᵛ. Along with Ippolito (see above), his name was among the twenty-two members of the Balbani family suspected of Reformed sympathies.

[58] On the harshness of the repression of sodomy in Calvinist Geneva, which welcomed many Lucchese exiles, see Crompton, *Homosexuality & Civilization*, 324–328; on

the desire to shake off the many precepts that now constituted Christian morality sometimes inspired an instinctive fondness for the new confessions; presented through the deforming lens of anti-Lutheran propaganda, the Reformed confessions could be mistakenly interpreted as advocates of sexual liberty. After all, Catholic polemicists painted Luther as a sodomitic swine, or, at best, a man who wanted reforms so that he could have sex with nuns without guilt. It is thus possible that Italians saw the Lutheran and Calvinist invitation to interpret the Gospel individually as a way to allow for greater sexual freedom.[59] There is no evidence, however, of such a fanciful reading of Reformed thinking in Lucca or, indeed, of any other heresy that provided doctrinal justification for free sexual behaviour or stressed the moral irrelevance of sex for purposes of attaining eternal salvation.[60]

One case might be an exception. Giuseppe Jova (or Giova, 1506–post 1569) appears in the Office of Decency's records for 1548. This young intellectual from Lucca, who was Vittoria Colonna's secretary, was well connected to the spiritual fellowship that formed around Juan de Valdés in 1530s Naples.[61] His appointment in 1546 as Chancellor of Lucchese schools, in spite of his having already been investigated for heresy,[62] shows that the ruling class tacitly acquiesced to the ideals of religious and civic humanism in this first phase of the spread of Reformed ideas in Italy. His flight to Lyons in 1561 is a tangible sign of the sudden change in climate following the repressive policies adopted by the Roman Curia from the 1540s onwards.

After his move to France, Giova soon joined the Prince of Salerno, Ferrante Sanseverino, (whose court he had previously frequented).[63] Sanseverino had taken refuge in France in the early 1550s under the protection

---

contempt for the 'unmentionable sin' in Reformation Germany and Switzerland, see Puff, *Sodomy in Reformation Germany and Switzerland*.

[59] Switzerland and Geneva have a special place in the Italian imaginary as lands of sexual liberty. On these visions (which are highly 'projective'), see Romeo, *Amori proibiti*, 89–95.

[60] On sexual heresies, see Romeo, *Amori proibiti*, 63–111. One important case was studied by Dall'Orto, "Adora più presto un bel putto, che Domenedio." There was also the famous case of Antonio Rocco, a heterodox interpreter of Aristotelian naturalism, who celebrated love for boys in *L'Alcibiade fanciullo a scola*. Rocco, *Alcibiade*; Cavaillé, "*Alcibiade* enfant à l'école"; Fasoli, "Bodily 'Figurae.'"

[61] Adorni-Braccesi, «*Una città infetta*», 74–75, 95–97.

[62] Tabacchi, "Giova, Giuseppe." On public education in Lucca, see above, Chapter 6, 112–113.

[63] Adorni-Braccesi, «*Una città infetta*», 95–97.

of Catherine de' Medici. The Prince had been forced to escape the legal clutches of the Viceroy of Naples, who branded him a rebel and a heretic for attempting to subvert the entire political balance of the Italian peninsula by allying with the French to drive the Spanish out of southern Italy. The short-lived alliance between the deeply Catholic Henry II, King of France, and the German Protestants might have raised hopes that Sanseverino could play a similar role for Italy to the one performed in Germany by Maurice of Saxony. In order to succeed in his intentions, he even planned to land on the Neapolitan coast with French and Turkish troops.[64] His willingness to join forces with Suleiman must have confirmed many chilling stereotypes about the destructive potential of political and religious subversion. In 1552, Sanseverino was thus declared an insurgent and accused of heresy, sheltering bandits, and indeed sodomy.[65]

In the 1530s, long before religious beliefs upset the political balance in Lucca and forced Jova into exile, "the agreeable Giovio of Lucca" had become a member of the Accademia dei Vignaioli in Rome.[66] This literary circle was "the most conspicuous group expression" of the Bernesque literary and poetic movement that frequently addressed the subject of homoeroticism in the form of pederasty.[67] It is not improbable that non-conformist sexual moral behaviour formed part of this cultural milieu frequented by the young Jova in Rome.

This experimental open-mindedness was extremely different, however, from the climate that was, at that time, sowing the seeds of heterodoxy in Lucca. As we have already seen, in the early sixteenth century, Lucchese humanism was mainly characterized by an Erasmian framework.[68] The governing elite saw education and the study of literature as essential instruments for building civic harmony.[69] One leading figure in the Erasmian movement

---

[64] Adorni-Braccesi, «*Una città infetta*», 221–222.

[65] Caponetto, "La repubblica di Lucca nelle orazioni di Aonio Paleario," 15–16.

[66] "l'ameno Giovio da Lucca"; Romei, *Da Leone X a Clemente VII*, 206, 238. I thank Simonetta Adorni-Braccesi for this important information.

[67] "la più appariscente manifestazione aggregativa"; Romei, *Da Leone X a Clemente VII*, 233–234. Same-sex attraction and misogyny were major themes in Francesco Berni's early poetic output. The male eros was legitimized by references to Classical poetry, but there were also precedents in the vernacular tradition, especially when male complicity was reflected in a bitter hatred of women and misogyny. Romei, "Introduzione."

[68] Adorni-Braccesi, «*Una città infetta*», 53–77.

[69] Erasmian intellectuals with Reformed sympathies, such as Ortensio Lando and Aonio Paleario, saw the religious and moral behaviour (*pietas*) of the Lucchese patriciate

Straccioni Uprising of 1531–32 led by the city's weavers. With the suppression of the Poggi conspiracy the city managed to prevent one ruling family from asserting itself above the others. With the quelling of the Straccioni Uprising that almost undermined the traditional middle-ground ideals that inspired the republican ruling class, the ruling elite partly assimilated the urban middle classes and neutralized their subversive potential by granting moderate recognition of their right to representation in the governing bodies.[78]

Along with political and religious crises, the middle of the sixteenth century also saw the end of a period of relative prosperity for Lucca, ushering in a serious decade-long economic crisis. In May 1552, after the collapse of some other minor businesses the Cenami, Parensi, and Saminiati company, one of the biggest in Lucca, with offices in Lyon and Antwerp, went bankrupt; the ensuing economic crisis was accompanied by serious famine that lasted for years, debilitating the city and making the government worry constantly about an imminent bread revolt.[79] While this was going on, the same political elite that had broadly endorsed the Reformation jealously safeguarded their monopolistic control over political power, keeping members of families that had become involved in the political life of the city on the margins. This was the backdrop for the conspiracy hatched by Lorenzo Dal Fabbro in the 1570s, a plot that aimed to install the Inquisition in Lucca, destroy any remaining Reformed groups, and undermine the government vis-a-vis Catholic authorities.[80]

On the occasion of the apostolic visit of Giovanni Battista Castelli, bishop of Rimini, to the diocese of Lucca in 1575, Lorenzo Dal Fabbro, a young silk merchant who had recently become a man of means,[81] denounced about ninety people as heretics. He was supported in this by ten or so fellow citizens (artisans and young clerics) and had the significant help of the patrician Gherardo Penitesi. A court case ensued that dragged on for several years and involved both the inquisitor of the nearby city of Pisa and the tribunal of the Holy Office of Rome. The tenacity of the Lucchese government in defending its right to judge its citizens without outside interference is shown by the sensational imprisonment of some of Castelli's confidants, leading to the arrest, in Rome, of three citizens of Lucca, the Standard-Bearer of Justice and

---

[78] Berengo, *Nobili e mercanti*, 83–146. Berengo, *Nobili e mercanti*, 243–245.

[79] Adorni-Braccesi, «*Una città infetta*», 220.

[80] Adorni-Braccesi, "Una città 'infetta,'" PhD thesis, 509.

[81] Adorni-Braccesi, «*Una città infetta*», 381.

two members of the Magistrate of the Secretaries (*Magistrato dei Segretari*). The entire city was suspected of heresy. Fifty-seven suspects belonged to families already well known to the episcopal court and the Office of Religion for their heterodox sympathies. Alongside 'average' and artisan families, some of Lucca's major families — especially those with members in exile in Geneva — could now count three generations of dissidents.[82]

One informant confessed to the inquisitor of Pisa that he had been heavily pressured to "join the seven, eight, or more people who had agreed to denounce and accuse the heretics, sodomites, and bad Christians in Lucca to Monsignor Visitor so that the honour of God will shine through as a consequence."[83] Lorenzo Dal Fabbro, however, also had a reputation as a sodomite. He regularly attended the convent of San Francesco, claiming that he took communion and confessed there every week. He associated with a group that was accused of "dishonestly seducing," under the pretext of religion, young males aged between fourteen and twenty-one. Such suspicions predated the conspiracy and related to the penitential practices adopted by these 'zealots.'[84] One witness who accused Dal Fabbro at the Office of Religion said that he had heard stories from a youngster named Bastiano who had refused an invitation from Dal Fabbro and another man by the name of Francesco Fantucci to join a company of penitents, unreservedly labelled as a den of "buggers, bigots, hypocrites," in the knowledge that other adolescents had been seduced by them. Whether or not the accusation was true, the informant condemned the practice as "totally against good religion" and not a "devout act of piety," but a "bad opportunity for superstition and sin, and dishonest scandal with the corruption of youngsters."[85]

Once again, the judicial authorities in Lucca did not exploit the accusation of sodomy; there is no trace of any proceedings against the conspirator or his accomplices in the records of the Office of Decency (or, at least, what remains of them). The Lucchese ruling class and its institutions rejected

---

[82] Adorni-Braccesi, "Una città 'infetta," PhD thesis, 381–385.

[83] "far parte dei 7–8 o più che erano loro d'accordo a denunciare e accusare a Monsignor Visitatore li heretici, sodomiti e mali christiani di Lucca affinché ne risultasse l'honor di Dio sopra di ciò"; Adorni-Braccesi, "Una città 'infetta," PhD thesis, 516.

[84] "sedurre dishonestamente"; Adorni-Braccesi, "Una città 'infetta," PhD thesis, 511, 534 n.

[85] "bucaioli, collitorti, hypocriti"; "molto contraria alla buona religione"; "atto divoto di pietà"; "brutta occasione di superstizione e peccato, e scandalo dishonesto a corruttela dei giovani"; Adorni-Braccesi, "Una città 'infetta," PhD thesis, 528.

the irrational violence that pitted Catholics against Protestants. The medieval ideal of civic religion and peace, discussed in Chapter 3, created fertile ground for Reformed ideas to take root among the city's elite and throughout the Republic. One of the dominant features of the Magisterial Reformation in Europe was, indeed, an urban-based character.[86] It was easy for the more dynamic elements of the city's mercantile class to establish lasting connections with their peers in France, Germany, and, above all, Switzerland.[87] However, unlike in other European social contexts, in Lucca these social characteristics allowed the Reformation to thrive. The rupture Reformed ideals created in Lucca was not in terms of the internal dynamics of city life but a result of changes in the equilibrium of the Italian political arena wrought by the Catholic reaction to the spread of Protestantism.[88] The favoured ideal for the survival of the Republic of Lucca was civic peace, with harsh compromises required on both Catholic and Reformed sides. Repressive violence was unleashed only to repress radical, anarchic, and outrageous forms of unbelief that, as we will see, became woven into the conflict between Catholics and supporters of a Protestantism imbued with civic and Erasmian humanism.

---

[86] Moeller, *Imperial Cities and the Reformation*; Mommsen, Alter, Scribner, *Stadtbürgertum und Adel in der Reformation (The Urban Classes, the Nobility and the Reformation)*.

[87] On exile in Geneva and the Italian Reformed community there, the essential study is still Pascal, *Da Lucca a Ginevra*. Simonetta Adorni-Braccesi has also made some fundamental contributions to this field: "Le Nazioni lucchesi"; "Tra fuga e partita"; "Strategie politiche e proselitismo religioso." On the international dimension of Calvinist community networks, see Grell, *Brethren in Christ*.

[88] For a precise summary of the balance between continuity and rupture within the phenomenon of the Reformation, see Po-Chia Hsia, "Looking Back from the Reformation."

CHAPTER 9

AFTER TRENT

The Council of Trent concluded its work on 4 December 1563 after a troubled history spanning almost twenty years. Established to deal with the rift in Christian Europe caused by the spread of the Reformation, the Council ended with the victory of the most intransigent branch of papal inflexibility at the top of the ecclesiastical hierarchy. With the internal battle in the Church won, the papacy started pressing secular authorities in countries where Roman Catholicism had a privileged status to recognize the Church's primacy by adopting the Tridentine decrees. The difficult challenge of the general implementation of these decrees was, however, only partially successful. In addition to internal conflicts over the process itself, secular authorities were generally skeptical about accepting the new level of supremacy that the Church sought in the Catholic arena.

Due to its unusual political structure and the broad endorsement of the Reformation by a significant segment of its ruling class, the Republic of Lucca offers an ideal vantage point for understanding the conflicts between civil and ecclesiastical institutions following the Council. One dogged supporter of post-Tridentine discipline was the bishop of Lucca, Alessandro I Guidiccioni (r. 1549–1600), who was close to the cardinal archbishop of Milan, Carlo Borromeo (r. 1564–1584), one of the most prominent examples of the commitment to the Counter-Reformation in terms of hierarchy and discipline. Guidiccioni's efforts to implement Tridentine reforms, however, met with frequent opposition from the diocesan clergy, the ruling class, and, indeed, the faithful.

A detailed analysis of such local cases of reforming bishops as we have in Lucca or Milan leads to a critical reassessment that questions the historiographical concept of 'confessionalization.'[1] In his *Konfessionsbildung* (1985), Ernst W. Zeeden underlined the structural similarities between the three main Christian confessions (Lutheranism, Calvinism, and Catholicism),

---

[1] This was the result of the overlapping of two concepts, 'confessionalism' and 'social disciplining,' developed in German historiography from the late 1950s onward. There is an excellent overview in Lotz-Heumann, "The Concept of 'Confessionalization.'"

each of which, in their efforts to win over the faithful, established coherent systems of beliefs, rituals, doctrines, personnel, and institutional organizations. Years later, Benjamin Kaplan identified the essential characteristics of 'confessionalism' (which is different from 'confessionalization') as a tendency to favour the internalization of church teachings using highly dichotomous ideological frameworks in order to create a uniform and essentially theocratic society.[2] 'Confessionalization' (a concept developed by Wolfgang Reinhard and Heinz Schilling) is instead the theory that links confessional phenomena to the process of state-building in early modern Europe. The formation of an increasingly complex state and a bureaucratic machinery formed the basis of the theoretical considerations by Gerhard Oestreich, who in the 1960s coined the term 'social disciplining'.[3] The insights developed by these historians helped to change the way that the Early Modern Period is now viewed. As a result, religious history freed itself from confessional divisions, broadening its horizons to analyze the common dynamics that influenced both the Catholic and Reformed worlds. The concepts of 'confessionalization' and 'social disciplining' helped to integrate the study of religious history into political and institutional history, casting new light on the social and political repercussions of religious phenomena.[4]

Yet, as John W. O'Malley noted, "every lens is also a blinder."[5] Like all 'ideal-type' models, 'confessionalization' operates as a self-fulfilling prophecy: "it puts a net on the sources that will capture only what the net will hold, letting everything else slip through."[6] Already in the late 1980s, Ronnie Po-Chia Hsia recognized the radical heuristic importance of the concepts of 'disciplining' and 'confessionalization,' but offset the monolithic view of power that these interpretative models tend to reinforce. In the Early Modern Period, civil and ecclesiastical institutions were often in conflict, pursuing different objectives. In a hierarchical society in which power and its validating legal

---

[2] Kaplan, *Divided by Faith*, 369.

[3] On 'social disciplining,' see Oestreich, *Neostoicism and the Early Modern State*; on 'confessionalization,' see Reinhard, "Reformation, Counter-Reformation, and the Early Modern State"; Schilling, *Religion, Political Culture, and the Emergence of Early Modern Society*; Reinhard, Schilling, *Die katholische Konfessionalisierung*; Schilling, "Confessional Europe." Paolo Prodi made an original and important contribution regarding the Italian context in Prodi, Penuti, *Disciplina dell'anima*; Prodi, *Papal Prince*.

[4] O'Malley, *Trent and All That*, 138.

[5] O'Malley, *Trent and All That*, 125.

[6] O'Malley, *Trent and All That*, 138.

system were spread out over many centres, the implementation of any reform project in the religious or political field had to go through a challenging process of negotiation. As if these institutional dynamics were not enough, after the outbreak of religious conflict in Europe common people exerted agency in reorganizing civil and ecclesiastical power; they supported, passively resisted, or actively opposed top-down attempts at social reform.[7]

One of the harshest critics of the paradigm of confessionalization is Ulinka Rublack; in reference to the context of Reformed Europe, she dismissed as overly simplistic the idea of a "Europe-wide alliance of the early modern 'state' and the Reformed churches indoctrinating and disciplining the Christian populace."[8] Rublack also opposed the theological interpretation that saw Protestantism as a 'rationalizing' factor in European history, pointing out that "Protestantism in no way clearly contributed to a rationalization of belief-systems and a 'disenchantment of the world' from 'magical sensual elements.'" According to Rublack, the Protestant focus on the biblical word (the Logos) did not make Calvinism and Lutheranism more 'rational', but led to Reformed religion's "super enchantment" with the world, with the senses and the body deeply involved in the liturgy and with obsessive references, especially in preaching, to the Antichrist, to demonic presences, to providence, and to eternity, all with their everlasting rewards and punishments.[9]

The following three chapters will seek to understand how the Catholic Church organized its efforts to stem the spread of heterodoxy in Lucca and explore the impact of these efforts had on the monitoring of sexual behaviours. The surveillance of sexuality played a key role in the attempt of Catholic authorities to establish a growing influence over both the conscience and the bodies of believers. As we will see, Bishop Alessandro I Guidiccioni (r. 1549–1600) was fully aware of the need to align the practices of the faithful so that they internalized a rigidly defined doctrinal creed. It is thus evident that 'ideal-type' constructs such as 'disciplining' and 'confessionalization' reflect the dynamics of this historical context, at least when considering Bishop Guidiccioni's intentions. As we will see, however, his plans and their practical application were two separate matters.[10] The case of Lucca clearly reveals that, even within the Church, it was difficult to mediate between the Roman Curia,

---

[7] Hsia, *Social Discipline*, 153–142.

[8] Rublack, *Reformation Europe*, 145.

[9] Rublack, *Reformation Europe*, 10–11.

[10] This discrepancy between theory and practice was also evident in the efforts of cardinals Carlo and Federico Borromeo in Milan; see de Boer, *Conquest of the Soul*.

the bishoprics, the inquisitorial courts, and the religious orders, above all the mendicant ones.

In the post-Tridentine period the foundations were laid for social changes that were to have a lasting impact on the daily life of common people in Catholic countries. The parish gradually became the fulcrum of religiosity and the associative life of believers.[11] This anthropological change influenced society, social contexts, and socializing habits for centuries to come in both rural and urban areas of Catholic Europe. Radical change also affected the rules governing marriage, dispensing with centuries of customary practices and imposing the ideal of premarital chastity, an element that is still unquestioningly regarded as an original constituent element of Christian ethics in public debate by both critics and supporters of 'traditional' Catholicism.

The central role played by marriage in society led to much more rigid surveillance of the multiple forms of sexual relations that, as we have seen in the previous chapters, existed in Europe in the late Middle Ages and the Early Modern Period. Any expression of desire that was not framed within marriage was subjected to growing ostracism; transgressions, including sodomy, could survive only at the cost of an increasingly guilty and embarrassed silence. In Lucca, this policy affected the procedures of the Office of Decency; the characteristic pragmatism that the Office showed during the first seventy-five years of the sixteenth century gave way to stricter moralism. While penalties for sodomy became harsher, there was, however, a significant reduction in the number of court cases involving sodomy. In the meantime, the dynamics of trials became increasingly similar to those of the tribunals of the Inquisition, as we shall see shortly, with an adopted rhetoric peppered with references to truth, divine love, benevolence, and repentance. In the minds of the Officers, divine love was also expressed — in a morbidly explicit way — through the practice of torture, which was employed with increasing frequency and using previously unknown means.

The episcopal court in Lucca was mainly concerned with monitoring the clergy, so its impact on the laity was relatively light. One reason for this might be that Lucca managed, though not without much effort, to prevent the Office of the Inquisition from establishing itself in the Republic. The ideals of civic religion in Lucca, with its local, community-based profile, created fertile ground for the spread of Reformed ideas that served to resist the process of political centralization desired by the Roman Curia. This

---

[11] O'Malley, *Trent and All That*, 135.

combination of factors — from the medieval tradition to Calvinism through the mediation of humanistic and Erasmian ideals, and this resistance to centralization — means that extreme caution is needed when using teleological narratives that advance a default idea of modernity taking hold in gradual stages. In the case of Lucca, which forces had a 'modernizing' effect and which resisted change? In Lucca, 'modernity' was imbued with the city's medieval past, so the city resisted the attempts of the Catholic Church to implement what, following the 'social discipline' and 'confessionalization' models, could conversely be interpreted as 'modernization.'

On 27 October 1564, the Lucchese Elders (*Anziani*) sent a letter "to [their] various ambassadors in other cities." The mobilization of the Republic's diplomatic corps was prompted by the government's concern over pressure from Bishop Alessandro I Guidiccioni, "who desired to start publishing some of the constitutions and decrees of the Holy Council of Trent." The ambassadors had to inform the Elders on what other governments were doing "before any publication [in Lucca] is made." This involved reporting on the terms in which the decrees of the Council of Trent were being discussed in other political arenas and whether steps were being taken to "start to implement anything deliberated there." The Elders clearly wanted to take advantage of the experience of other governments in order to find a politically workable path for Lucca when trying to mediate between defending the Republic's independence and the need to respond to the insistence of Rome. The request to the ambassadors to act in total secrecy is a sign of both the high stakes involved (especially the risks the Republic would face by acting publicly) and the impossibility of coordinating a plan of resistance with other Italian cities.[12]

The reports from Lucca's ambassadors were soon received. In November, Giambattista Santucci wrote from Ferrara to inform the Elders on local worries about requests from the Holy See. Besides the specific Tridentine measures on the regulation of the clergy, people in Ferrara were greatly concerned by the decrees touching on nuns; above all, Santucci reported, it

---

[12] "ai vari ambasciatori in altre città"; "che desiderava cominciare a far pubblicare alcune costituzioni et decreti del sacro Concilio di Trento"; "avanti che si vengha a pubblicazione alcuna"; "cominciato a mettere in essenza alcuna cosa deliberata da quello"; ASL, Offitio sopra la Giurisdizione 68, *Pubblicazione del Concilio di Trento*, unnumbered folio, 27 October 1564.

seemed "strange and almost impossible [in Ferrara] that all those constitutions must and can be observed," especially "with regard to marriage and
concubinage."[13]

The Republic of Lucca also recognized the momentous scope of the
changes to marriage regulations that Rome wanted to impose. The Council of
Trent had, in fact, introduced a new framework into the body of consolidated
traditions that had heretofore governed and acknowledged marriages. Before
Trent, the contracting of a marriage was generally a process regulated by a
complex set of rituals and events that spread over an extended period of time,
not just days, but months and sometime even years. Western Christian tradition had established a specific moment, the 'betrothal' or pledge to marry that
was spoken in the future tense (*per verba de futuro*) and served as a way to
formalize the beginning of the long process leading to an eventual union with
the physical transfer of the bride from her paternal to her matrimonial home
(and bed). The presence of a priest was not required at any stage of the long
process, though a priest was often called to bless the couple or the nuptial
bed, wish the bride and groom good luck, and ward off the devil's schemes or
any reversals of fortune. The celebration of Mass was optional and sometimes
occurred long after the conclusion of the process.

The betrothal that started the process had an immediate binding effect,
with the result that the withdrawal of one party from the agreement led to a
penalty or an obligation of compliance. The process did, however, vary from
place to place and from social class to social class. In Venice, for example,
working-class youngsters had sex after a simple vow and often inverted the
stages of marriage by promising to 'regularize' carnal relations that sometimes
had started with an 'irregular' sexual relationship or even outright coercion
or rape.[14]

The simple vow exchanged by the couple in the present tense (*per verba
de praesenti*) with words such as "I am yours" was, in fact, the crucial moment
when, in the eyes of the Church, the sacrament of marriage came into effect.
The simplicity of the vow could lead to many problems, not the least of which
were clandestine marriages (with all their legal, economic, and personal
consequences).

---

[13] "strano et quasi impossibile che si debbino e possino osservare tutte quelle costitutioni"; "circa i matrimoni et concubinari"; ASL, Offitio sopra la Giurisdizione 68, *Pubblicazione del Concilio di Trento*, unnumbered folio, 27 October 1564.

[14] Pelaja, Scaraffia, *Due in una carne*, 113.

The Council of Trent thus set out to solve the problem of clandestine marriages by imposing radical changes to centuries-old marriage practices and customs. The Church's definitive legislation on weddings was approved on 11 November 1563 with Trent's *Decree on the Reform of Marriage* (*Decretum de reformatione matrimonii*). The decree's first chapter, *Tametsi*, dealt directly with clandestine marriages by establishing that all weddings, from that moment on, had to be publicly announced in church three times before the wedding (the so-called publishing of the banns), had to be celebrated in a church in the presence of the parish priest and witnesses, and that at the end of the ceremony the priest had to record the new couple in a register, thereby giving the sacrament its civil value. In terms of Canon law, this marked the completion of a process to deal with clandestine marriages first advocated at the Fourth Lateran Council (1215). But the Church also introduced some fundamental breaks with the past.[15] For example, by making no pronouncements on betrothals, the promise to marry that in many cases — especially among the working classes — was the only 'formal' act that authorized the sexual relationship and conjugal life, the Council totally devalued this stage in the process by tacitly attributing only legal, and no sacramental value to it. While promises of future intent remained a common practice in many contexts even after Trent, the rite celebrated by a priest was now the only way to ratify the validity of a conjugal bond. The Church's new regulations and its renewed emphasis on the doctrine of freely given consent by the two persons who were joining themselves in marriage thus destabilized the traditional systems of family control over marriage.

The discussions triggered by these decrees also concerned the etiquette and role of sex within marriage. In its first thousand years, Christianity followed Roman legal views and saw the mutual consent given by the bride and groom as the essential element in a marriage, but then, after the first millennium, it began to see sexual intercourse as the essential element of a Christian marriage that determined its validity and indissolubility. In an attempt to reconcile these contrasting positions, the twelfth-century canonist Gratian counterposed the concept of *matrimonium initiatum* (a marriage that has started), expressed by the consent of the two partners, with the concept of *matrimonium ratum* (a marriage that had been 'ratified'), expressed by the act of intercourse. As late as the sixteenth century, however, canonists continued

---

[15] Lombardi, *Storia del matrimonio*, 21–81; Pelaja, Scaraffia, *Due in una carne*, 111.

to hold divergent opinions on the matter.[16] The Council of Trent abolished the concept that the legal validity of a presumed marriage rested on intercourse alone, claiming that the sexual act was not sufficiently public to guarantee 'present' commitment.[17] The historical repercussions of this doctrinal decision against intercourse and in favour of the exchange of vows are extremely complex. On the one hand, it attributed great importance to the reciprocal willingness of the parties, helping to lay the foundations for the present-day Western notion of marriage featuring — at least in theory — two legal subjects joined by a voluntary pact. On the other hand, it extended the Church's control over the pre- and post-marital sex lives of generations of Catholics, triggering the condemnation of any expression of sexuality not involving a man and a woman who are married to each other. While procreation did not necessarily have to be the ultimate aim of intercourse, the faithful were bound — and indeed still are in Catholic teachings — by the imperative not to exclude it.

The interest in marriage shown by Church authorities was a strategic response to the Protestant emphasis on the matter. Luther had vehemently criticized the requirement that clergy remain celibate, which he saw not only as an impossible objective but also as one of the main causes of the moral corruption of the Church of Rome. His view that the clergy could and should marry not only revolutionized the life of (Protestant) clergy, but also modified the hierarchy of values that, from the Patristic Age onward, had established the superiority of the clergy by identifying them with the purity of chastity in contrast to a world that was at the mercy of sexual urges and, thus, sin. Luther's innovation was accompanied by an affirmation of marriage as the main and essential structural element of society, as the only institution that could control the 'malevolence' of lust and thus serve the interests of order and the common good.[18]

Lutherans thus resolved the contradiction of marriage — a highly dignified institution stained by the weakness of the flesh — by denying its sacramental status and reducing it to a rite, an earthly ritual and matter. This, however, did not make marriage completely secular, nor did it constitute an official sanction of sexual pleasure within its confines. Civil institutions were now responsible for ensuring that the conjugal pact was used to lessen the

---

[16] Pelaja, Scaraffia, *Due in una carne*, 107–108.

[17] Pelaja, Scaraffia, *Due in una carne*, 116–117.

[18] Wiesner-Hanks, *Christianity and Sexuality*, 61–66.

grip of carnal desire because it was believed to be part of God's design. Social order and divine order had to coincide. Domestic discipline, respect for patriarchal authority, and the role of parents in providing a religious *education* for their children all played a central role in the new protocol for Protestant marriage.[19] Although there were some differences (the role of sex in conjugal life, for example, was viewed with greater suspicion in Calvinism than in Lutheranism), there was a similar concept in the different Protestant confessions, especially those that had forged an organic relationship with political power and become institutionalized.[20]

The way in which the Catholic Church decided to regulate sexual desire is closely linked to the polemical way in which moral theology reacted to the fundamental assumptions of the Reformed Churches. By totally renouncing faith in the ability of works to guarantee eternal salvation, Luther placed salvation in the believer's trust in God alone and the sacrifice of his son, Jesus Christ. Although the main movements in the Magisterial Reformation did not embrace antinomian ideas, which justified total indifference to moral actions by believers convinced of their salvation, the notion of individual will was surrounded by substantial suspicion. By contrast, the Catholic Church recognized the fundamental importance of believers cooperating in the salvific work of God operating through grace. However, this optimistic attitude towards free will generated some damaging side effects with regard to sexual morality. The fact that believers constantly entertained sinful urges and thoughts posed the serious problem of how to assess, in moral terms, the 'consent' given to desire. For how long could these urges remain in the tormented soul of a follower of Christ without constituting a sin?[21]

This question was at the cornerstone of the controversy surrounding morose delectation (*delectatio morosa*), the pleasure of using the mind and imagination to savour acts prohibited by the law of God. This pleasure intensifies when the reason "does not dispelled it as quickly as it should be, or worse, it knowingly accept it. In both of these cases it is a mortal sin, even if it is not performed or entertained as an external act."[22] The most radical movements

---

[19] Wiesner-Hanks, *Christianity and Sexuality*, 151–160.

[20] Wiesner-Hanks, *Christianity and Sexuality*, 64.

[21] Lucà Trombetta, *La confessione della lussuria*, 16–17.

[22] "in non discacciarla tanto presto, quanto dovrebbe, o quel che è peggio, in deliberatamente accettarla [...] in amendue questi casi è peccato mortale, anchor che non si faccia, né si proponga di fare la opera esteriore"; Azpilcueta, *Manuale*, Chap. 11, par. 10. The passage is discussed by Lucà Trombetta in *La confessione della lussuria*, 21.

in Catholic moral theology thus saw will and desire as more important than the act itself. In theoretical and practical works for confessors and penitents, the instruction was to focus on the source of external acts during an examination of conscience, rather than on the acts themselves because this was the moment when the will subscribed to evil, even if only through negligence.[23] By accepting the premise that sins of thought were of the same nature as empirical actions, the most rigid theologians imposed the same penitential discipline. Consequently, because a sin committed in thought had identical consequences as a sin committed in deed, Catholics were constantly teetering on the precipice of the eternal abyss of hellfire.[24]

Compared to medieval manuals for confessors, therefore, the difference lay not in the categories themselves, but in the attention given to detail and to the innermost aspects of desire.[25] The proliferation of penitential literature and the aforementioned manuals stemmed from the need to create a uniform language and a common grammar to govern an intrinsically chaotic and elusive reality. The coherence of discourse had to be reconciled with the contradictory nature of individual behaviour. There was a circular relationship between confessional theory and practice; as well as being the specific target of doctrinal formulations, confession supplied the 'empirical' material from which theologians derived information and made requests to adapt casuistry to changing social demands. The development of the new science of casuistry was connected to the gradual understanding and internalization of penitential practices.[26]

Managing lust raised huge problems at this point. Indeed, the Catholic Church focused on reassessing the role of sex in marriage just as much as it focused on conserving the sacred nature of matrimony itself. When the married status reacquired its dignity as the expression of a Christian vocation, the subject of sex between spouses raised the interest of moral theologians. Although for centuries Catholic theologians had taught that the conjugal act was not free from sin (albeit venial), in the second half of the sixteenth

---

[23] Lucà Trombetta, *La confessione della lussuria*, 20–21.

[24] Lucà Trombetta, *La confessione della lussuria*, 118–119.

[25] Lucà Trombetta, *La confessione della lussuria*, 32.

[26] Lucà Trombetta, *La confessione della lussuria*, 67–68. My intention is not to express a judgement on the science of casuistry in and of itself but on its impact on the development of a Catholic attitude towards sexuality that can openly be defined as paranoid. For an overview of casuistry and its intellectual fecundity in a comparative context, see the recent work by Ginzburg and Biasiori, *A Historical Approach to Casuistry*.

century a trend of thought developed that interpreted marital sex and any resulting pleasure in a largely positive light. This led to a series of discussions on
case and circumstance that transformed internal debates into sex education
manuals with minutely detailed considerations of situations, behaviour, and
positions, all this in an attempt to define the often extremely flexible limits of
what was or was not licit. The licitness of conjugal sex led to the authorization
of what would now be called foreplay and sexual fantasies: fondling, genital
stimulation, and obscene words and images were all allowed as preparation
for coitus. The only categorical prohibitions were the discharge of sperm outside the vagina, which contradicted the ultimate aim of sex, and anal penetration. Some, however, still claimed that sodomitic foreplay constituted only
a venial sin if it was intended to lead to vaginal penetration.[27] This increase
in sex-based discourse raised profound concerns among some theologians
who harshly condemned the more accommodating and permissive trends
and branded them as lax. Sex, however, was still discussed in a copious output
of texts.[28]

From the late Middle Ages on, sexual behaviour was considered in a
predominantly merciful way that saw humanity as intrinsically fragile and
sinful. Because this centred on the extended social dimension of the Christian community, certain transgressions could be, and had to be, tolerated in
order to guarantee the conservation of the social order.[29] However, when the
spiritual dignity of marriage was recognized, thereby reducing the division
between clergy and laity, the Church began to scrutinize sex in an increasingly obsessive fashion. As soon as marriage became a vocation, sex could be
tolerated only as a tool to achieve the holiness of a Christian life.

The Tridentine decree on marriage set in writing the prohibition of premarital cohabitation and sex.[30] It is easy to grasp what this landmark change
meant in a society in which the marriage market was so restricted. As we
have seen, for the upper classes the constant increase in the cost of dowries
imposed a limit on the number of daughters who could marry, forcing other
daughters into the cloister. On the male side, the tradition of preserving family property through the primogeniture system meant that, in most cases,

[27] Pelaja, Scaraffia, *Due in carne*, 122.

[28] Quantin, "Le Saint-Office et le probabilisme"; Stone, "Scrupolosity and Conscience."

[29] On the transition from the social and collective dimension to an emphasis on individual conscience, the fundamental work is still Bossy, *Christianity in the West*. On the
Catholic perspective, see Prosperi, *Tribunali della coscienza*.

[30] Pelaja, Scaraffia, *Due in una carne*, 111.

the designated male heir was the only son who married, maintaining his spinster sisters and bachelor brothers on family properties. Among the working classes, many were denied access to marriage, whether because of their inability to raise the necessary income to maintain a family, their professional position (in some contexts apprentices could not marry), or (especially in the case of peasants) the difficulty of balancing the number of working hands with the number of mouths to feed. As we saw in Chapter 3, there were many reasons that justified moderate tolerance of sexual relations that had not been consecrated by marriage. While cohabitation by a man and a woman of the working classes often constituted a bond of solidarity that guaranteed survival for both, concubinage was a practice that was unofficially accepted for most younger offspring who were unable to marry.[31]

Behaviours that society had managed to come to terms with, such as cohabitation, concubinage, prostitution and, to a certain extent, sodomy, now had to be hidden from view. This was reflected in the rhetoric used by preachers and moralists when addressing the faithful. The resulting situation was paradoxical; whereas casuistry produced an increasingly detailed and elaborate discourse on sexuality, in the public sphere sex was relegated to an embarrassing silence. As the duties of confessors became more specialized, an increasing distinction was made between works for penitents and manuals for training the clergy. Sexual issues were hinted at in the former and explored in depth in the latter.[32] It was probably the intrinsic difficulty surrounding lust — it required great effort to define and special care in formulating exhortations — that led it to become the focus of confession during the seventeenth century.[33]

When it came to extramarital sexuality, discussion focused on whether there was 'parvity of matter', that is, trivial or insignificant culpability in lascivious pleasures. According to this moral theological term, the violation of divine precepts was only a venial sin when the matter in question was not very serious (such as stealing a pin or swearing out of anger). In taking a stand against lax tendencies, however, hardline theologians totally rejected the possibility that parvity of matter could be applied to sins of lust.[34]

---

[31] Romeo, *Amori proibiti*.
[32] Lucà Trombetta, *La confessione della lussuria*, 70–71.
[33] Lucà Trombetta, *La confessione della lussuria*, 76–77.
[34] Lucà Trombetta, *La confessione della lussuria*, 36–59.

The debate also influenced the spiritual guidance provided to betrothed couples. More permissive thinkers argued that they should be treated differently from unmarried people and that, as long as they were discrete, it was acceptable for them to enjoy spending time together talking and indulging in affectionate acts such as kissing. These opinions were countered by those who were suspicious of any expression of human affection, especially by Alfonso Maria de' Liguori (1696–1787), who in the eighteenth century became the Catholic point of reference for regulating morality, wrote in his 1757 instruction manual for confessors.

These radical changes were met with general resistance. Some questioned whether the delegates at Trent had been fully aware of the revolutionary scope of their decisions.[35] Even the higher clergy themselves seem to have realized that it would be impossible to implement conciliar decrees in the short term. In his letter of November 1564 from Ferrara, the Lucchese ambassador Giambattista Santucci wrote that "the superiors, *and also* prelates" in Ferrara expressed many doubts, underlining that

> in other times [...] these same constitutions were made, introduced, and initiated with great rigour. Nevertheless, they gradually lost shape and fell into disuse, and it seems that the same thing is about to happen once again.[36]

However, instead of pushing for more inflexibility the clergymen Santucci mentioned firmly believed that many chapters needed to be moderated and that, although concerted action could be taken at the beginning, success would be "short-lived and slow."[37]

Although the government of Lucca initially adopted delaying tactics, it was eventually forced to accept the Tridentine decrees for reasons of political realism and the need to placate Roman suspicions about Lucchese orthodoxy.

---

[35] Bossy, *Christianity in the West*, 25.

[36] "i superiori, *etiam* prelati" "per altri tempi [...] si sono fatte queste medesime costitutioni et introducte et principiate con gran rigore, et non di meno si sono a poco a poco allargati et andate in desuetudine, et par che accennino che sia per intervenire il medesimo questa volta anchora.; ASL, Offitio sopra la Giurisdizione 68, unnumbered folio, 2 November 1564. By "in other times" Santucci may be referring to the Fourth Lateran Council of 1215 and its decrees.

[37] "brevi et lenti"; ASL, Offitio sopra la Giurisdizione 68, unnumbered folio, 2 November 1564.

Bishop Alessandro I Guidiccioni first locked horns with the city government over his support of Rome's attempts to install the Inquisition in Lucca. After going into voluntary exile from his Episcopal See (1556–63), he returned home with a more collaborative attitude towards the local government.

One of Guidiccioni's first undertakings upon his return was the reform of the clergy in his diocese to bring them in line with the Council's suggested model of pastoral care. In December 1564, at the end of an orderly procession in which all the clergy in the diocese, gathered for the first synod in Guidiccioni' episcopate, had paraded along the city streets, the reforming bishop "published and stated the orders of the Holy Council of Trent" that "everyone accepted" and to which everyone "swore their obedience."[38] In promulgating the Tridentine decrees, Guidiccioni was acting with the full compliance of the government of Lucca which, nearly a month earlier, on 17 November 1564, had declared that "the decrees of the Holy Council of Trent are understood and accepted by [...] our Council" and that they had to be publicly proclaimed.[39] The following year, after pressure from Cardinal Carlo Borromeo (Guidiccioni's friend and the inspiration behind the new policy launched by the Lucchese episcopate), Pope Pius IV awarded Lucca the 'Golden Rose,' a papal decoration traditionally reserved for sovereigns who had distinguished themselves in defending the prerogatives of the Church. The political significance of Pius IV's gesture was clear; he intended to send a clear message to an Italian state with close ties to the Reformation.[40] In 1567, Bishop Guidiccioni provided further proof of his commitment to Tridentine reforms by printing a pedagogical pamphlet addressed to the priests of his diocese (*Alli sacerdoti della sua diocesi*).[41] He then conducted regular and thorough visitations of the parishes and ecclesiastical institutions in his diocese.

After the diocesan synod of 1564, Guidiccioni convened a second synod four years later, after the end of which he drafted and published a list of regulations (*Constitutiones Synodales*) to facilitate the introduction of the Tridentine disciplinary decrees (*Lucensis Ecclesiae constitutiones synodales*, 1571). The synodal regulations were then revisited and printed in a

---

[38] "pubblicati e dichiarati li ordini del sacro Concilio di Trento"; "tutti accettarono"; "giurarono la loro osservanza"; Civitale, *Historie di Lucca*, 2:614.

[39] "i decreti del Sacro Concilio di Trento s'intendano e siano accettati dal [...] nostro Consiglio"; "fare pubblico bando"; Adorni-Braccesi, "Una città 'infetta," PhD thesis, 377.

[40] Adorni-Braccesi, "Una città 'infetta," PhD thesis, 378.

[41] Guidiccioni, *Alli sacerdoti della sua diocesi*. See Ragagli, "La Repubblica e il Sant'Uffizio," 78–79.

vernacular edition as "rules for all types of priests" (*Regole per le classi de' sacerdoti*, c. 1577); the vernacular version was clearly meant to compensate for the ignorance of Latin on the part of rural parish priests. The *Regole* was reprinted at least two more times, in 1580 and 1588.[42]

Along with other works, the *Regole* was one of the basic texts priests in the diocese had to have in their possession; being found without it during a pastoral visit led to the imposition of precise penalties.[43] The 1588 edition was accompanied by "some warnings for the people," evidence of a desire to address the ignorance of both the clergy and the common folk. The sacrament of confession took up the most space in the *Regole*, with instructions to priests and the laity.[44] In addition to urging priests to comply with all of the formal conditions that conferred validity and due solemnity at the completion of the ritual obbligations, the bishop was concerned that all believers should be confessed by their parish priest, granting exceptions only in rare cases.[45]

It is clear that the regulations on confession were meant to monitor the orthodoxy of believers by establishing widespread and thorough control and preventing them from skirting their sacramental duties. The regulations declared that the sacrament of confession could not be given to usurers or "women who come to confession with curls, wearing a lascivious or lavish dress, adorned with frivolous ornaments, or without a veil or other cloth over their shoulders, breasts, and heads, covering at least all of their foreheads." Above all, however, the parish priest could not "absolve any person who refuses to reveal to us those suspected of heresy and those who kept heretical books or writings, or practised with heretics, and who cast spells or charms."[46] Physicians who had treated sick people who were known to have refused confession had no right to ask for God's forgiveness through the mediation of the Church. Indeed, believers were warned that "those who do not wish to be abandoned by their physician must first go to their

---

[42] Adorni-Braccesi, "Guidiccioni, Alessandro," s.v.

[43] Adorni-Braccesi, "Una città 'infetta,'" PhD thesis, 396.

[44] Guidiccioni, *Regole per le classi de' sacerdoti*, 67.

[45] Guidiccioni, *Regole per le classi de' sacerdoti*, 78–79.

[46] "le donne che si presentano alla Confessione con ricci, in habito lascivo, o sontuoso, o con vani ornamenti, et senza velo, o altro pannolino sopra le spalle, e'l petto, e in capo che le copra almeno tutta la fronte"; "assolvere alcuna persona che ricuserà di manifestare a Noi i sospetti d'heresia, et quei che tenessero libri, o scritture heretiche, o praticassero con Heretici, et che fanno incanti, o malie"; Guidiccioni, *Regole per le classi de' sacerdoti*, 79–80.

priest."[47] Although the obligation was limited to confession and communion at Easter, in his writings Bishop Guidiccioni favoured frequent recourse to the sacraments.[48]

Guidiccioni urged priests to determine which sins constituted 'reserved cases' (that is, sins that could not be absolved through confession) by consulting a copy of the bull *At the Table of the Lord* (*In Coena Domini*) that they ought always to have at hand.[49] He also encouraged the faithful to stay informed about these exceptions through the far-from-simple task of understanding the complex structure of the respective areas of jurisdiction of the different religious authorities.[50] According to the list included in the *Regole*, the episcopal court was always responsible for blasphemy, "affronts against images of God and the saints and their relics with violence or filth" such as "the pollution of the church or cemetery with blood and with the effusion of the human seed," refusal to observe Lent, violence towards clerics, lack of respect for the authority of parents and elders, murder or serious violence, mistreatment of children, failure to observe the new conciliar measures regarding marriage. Last but not least, the *Regole* assigned to the episcopal court responsibility for those who "had carnal relations with religious persons, or with relations up to the second degree, with a godmother or goddaughters; abducted and raped virgins by force, or had carnal relations with animals, and the *sin against nature.*"[51]

---

[47] "chi non vuol essere abbandonato dal Medico, ricorra primieramente al Sacerdote"; Guidiccioni, *Regole per le classi de' sacerdoti*, 138.

[48] Guidiccioni, *Regole per le classi de' sacerdoti*, 129–130.

[49] Guidiccioni, *Regole per le classi de' sacerdoti*, 78.

[50] Guidiccioni, *Regole per le classi de' sacerdoti*, 135–136.

[51] "la polluzione della Chiesa, o Cemeterio, con sangue, et con la effusione del seme humano"; "haver usato carnalmente con persone religiose, o con parenti fino nel secondo grado, con commare, o figliocce; rapito stuprato vergini per forza, o usato con animali, et il *peccato contro natura*"; Guidiccioni, *Regole per le classi de' sacerdoti*, 136–138. Emphasis added.

CHAPTER 10

THE IMPACT OF RELIGIOUS REFORMS ON THE JUDICIAL PRACTICE OF THE OFFICE OF DECENCY

The surveillance of sodomy was part of the reform plan implemented by the bishop of Lucca. In practice, however, sodomy was never prosecuted with excessive zeal by the episcopal court. As a crime of mixed jurisdiction (*mixti fori*), both secular and ecclesiastical courts could act on the principle of prevention, with the competent court established as the one that had initiated the proceedings. The episcopal court launched proceedings against lay persons only occasionally. My first (although, admittedly, not thorough) examination of the documents held in the "Criminal" section of the Episcopal Archive of Lucca revealed only one case in which an independent process was started. This was a case against two young men who had accused each other of many consensual sexual relations. Unfortunately, the fragmentary nature of the records makes it impossible to know how the pair were intercepted by the episcopal court, or, indeed, the sentence they received. The trial depositions do, however, show that the procedural practice of the episcopal court was extremely similar to that of the Office of Decency.[1]

In surveying the records of the episcopal court, normally overseen by the bishop's vicar, we find not only that it had very little interest in controlling the sodomitic behaviour of the laity, but also that there were very few cases of priests and friars indicted for the crime. In 1550, the priest Benedetto da Panicale was accused and convicted of committing sodomy on many occasions with various young and adolescent men. He was to be imprisoned for a minimum of one year and a maximum to be established with the approval of the bishop, and encouraged to sit out his sentence patiently, since attempted escape would lead to three years of forced labour on the galleys.[2]

---

[1] ASDL, Criminale (provisional no. 1090), 1575–76–77, fol. 55ʳ, 25 September 1575. When I consulted the Criminale records, the collection was being reordered so its volumes had provisional numbers assigned to them by the staff; the volume numbers may now have changed, but the chronological sequence of the volumes remains unvaried.

[2] ASDL, Criminale (provisional no. 78), 1551, fols. 29ʳ–30ᵛ, May 1550.

Despite the episcopal court's lack of interest in prosecuting sodomy, a document found among its records reveals that some of the diocesan clergy were familiar with sodomitic practices. On 12 December 1581, a cleric at the seminary of Lucca, Giuseppe di Silvestro, went to the bishop's vicar to denounce a serious altercation he had had with Father Nicolao di Domenico, a "major acolyte" at the cathedral church of San Martino. Giuseppe explained that one evening, at around eleven o' clock when he was returning to his rooms, the priest had followed him and when "he was going through the cloister of San Martino, he made certain gestures towards me with his hands that I did not like." After telling him "to go and do those things elsewhere," he added that "such gestures are normally done to whores like you" [i.e., the priest]. When Fr. Nicolao replied that Giovanni was a whore and not he, the pair came to blows, but fortunately another cleric at the seminary who had witnessed all this put himself between them and separated them. Giuseppe then explained that Father Nicolao's gestures, consisting of "certain circles like an 'o'", were clear allusions to anal sex: "I think that [...] he meant that I was a male whore."[3]

On other occasions, the episcopal court acted against clerics in response to pressure from the Office of Decency. In 1553, a nine-year-old boy appeared before the Officers to denounce with impunity the abuse he had been sub-jected to by a priest, Fabrizio da Camerino.[4] The Office's records do not docu-ment the trial proceedings, but the outcome can be found in the archive of the episcopal court, to which the case was transferred. Taking into account the priest's escape (it is not known whether this was facilitated by Church institu-tions), the vicar decided to sentence him *in absentia* to suspension from all priestly functions (*a divinis*) for a period of three years and permanent exile.[5] In practice, therefore, the episcopal court in Lucca significantly reduced the severity of penalties imposed by canon law, which, after the Third Lateran Council, prescribed demotion (involving the removal of all clerical benefits) and lifelong confinement in a monastery for clerics found guilty of sodomy.[6]

---

[3] "accolito maggiore"; "ei passeggiando nel chiostro di S. Martino mi faceva certi atti con le mani che non mi piacevano"; "che andasse a fare quelli atti altrove"; "questi atti si sogliono fare alle bardasse pari tuoi"; "che io ero bardassa et non lui"; "si misse in mezzo tra noi et ci spartì"; "certi circoli come *o*"; "io penso che [...] volesse significare che io ero bardassa"; ASDL, Criminale 14, 1579–80, unnumbered folio, 12 December 1581, deposi-tion of Giuseppe di Silvestro, cleric at the Seminary of Lucca.

[4] "animo conseguendi impunitatem"; Onestà 1, 1553, fol. 29ᵛ.

[5] ASDL, Criminale (provisional no. 11), 1553, fol. 30ʳ⁻ᵛ.

[6] Goodich, *Unmentionable Vice*, 35–39.

Some cases involving clerics were conducted jointly by the episcopal court and the Office of Decency. In 1570, a man went to the Officers to report the sexual abuse his sons had suffered at the hands of their tutor, a priest named Piero da Pescia.[7] The latter denied the accusations brought against him by telling the bishop's vicar, in charge of the episcopal court, that the boys had accused him out of animosity because he had punished them severely for molesting an old woman who had paid him a visit by constantly putting their hands on her breasts.[8]

When the priest complained that his pupils always teased him, accusing him of being in love, the episcopal judge asked him to clarify whom the boys said he was in love with, insinuating that the boys were alluding to an amorous attachment to one of their classmates. The priest ignored the insinuation and replied that he did not know because they had never told him.[9] The following day, the Office of Decency collected statements from many of his pupils, all of whom willingly repeated detailed accounts of similar sexual abuse.[10] From that point on, further interrogations by the civil court took place in the presence of the bishop's vicar who, for his part, continued to challenge the defendant's constant denials. After many interrogations and prolonged torture, the priest finally yielded ("I want to tell the truth") and confirmed the accusations brought against him by the boys.[11] Although the priest was sentenced by the episcopal court, the proceedings conducted by the Office of Decency continued because one of the victims had also accused another rapist, a layman, who was summoned, interrogated, and severely tortured, before being released a few days later.[12]

There was a similar case in 1573 involving Benedetto di Ponzio dal Borgo, a priest who provided teaching and household administration to Messer Francesco di Fano, a "professor of humane letters" who was responsible for the *education* of four boys boarding with him.[13] The denunciation was made in early May by Pier Andrea di Olmo di Baccio, aged around ten, who claimed that he had been molested not only by the priest, but also by one of his friends and five other youngsters. While the Officers interrogated the young people

---

[7] Onestà 1, 1570, fols. 3ʳ–8ʳ.

[8] "questi putti li mettevano le mani in seno"; ASDL, Criminale 12, 1570, fols. 7ᵛ–8ʳ.

[9] ASDL, Criminale 12, 1570, fols. 7ᵛ–8ʳ.

[10] Onestà 1, 1570, fols. 4ᵛ–6ʳ.

[11] "io voglio dire la verità"; ASDL, Criminale 12, 1570, fol. 11ʳ.

[12] Onestà 1, 1570, fols. 7ᵛ, 9ʳ, and 11ᵛ.

[13] "professore di umane lettere"; Onestà 2, 1573, unnumbered folio, 13 May 1573.

mentioned in Pier Andrea's first deposition,[14] the vicar questioned the priest, Benedetto, who for over a week denied the accusations brought against him. He, too, argued that the allegations were an act of spite by the boy who had been rightfully punished him many times for his disobedience.[15]

While in the previous trial the vicar attended the interrogations of the lay defendants, in this case the Officers of Decency participated in the sessions at the episcopal court. After the usual procedure of counter interrogations, during *strappado* torture Benedetto admitted that all of the accusations against him were true. He subsequently repeated this confession before the Officers and some of the Elders of Lucca (the *Anziani*). In this case, the sentence was curiously divided between the religious and civil institutions: the priest paid the seminary a fine of twelve *scudi*, the same amount imposed on lay adults under the age of fifty by the Office of Decency, but he was also sentenced to a year's imprisonment to be served in Lucca's main jail, the Carcere del Sasso, situated in the ancient Roman amphitheater.

As far as relations between the ecclesiastical and secular courts are concerned, there does not seem to have been any jurisdictional conflict over sodomy — the 'crime' was and remained in the purview of secular authorities. That is not to say that the Church did not concern itself with 'the sin against nature,' but its position on this is not easy to determine, especially in the wake of the crisis triggered by the spread of Protestantism. Despite the frequent association between religious heteredoxy and sodomy that we have already discussed in Chapter 8, the crime was not mentioned in texts for inquisitors published in Italy during the same period. Although it was considered a crime that bore the stench of heresy, still the two categories did not completely overlap from a theological perspective. Sodomy did feature, however, in Spanish manuals and their Italian translations, an indication of the difference between the control strategies of the two Inquisitions. Some of the Iberian manuals did, in fact, include sodomy among the crimes under the jurisdiction of the Inquisition and, by extension, the Church. The Roman Holy Office generally ignored sodomy. But not so Pope Paul IV Carafa who, on 25 November 1557 included sodomy among the crimes falling under the Inquisition's jurisdiction. His decision, however, remained a dead letter; the only non-normative sexual behaviours regularly prosecuted by the Holy Office were bigamy and solicitation in the confessional. Michele Ghislieri was one of the delegates of

---

[14] Onestà 2, 1573, fols. 2^r–5^r.

[15] ASDL, Criminale 16, 1573, fols. 138^r–142^r.

the Roman Inquisition who, during Paul IV's pontificate, investigated sodomy. After becoming pope, with the name of Pius V (r. 1566–72), Ghislieri went back to the issue. His bull *Cum primum* (April 1566), a general measure against bad habits, condemned those who did not respect divine worship, blasphemers, simoniacs, concubines, and those tainted by the sin of sodomy. The pope encouraged increased severity in the punishment for this crime, even for clerics; according to previous jurisprudence, after being demoted from the clergy, the guilty were handed over to the secular authority for the execution of the sentence, which generally meant capital punishment. Two years later, Pius V returned to the subject with a bull exclusively devoted to sodomy (*Horrendum illud scelus*, August 1568). The measure further clarified that all those guilty of sodomy, whether priests or secular or regular clergy of any rank and dignity, were to be deprived *ipso facto* of all their clerical privileges for any office and dignity, as well as of all ecclesiastical benefits. After being declassed by an ecclesiastical judge, the convicted were then to be transferred to the secular authority for the implementation of the death penalty. However, in spite of Pius V's two bulls, the judges of the Holy Office were not eager to extend the inquisitorial jurisdiction over the crime of sodomy. On 12 October 1600, during a session in the presence of the pope, the cardinal-inquisitors established that the Holy Office would not proceed against sodomy.[16]

Despite the uncertainties and fluctuations of the Holy See and its Tribunal, the Council of Trent had a significant impact on the Church's attitude towards sodomy, which was reflected also in the way that sodomy was dealt with in Lucca. In a climate in which pastorals addressed to the people and for the formation of the uneducated clergy started to avoid overly explicit references to sex, limiting themselves to instilling a general fear of all practices not sanctified by marriage and the purpose of procreation, the coarseness that had been employed by fifteenth-century preachers to shock the faithful soon became a distant memory. The fear was that sexual fantasies would be stimulated rather than placated.[17] By stressing in his *Rules* (*Regole*) for priests that the clergy of Lucca should take care "not to teach the sin to those who do not know it, such as women, children, and the like through imprudent and impertinent questions,"[18] Bishop Guidiccioni showed that he was perfectly

---

[16] Scaramella, "Sodomia," 1445–1446.

[17] Canosa, *La restaurazione sessuale*, 117–118.

[18] "di non insegnare con imprudenti, et impertinenti interrogazioni il peccato a chi nol sa, come a donne, a fanciulli, et simili"; Guidiccioni, *Regole per le classi de' sacerdoti*, 70–71.

in tune with the pastoral concerns of those attempting to reform habits in accordance with the desires of the Council of Trent.

An analysis of the data regarding the Office of Decency reveals a shift away from the late communal model that imposed mild but far-reaching regulations on non-procreative forms of sexuality. From the 1580s onward, the Office's workload decreased dramatically, becoming almost insignificant by the end of the century (see Table 5). Although there was a gradual drop in the number of individuals charged and tried, the amount of paperwork produced for every trial grew exponentially, as did the number of witnesses and the repetition of interrogations. For example, while only six convictions were handed down between 1591 and 1599, the actual volume of hand-written trial records is just as thick as those from previous years. In all likelihood, the increasing scrupulousness used in conducting investigations was the result of the choice to gradually hand down harsher sentences. After the 1572 case of old Girolamo Nucchelli, whose death sentence was commuted to house arrest for the rest of his life,[19] the first sentence applied in accordance with the Statute penalties was given in 1581 to a thirty-five-year-old Florentine accused of sodomizing several times a seventeen-year-old Lucchese named Agostino.[20] The Florentine was sentenced to exposure in the pillory, two years' imprisonment, and a one hundred florin fine. Previously, much milder sentences had been imposed on his peers in keeping with the common practice of 'negotiating' the punishment. Instead, only a year later, in 1582, a fine of twenty *scudi* was given to two minors, Alessandro Ciuffarini and Stefano di Battista Franciotti, both under eighteen years of age.[21] Ciuffarini was also warned that he would receive a second conviction if he were later to be named by others whom he had failed to mention, a circumstance that had not previously led to an increase in penalty.

In 1583, some changes in direction were approved in a new law, a complex measure whose effects are not immediately obvious. The annual election of the Officers of Decency was confirmed, but with the proviso that one member had to be a doctor in law — an indication that the government was trying to increase the 'professionalism' of the institution. The wording of the Statutes, which clearly defined sodomy as "that rape against nature that *is done to men*," was extended, in keeping with common procedure, to

---

[19] See above, Chapter 4, 76–82.
[20] Onestà 3, 1581, fol. 5ʳ.
[21] Onestà 3, 1582, fol. 11ʳ⁻ᵛ.

refer to "any person of any status, rank, *sex*, or circumstance" who fell "into this truly abominable sin [...] actively or passively."[22] The level of penalties for first offences was reviewed and lightened to reflect the Office's practice; for offenders under twenty-five years of age, the revised Statutes largely followed the sentences that were generally imposed by the Officers through the negotiation of the sentence (Table 6).

While the situation for first offenders was somehow made lighter, for repeat offenders it became more serious. On a second conviction, those under eighteen year of age had their fines doubled, while those aged between eighteen and twenty-five were to be imprisoned for a year and those over twenty-five given the death penalty. On a third conviction, the death penalty was prescribed for all offenders. In short, while the laws were adapted to the practice of reducing sentences for the eighteen to twenty-five age group, the circumstances for those over the age of twenty-five worsened dramatically. The most significant change in the 1583 provisions was in the determination of aggravating circumstances, most specifically in the regulation that if "any person committed that crime with rupture and effusion of blood in the passive partner," the penalties reserved for people over the age of twenty-five would be applied even to younger offenders — that is to say, they would pay for the crime with their life.[23]

The Office's records show that the new measures were adopted effectively. On 18 June 1585, eighteen-year-old Paulo di Nicolao da Piazzana was sentenced "to remain in the prison in the palace alone in a cell for one month so that no one can associate with him *in accordance with the new law*."[24] A few months later, the same penalty was imposed "in accordance with the order of the law" on a seventeen-year-old confessed offender named Paulino.[25] A few days after Paulino's sentencing, the notary recorded the order to implement the new directives in a small dossier of unnumbered sheets:

---

[22] "quello stupro che contra natura *farsi nel maschio*"; "qualunque persona di qualunque stato, grado, *sesso*, ò condizione"; "in questo sì abominevol vizio [...] attivamente, o passivamente"; *Leggi e decreti*, Chap. 107. Emphasis added.

[23] "qualunque persona commettesse tal delitto con frattura et effusione di sangue nel patiente"; *Leggi e decreti*, Chap. 107.

[24] "a stare nelle carceri del palazzo in un fondo solo che nessuno possa praticare seco *segondo la forma della nuova legge* per un mese"; Onestà 3, 1584, unnumbered folio (18 June 1585). Emphasis added.

[25] "segondo l'ordine della legge"; Onestà 3, 1585, unnumbered folio (5 October).

any person committing this crime or sin with rupture and effusion of blood [...] if he is older than twenty-five years, he will lose
his head and die and [...] every time that this crime occurs for
which the death penalty is imposed, the Office of Decency must
send the proceedings that have taken place to the Podestà, who
is obliged under pain of a hundred *scudi* [...] to give and execute
the sentence within a period of fifteen days starting from the day
when the trial records are delivered.[26]

This seems to have come to fruition immediately, because the same
collection of papers contains the proceedings of a trial, also forwarded to
the Podestà, requesting justice for a seven-year-old male rape victim. It was
noted in the margin that the ages of the offenders had been checked, with all
three being over twenty-five; at the same time, a surgeon had confirmed the
presence of a rupture in the child's anus with an effusion of blood. Although
there is no record of the execution of the sentence, given the set of circumstances, it can be assumed that the death penalty was applied.[27]

The measure, however, was not meant to punish more severely only the
anal rape of boys and men, but of women, too: in the following years two men
received the death penalty for their anal rape of women. In the first of these
cases, Lorenzo Pieri was found guilty of having anally raped two women, both
of whom he brutally assaulted in their homes during violent nocturnal break-
ins.[28] On 20 April 1591, "the Lord Podestà [...] sentenced the aforementioned
Laurenzio to the death penalty [...] and then to be burnt."[29]

The increased severity of the Officers' penalties at the end of the
sixteenth century cannot be explained by cases involving brutal violence,
either. The last man sentenced to death was the soldier (*sbirro*) Muzio da
Ascoli who, according to his 1595 trial, had formed a relationship with the

---

[26] "qualunque persona commettesse tal delitto, o vizio con frattura et effusione di
sangue [...] se sarà maggiore di anni 25 cada in pena della testa in modo che muoia et [...]
ogni volta che occorra caso per il quale venga da impuorsi la pena della morte debba
l'Offizio del'Honestà mandare il processo che haverà formato al podestà il quale sia tenuto
sotto pena di *scudi* cento [...] haver data et esseguita la sentenza in termine di 15 giorni
correnti dal di che sarà consegnato il processo." Onestà 3, 1585, unnumbered folio.
[27] Onestà 3, 1585, unnumbered folio (21 October).
[28] See below, Chapter 12, 230–231.
[29] "il Signor Podestà [...] condannò il soprascritto Laurenzio alla pena del capo [...]
et ad esser poi abbrugiato"; Onestà 3, 1591, fol. 3ᵛ.

prostitute Maria della Spezia. It is not entirely clear why the Officers were so harsh against him. Although it was probably the lesions in the woman's anus, it is also true that these could have been caused by the 'French disease' and not by Muzio's violence. That, after all, was Muzio's alleged reason for ending their sexual relationship while still continuing to help her financially. Whatever the truth may have been, violence was never mentioned during the trial. The soldier's defence was based on his argument that Maria had made her slanderous accusation in order to punish him because he had stopped providing her with financial assistance; he admitted to the judges that he no longer wanted to give her money because he was jealous of her; as he put it, she continued to work as a prostitute when he wanted her "not to do service to anyone other than me."[30] However, he also stated that they had later made peace, "having had compassion for her because of the love that he previously felt for her."[31]

It was this statement that made his version of events seem improbable in the eyes of the Officers. If they had smoothed things over, the Officers reasoned, "Maria had no reason to accuse him out of spite as he says." The Officers therefore concluded that all of the accusations against him were true: "it has to be believed that this is the truth and that the defendant should *freely* confess."[32] Maria, who was accused of committing sodomy with many of her clients, was banished for life from the city and territory of Lucca, while Muzio was sent to the Podestà to be tortured and receive the death penalty. The sources do not initially reveal his sentence.[33] His position might have been worsened by his defiant attitude towards the institution; as we saw in Chapter 2, he criticized the practice of torture by openly stating that his confession had been coerced and by asking that his statement go on the record, insisting that he wanted "justice, and not mercy."[34] The records also show that shortly before his trial at the Office of Decency, Muzio had been imprisoned for a month for violence against an apprentice, a sentence that he was probably still serving in the city prison at the time of Maria's trial. The records, however, do

---

[30] "che non facesse servizio ad altri che a me"; Onestà 4, 1595, fol. 17ʳ.

[31] "havendo hauto compassione a lei per l'amor che li portava prima"; Onestà 4, 1595, fol. 18ʳ. Emphasis added.

[32] "Maria non aveva adunque occasione di accusarlo per dispetto come dice"; "bisogna necessariamente credere che sia così la verità et esso constituto dovrebbe *liberamente* confessarla"; Onestà 4, 1595, fol. 18ʳ. Emphasis mine.

[33] Onestà 4, 1595, fol. 29ʳ⁻ᵛ.

[34] "giustizia, et non misericordia"; Onestà 4, 1595, fol. 16ᵛ.

not state that the second conviction was the aggravating circumstance that justified the court's decision to issue the death penalty.

Muzio appealed from prison to the General Council of Lucca asking for clemency: "Muzio di Piero da Ascoli requests to be freed from the torture and the death penalty against him to be executed by the Lord Podestà *for having practised the sin of sodomy with Maria, a prostitute from the mountains around Genoa*."[35] The Officers provided the Council with a factum, "giving it information about everything so that it could order what had to be done in the aforementioned case."[36] The pardon was granted, but at the cost of "being sent for constant punishment in Prince Doria's galleys for the rest of his life."[37]

The month before, the General Council had ruled on another convicted sodomite, Baldassarre della Vedova, who was banished for life from the city and territory of Lucca on pain of death, starting on 31 October 1588. The records of the proceedings against him have not survived, but it is certain that this was his second conviction; in 1579, he had already been found guilty by the Office of Decency of anal intercourse with thirteen-year-old Borromeo di Bernardo Borromei.[38] Baldassarre's petition in 1588 was accepted, and the legislative assembly approved an extension to a previously granted year-long safe-conduct allowing him to re-enter the city walls without the death penalty becoming enforceable.[39] In 1598, a forty-two-year-old innkeeper was also sentenced to permanent exile after confessing his guilt, having already served a year in prison in complete isolation.[40] Therefore, two death sentences were definitely delivered between 1585 and 1599 (although one was commuted to life on the galleys), along with another that remains to be confirmed in the records of the Podestà (but which was in all likelihood applied, given the circumstances). In addition, two sentences of permanent exile were handed down. Considering the sharp decrease in accusations and suspects during the

---

[35] "Muzio di Piero da Ascoli domanda esser liberato dal tormento et pena della morte contra esso da esseguirsi dal Signor Podestà *per havere usato il vitio sodomitico con Maria meretrice dalle montagne di Genova*"; Onestà 4, 1595. Emphasis added.

[36] "dandoli notizia di tutto acciocché potesse comandare quanto si havea da fare nella soprascritta causa"; Onestà 3, 1595, a file of unnumbered folios now bound between fols. 102ᵛ and 103ʳ. Emphasis added.

[37] "essere mandato al tormento perpetuo delle galere del Signor Principe Doria per tutto il tempo della sua vita"; ASL, CG 79, 414 (28 December 1595).

[38] Onestà 2, 1579, fol. 64ʳ.

[39] ASL, CG 79, 371 (29 November 1595).

[40] Onestà 4, 1598, fol. 90ʳ.

same period, it is clear that the reduced scope of persecution led to increased severity in punishment.

We have already seen that the brief proceedings of the 1550s and 1560s gave way to far more complex and drawn-out criminal procedures in the decades that followed. The number of interrogations and witnesses called to testify increased, questions became more detailed, and judges paid more attention to identifying any contradictions in statements by repeating the same questions over again. The pressure from the judges' questions was sometimes so intense that it was difficult for defendants or the witnesses to provide coherent answers. Any inconsistencies led the judges to challenge the statements or to ask unrelenting questions about irrelevant details so that the overall reliability of the accused or of the witnesses could be discredited when they contradicted themselves. Once their trustworthiness on trivial matters had been challenged, it was easy to dismantle their statements about events directly related to the trials. As one judge stated in 1592, "Since he lied about this [...] he lied about the other things."[41]

'Truth' is a word used increasingly often in statements by the Officers in the last thirty years of the sixteenth century. Although the Office of Decency was a civil magistracy, the rhetoric of trials gradually assumed an extremely similar tone to that adopted by Church inquisitors. The court seems to have assumed that it was already in possession of the truth, so the purpose of the criminal proceedings was simply to extort it from the accused or the witnesses: "think carefully and tell us what you did, otherwise you will be made to do so by force."[42] Given that a conviction could not be made without a confession, any expedient was legitimate in order to persuade an offender to confirm the allegations levelled against him. The Officers always began with persuasion, stressing the freedom of the defendant: "it is known that you have told lies thus far, so make up your mind to tell us *freely* who ruptured your arse."[43] They then underlined their own kindness, showing their 'love' by delaying recourse to torture: "think about *lovingly* telling us the truth about those who sodomized you, otherwise we will proceed with a rigorous examination."[44]

---

[41] "Siccome ha detto il mendacio in questo [...] l'ha detto nell'altre cose"; Onestà 3, 1592, fol. 44ᵛ.

[42] "pensi bene et dichi quello che ha fatto altrimenti si li farà dire per forza"; Onestà 3, 1582, fol. 17ʳ.

[43] "si conosce che finora ha detto le bugie et perciò si resolvi di dire *liberamente* chi li ha rotto il culo"; Onestà 3, 1595, fol. 110ʳ. Emphasis added.

[44] "pensi di dire *amorevolmente* la verità di quelli che l'hanno sodomitato altramente si procederà con lui a rigoroso examine"; Onestà 3, 1596, fol. 116ᵛ. Emphasis added.

If exhortations to tell the truth made "in a loving way"[45] did not produce the desired effect, the Officers continued in the torture chamber, where, from the 1570s onwards, increasingly severe measures were employed. In 1572, a new technique was introduced that involved attaching a stick to the feet of the man under interrogation with his legs spread wide open[46] and while he was hanging defenceless from the *strappado* rope one of judges' assistants tied iron weights to his legs to intensify the pain.[47] Although persons being interrogated in this manner were first given a medical examination to determine whether they could withstand torture, the Officers sometimes abandoned all precautions protecting those in their custody and even used previously unknown methods of torture to extract a confession. In 1579, a seventeen-year-old boy was tortured on the rack "where he had to remain with the approval of the honourable Office and not be removed from it until a decision was made by the Office"[48] Also known as 'the goat', the rack was used to stretch the victim's limbs. Ten years later, the Office imposed the "torment of fire", which consisted of exposing a victim's oiled feet to a source of heat. Accused of raping the female prostitutes who were tried in 1588 (see Chapter 6), Paulo Landucci was tortured for a quarter of an hour until the session was suspended "because the soles of his feet appeared red-hot and blistered," and was taken back to prison in tatters.[49]

Resistance to torture, as we have seen, led suspects to be released from prison without a conviction; the harsher the ordeal, the more unbreakable the defendant's moral integrity appeared in the eyes of the judges. As the years passed, the Office's records featured an increasing number of examples of poignant devotion to Christianity expressed by subjects while resisting 'rigorous examination.' Factors such as invocations to God, the Virgin Mary, and Jesus Christ, along with the ability to bear pain with the spirit of a martyr (placing oneself in divine hands), gradually influenced revisions to the accusatory procedure to the detriment of those under investigation. On 3 February 1570, a defendant cried out "Lord, Lord I didn't do it" and "Saint Mary

---

[45] "a dire la verità all'amorevole"; Onestà 3, 1596, fol. 116[v].

[46] "un bastone ai piedi con le gambe larghe"; Onestà 2, 1572, fol. 52[r].

[47] Onestà 2, 1572, fol. 40[v].

[48] "dove ci si doveste stare a beneplacito di esso spettabile Offizio et di quello non lo levare se non col partito di detto Offizio"; Onestà 2, 1579, fol. 20[r].

[49] "tormento del fuoco"; "apparendo le suole dei piedi assai infocate e aviscicate"; Onestà 3, 1588, unnumbered folio (deposition of Paulo Landucci, 4 July 1588).

of Loreto, help me" while hanging from the rope during an interrogation.[50] In the last decades of the sixteenth century, these sort of cries can be found over and over again in the trial reports; at the same time, the notaries started to recur to a vehement religious rhetoric when noting down the depositions, referring more emphatically to godly punishments, divine chastisement, upright conscience and sin than they ever did in the past. A sergeant-at-arms named Remigio Garsia was one of many men denounced in 1570 by the young bath-house boy Giovan Battista. When the Officers urged him to tell the truth about the wicked acts they had committed, he responded: "my Lords, I am totally innocent of this sin, and I haven't done it in any way, and pray to God, may my soul and body be damned if I am lying."[51] When he was led to the place of torture, undressed, and tied up, he continued to repeat:

> I didn't do it, I call God as a witness of my innocence, and if I didn't do it, I pray you to help me. If this is not the case, God, give me any terrible sentence against my body and soul and those of my children. Otherwise, God, help my innocence and on my knees, I pray to God to show the judgement against me if I committed this sin and to help my innocence if I did not.[52]

His invocations continued even after the judges ordered that he be hoisted from the ground:

> he cried out: "alas," and then did not respond after being interrogated several times. After that, he said: "my Lords, I didn't do it, I didn't do it, and if this is not the case, may God show a miracle on my person. I can't say otherwise, and it isn't true."[53]

---

[50] "signore io non l'ho fatto […] santa Maria dell'oreto [sic] aiutami"; Onestà 1, 1570, fol. 9^r.

[51] "signori io sono innocentissimo di questo peccato, et non l'ho fatto in modo nessuno, et prego in damnazione dell'anima et corpo […] Idio"; Onestà 2, 1572, fol. 70^r.

[52] "io non l'ho fatto, chiamo Idio in testimonio dell'innocentia mia, et se io non l'ho fatto ti prego mi aiuti, et se è altrimente Idio fa contra di me dell'anima e del corpo mio et miei figlioli ungni sententia cattiva, se non Idio aiuti l'innocentia mia et inginocchiato pregò Idio che se ha fatto questo peccato monstra la sententia contra di me se non aiuta la innocentia mia." Onestà 2, 1572, fol. 70^r.

[53] "gridò: 'hoimé,' et dopoi interrogato più volte non rispondeva, et dopoi disse: 'signori io non l'ho fatto io non l'ho fatto, et se è altrimente Idio monstra miracolo sopra la persona mia io non posso dire altrimenti et non è vero.'" Onestà 2, 1572, fol. 70^r.

Remigio's steadfastness, also displayed during counter interrogation, broke the willpower of his young accuser, who finally admitted that one of his enemies had suggested making the allegations. Consequently, Remigio was released "as an innocent man."[54]

Although the government of Lucca fought to keep control over sexual mores firmly in its hands, it is clear that the civil tribunal of the Office of Decency radically changed its judicial practice after the adoption of the canons of the Council of Trent, borrowing strategies that were the hallmarks of contemporary Roman inquisitorial tribunals.

---

[54] "come innocente"; Onestà 2, 1572, fol. 70ᵛ.

CHAPTER 11

SODOMY AT SAN FREDIANO, THE BASTION OF RELIGIOUS DISSENT

The previous chapter showed that the assertion of post-Tridentine discipline had significant repercussions on the approach of the Republic of Lucca to controlling religious dissent and sexual morality. The next two chapters will focus on the various ways in which this change was resisted. Opposition to the rigorism of Bishop Alessandro I Guidiccioni spread out from different sectors of society in Lucca. While the next chapter will analyze forms of popular and institutional resistance, including the most radical expressions of religious heterodoxy from the perspective of the history of sexuality, the focal point of this chapter will be the persistence of dissent in the Augustinian convent of San Frediano. As the former bastion of Reformed ideas in the city, this religious centre continued to lay forceful claims to its independence from the Episcopal Curia. The resulting conflict provided the backdrop for a sexual misconduct scandal involving not only some of the Augustinian canons, but also the prior of San Frediano himself.

Having fostered the spread of Reformed preaching already in the 1540s, from the second half of the sixteenth century, the convent, which was governed by the Congregation of the Canons Regular of St. John Lateran, attracted special attention from the episcopal court. The bishop's interest was almost certainly triggered by ongoing rumblings of dissent. Drafted between 1551 and 1554, the *Acta Capitularia* (capitulary regulations) of San Frediano adopted a drastic stance against the spread of Lutheranism, including the prohibition both of books classed as heretical and of attitudes that were imprudent or even remotely similar to Reformed ideas. In their stance against the possible influence of Reformed ideas, the *Acta* must have been a response to the work and continuing influence of Pietro Martire Vermigli (1499–1562), the convent's Reformed prior from June 1541 to 12 August 1542 who, having been summoned to a Chapter Extraordinary of the Lateran Congregation to respond to suspicions that his passionate preaching in Lucca had aroused, found it advisable to flee first to Pisa and then, eventually, to Switzerland, where he established himself as an important Protestant theologian.[1]

If there was any debate on the matter of Vermigli and San Frediano in the General Chapters of the Canons Regular of St John Lateran, the decision not to record them was also probably deliberate. In 1552, Pope Julius III sent a letter to the General Chapter held in Ravenna. Although he expressed his satisfaction with the measures taken by the canons against heretics (especially against Lutherans), he also imposed the condition that convictions always had to be applied with the placet of the Holy See. The message was clear: the Congregation was not allowed to deal with cases of heresy internally or purely on its own initiative. At the same time, the pope warned superiors to keep a close eye on preachers, who were no longer allowed to voice 'ambiguous' opinions on prayers for the deceased, indulgences, the cult of saints, the authority of the pope, sacramental confession, or the Eucharist.[2]

It seems, however, that these resolutions did not fully stem the spread of heterodox ideas at San Frediano. A booklet entitled *Sopra il predicatore di San Frediano* (On the preacher at San Frediano) in the records of the Bishop's Court contains statements made in 1556 by several individuals who were still outraged by the heretical content of sermons preached by an unnamed Canon Regular at the convent.[3] The Servite Friar Jacopo was scandalized because the preacher at San Frediano did not start his sermon with the Ave Maria, "as everyone usually does."[4] Furthermore, following the publication of "certain indulgences for the liberation of Christians who were in the hands of the Turks," the friar stated that "those who took these indulgences went against the ones in the Testaments," which "caused quite a scandal."[5] The unnamed preacher's focus on justification through faith alone, however, raised

---

[1] On Pietro Martire Vermigli, better known in English as Peter Martyr Vermigli, see McLelland, *Peter Martyr Vermigli and Italian Reform*; McNair, *Peter Martyr in Italy*; and, more recently, Kirby, et al. eds. *A Companion to Peter Martyr Vermigli*.

[2] Guglielmi, *I canonici regolari lateranensi*, 121–122.

[3] These were the prior and a friar of the local Servite convent, a Carmelite, the cleric Rocco de' Nobili, and a layman Giovanni de' Nobili (a relative of the cleric). ASDL, Criminale 113, Sopra il predicatore di San Frediano, fol. 1ʳ.

[4] "come si usa da tutti"; ASDL, Criminale 113, Sopra il predicatore di San Frediano, fol. 1ʳ.

[5] "certe indulgentie per riscatto di christiani che erano in mano de' turchi"; "chi pigliava queste indulgentie haversa quelle testamentarie"; "dié scandalo assai"; ASDL, Criminale 113, Sopra il predicatore di San Frediano, fol. 3ʳ.

the deepest concerns among those present.[6] The matter must have caused outrage because, a few days later, the bishop himself visited the (still unnamed) preacher's cell and confiscated some prohibited books found in the room. The rumours that followed echoed the recent past, with speculation that this "might have been because the friar in question was a disciple of a certain Florentine, whom he named as Don Pietro Martire," that is, the prior who had fled to Switzerland in 1542.[7]

It was not only heresy, but also moral laxness that brought the Congregation to the attention of the episcopal court. In the 1570s, when the bishop was imposing discipline on the clergy and the faithful with renewed vigour by banning celebrations and dances, his vicar received a worrying denunciation. It said that in a "room in the house belonging to the friars of San Frediano" in nearby Santarlascio, a small hamlet just north of Lucca, "many peasants" and "married and unmarried countrywomen, and two girls from the city of Lucca" dined with the canons "in the same monastery" before abandoning themselves to dancing, inspired by the sound of "a lyre and a violetta."[8] The accuser went on to state that "in 1572 or 1573," "a friar from San Frediano, who had a woman with him" went to an *osteria* near Moriano, and "the friar disguised himself [as a layman] there in the *osteria* and took the clothes from a peasant."[9] It also seems that the canons took great delight in hunting, which was now prohibited to clergy, just as they did in gambling and female company.[10] It is impossible to know whether these rumours had any substance or were fuelled by malicious gossip, or whether the testimonies were manipulated to attack the religious institution that was closest to the heretical movement in Lucca and, as we shall see, most hostile to the bishop's authority.

---

[6] ASDL, Criminale 113, Sopra il predicatore di San Frediano, fol. 1ᵛ.

[7] "poterebbe essere stato perché detto frate è stato discipulo del fiorentino, quale dichiarò esser stato don Pietro Martire"; ASDL, Criminale 113, Sopra il predicatore di San Frediano, fol. 2ᵛ.

[8] "sala del palazzo de' frati di San Frediano [...] molti contadini [...] donne così contadine maritate come non maritate, et dui fanciulle dalla città di Lucca [...] nel medesimo monastero"; "una lira et una violetta"; ASDL, Criminale (provisional no. 109), 1575–76, fol. 168ʳ, 169ʳ.

[9] "l'anno 1572 o 1573"; "un frate di San Frediano, che havea una donna con lui [...] detto frate si era travestito li nell'hostaria et preso i panni da un contadino"; ASDL, Criminale (provisional no. 109), 1575–76, fol. 170ʳ. Moriano is a hamlet a few kilometres north of Lucca.

[10] ASDL, Criminale (provisional no. 109), 1575–76, fol. 170ᵛ.

Some years previously, there had been an outbreak of open conflict between the convent and the episcopate. In 1574, the bishop's vicar had collected statements against the prior of San Frediano, Don Ugo da Casoli, who was alleged to have launched an unthinkable attack on both the bishop and his vicar by saying that they were excommunicated for having consecrated the oratory of San Giovannetto, which was next to the homonym convent for women; the prior claimed full authority over this oratory and deemed any episcopal interference with it to be unlawful.[11] The idea that the bishop could not consecrate a church was certainly risky, especially since the relationship between the Canons Regular of the Lateran and the convent of San Giovannetto was unclear.

Sexual scandal had first damaged the reputation of San Frediano at the beginning of the sixteenth century, leading Pope Paul III to order its suppression. However, the canons managed to have the measure revoked and the convent regained its prestige by restoring internal discipline through the work of its prior, Don Illuminato da Pavia. However, in 1536, following another corruption case, they were forced to hand over control of San Giovannetto to the Franciscans.[12] The 1574 diplomatic accident happened after a fight in the oratory between worshippers ended in murder. The nuns of San Giovannetto asked the bishop to reconsecrate the sacred place, because it had been rendered impure by the bloodshed. At this point the prior of San Frediano, Don Ugo da Casoli, stepped forward to say he wanted to officiate the solemn ceremony of reconciliation himself and asked "His Most Reverend Holiness for consecrated water with which the prior would then conduct the ceremony and reconcile the church."[13] After the bishop's refusal and his subsequent celebration of the rite, a Franciscan friar who had asked for the intervention of the episcopate was summoned by Prior Ugo, who attacked him saying "many deranged things, using unseemly words, saying that the bishop was excommunicated for having reconciled this church under his control." The prior then said that he wanted liturgical celebrations to take place elsewhere in the convent, not in the oratory, but the Franciscan friar refused to accept so as not to violate the decrees on seclusion "against the order of the Holy Council" of

---

[11] ASDL, Criminale (provisional no. 108), 1574–75, fol. 30ᵛ.

[12] Gandolfi, "La riforma a Lucca," 34–37.

[13] "Sua Santità Reverendissima acqua consacrata con quale detto priore haverebbe poi fatta la cerimonia et riconciliata la chiesa"; ASDL, Criminale (provisional no. 108), 1574–75, fol. 32ʳ.

Trent.[14] The prior seemed not to care about that and continued to insist that, given the content of the bull *In Coena Domini*, the bishop should be considered *ipso facto* excommunicated "because His Most Reverend Holiness did not have the authority and could not interfere in their affairs."[15] In testimonies given to the episcopal court, Prior Ugo's mental health was questioned and the widespread hostility at the convent of San Frediano towards the bishop was noted: "he said lots of insane things and improper words against the episcopal dignity of the Most Reverend Monsignor, as did many other friars who were present there, with each one helping him to speak badly of the bishop."[16] This was not the full extent of the prior's attack, however, because many parishioners of San Frediano were given licence by convent superiors to disregard Lent,[17] while the canons refused to recognize the validity of absolution by the bishop in cases reserved to him. For example, a penitent who had gone to the episcopal palace after his wife had suffocated their son in bed (it is unclear whether this was a tragic mistake or a deliberate act) was threatened by Prior Don Ugo because, as a parishioner of San Frediano, "neither the bishop nor the vicar of Lucca could absolve him of that sin." Don Ugo forced the parents to make an ignominious public abjuration and repeated that the bishop had lost all of his authority by reconsecrating the church of San Giovanetto in violation of the bull *In Coena Domini*.[18]

The prior's attacks on episcopal authority continued when the bishop ordered convents to display a decree obliging religious orders to take responsibility for annually giving alms to the poor. When Prior Ugo was reprimanded for not having promoted the measure, he replied controversially that his convent did not require such a decree because "we give alms" not "out of a daring imposition on this convent, but driven only by the incentive of charity, seeing the great misery and poverty that can be found in this parish

---

[14] "molte et molte pazzie et parole inconveniente et che il vescovo era excomunicato havendo fatto tal reconciliazione d'una chiesa suggetta a lui"; "contra l'ordine del sacro concilio"; ASDL, Criminale (provisional no. 108), 1574–75, fol. 32ᵛ.

[15] "perché Sua Santità Reverendissima non haveva l'autorità né si poteva ingerire nelle cose loro"; ASDL, Criminale (provisional no. 108), 1574–75, fol. 33ʳ.

[16] "disse molte pazzie et parole inconvenienti contra la dignità episcopale di monsignore Reverendissimo come ancho facevano molti altri frati ivi presenti che ciaschuno l'aiutava dire male del vescovo"; ASDL, Criminale (provisonal no. 108), 1574–75, fol. 33ʳ.

[17] ASDL, Criminale (provisonal no. 108), 1574–75, fol. 33ʳ⁻ᵛ.

[18] "né il vescovo né il vicario di Lucca havevano potuto assolverlo di quel peccato." ASDL, Criminale (provisonal no. 108), 1574–75, fol. 33ᵛ.

of ours."[19] Although archival sources do not reveal the outcome of these bitter disputes, it seems that in the 1570s there were still serious anomalies surrounding the Canons Regular of the Lateran of Lucca. After 1556, there is no direct evidence of ongoing heresy, but testimonies collected reveal that towards the end of the century the convent of San Frediano still served more-or-less explicitly as an autonomous centre of spiritual aggregation in open conflict with the episcopal authority. The prior's claims, however, did not rest exclusively on the spiritual influence of the convent over a signinificant part of the population that had sympathized for the Reformation and now felt under threat. It was grounded on an established tradition of autonomy within the territories of the diocese of Lucca. The prior of San Frediano had been entrusted with quasi-espicopal powers since the late fourteenth-century. A Bull by Urbano VI (r. 1378–1389) honoured the prior with the privilege of wearing the "pontificals," that is, those garments and accessories that marked episcopal authority such as the ring, crosier, miter, and pectoral cross.[20] This privileged position corroborated the sense of independence of the convent and, after the spread of the Reformation in Lucca, contributed to exacerbate the conflicts between filo-Protestants and Catholics.

It was in this tense climate of competing authorities that sodomy cast its shadow over San Frediano. On 15 January 1579, sixteen-year-old Ottavio, son of Paolino Muratori, was interrogated by the Officers of Decency. He said that he had been placed as a child novice at San Frediano at about the age of eight. Although he claimed to be friends with many people at the convent — among whom Andrea Orsini, Battista Stiatta, Marchio Testore, Lorenzo Serdini, Giuseppe Vanni, and the painters Mercurio and Giovanni — he initially denied having sodomitic relations with them. After suffering the terrible torture of the goat he confessed and accused not only four unnamed individuals with whom he had had sex in the previous few months, but also three canons — Fra' Serafino da Vercelli, Don Ippolito Lombardo, and Don Jacopo da Piacenza — and the former prior, Gattinara, who allegedly had sexually abused him when he was a novice.[21]

---

[19] "noi facciamo elimosine"; "non per bravezza imposta a dicto monasterio, ma solo mossi da stimulo di carità, vedendo la gran miseria o povertà che si ritrova in questa nostra parrocchia"; ASDL, Criminale (provisonal no. 108), 1574–75, fol. 75ᵛ.

[20] Gagliardi, *Li trofei della croce*, 66–67. The Bull is in ASL, Diplomatico, San Frediano, 13 February 1396.

[21] Onestà 2, 1579, fol. 20ᵛ.

The depositions describe how the atmosphere at San Frediano changed according to who was the prior in charge. When Sandigliano was the prior, young Ottavio was not abused by this prior, let alone solicited, but was molested instead by a certain Don Serafino, who called him to his cell at dinnertime.[22] Prior Ugo da Casoli was just as respectful as Sandigliano, but also more concerned about monitoring the behaviour of his friars; he strictly forbade novices from setting foot in the convent.[23] According to Ottavio's statement, the climate changed when Gattinara was appointed prior. Five or six months after the new prior's arrival,

> after the feast of San Frediano, he [Ottavio] cleared away the church silverware and took it upstairs to Prior Gattinara, who asked how long he had served there and said that he was fonder of him than the other novices and that [...] he should go to see him because he wanted to give him something. He thus went to the prior in his cell and found him writing. He stopped writing, welcomed him in, and took him by the hand. He went to a chest [...] took out a surplice and gave it to him, saying, "take this, since yours is torn." He then locked the door and went over to him, asking him if he had ever done anything with anyone. When he said no, the prior said, "be a good boy, don't say anything and I'll help you." Meanwhile, he [Gattinara] started loosening his hose and, after laying him down on the bed, he sodomized him once and sent him away [...] telling him to keep quiet.[24]

When the episode reoccurred, it became increasingly clear that Ottavio's consent to sex would be rewarded with the "habit" (*vestizione*), namely,

---

[22] Onestà 2, 1579, fol. 21ᵛ.

[23] Onestà 2, 1579, fol. 22ʳ.

[24] "doppo la festa di san Frediano essendo sparecchiata la argentarìa di chiesa et portatola di sopra da detto priore Gattinara, domandato quanto tempo era che serviva et che li volea bene più che alli altri chierici, et che [...] l'andasse a trovare che li volea donare non so che, et così andò dal sopraddetto priore in cella, et trovò che scrivea, et lassato di scrivere disse sia il ben venuto, et lo prese per la mano et andò a una cassa [...] prese una cotta et nela donò dicendo 'piglia questa che la tua è sdrucita,' et subbito serrò la porta et andò da esso constituto domandandoli se havea da fare con nessuno, et esso constituto disse di non, et allora detto signor priore disse 'sia buon figliuolo et non dire nulla che io ti aiuterò,' intanto li cominciò a sciogliere le calze, et appoggiandolo a letto, lo sogdomitò una volta et così lo licentiò [...] dicendoli che stesse cheto"; Onestà 2, 1579, fol. 22ʳ⁻ᵛ.

admission into the Order. On the third occasion, the prior gave him some boxes full of sugared almonds. In the meantime, two other friars, Don Ippolito da Vercelli and Don Jacopo da Piacenza, adopted the same subterfuge as their superior in order to have sex with the boy.[25] The focus of Ottavio's accusations then switched to the laymen, at which point the trial changed direction and stopped pursuing the incrimination of the prior and the canons, probably because the Officers of Decency had no jurisdiction over them. In the end, the prior and the two canons seem to have gotten off scot free; no evidence of the case was found in the records of the episcopal court, despite a thorough examination of the records.

The whole affair remains shrouded in mystery. The fact that the young Ottavio confessed while under torture suggests that it was the Officers' desire to proceed that led to the sudden development of the case. Although purely speculative, it is possible that, once again, the secular court acted in order to ease the situation and resolve the matter without damaging the public reputation of the city. It seems that the rumours about Ottavio, the canons, and the prior had been circulating for some time. One of the accused laymen, the baker Paulo di Agostino Cristofori, stated that his friend, Don Domenico da Vercelli, a canon at San Frediano, had warned him to be careful because Prior Gattinara was planning to avenge a wrongdoing, namely that Paulo was alleged to have spread the rumours about young Ottavio. The baker went immediately to see the prior and found him in the company of some other canons. According to his deposition, when he asked for a tête-à-tête, Gattinara replied bluntly, "talk to me here." The baker then said in front of everyone: "my lord prior, I heard that you want to cause me trouble by saying that it was I who revealed what Ottavio did." The prior's response was to tell him to "go away and mind your own business." Out of respect for the place, the baker did not answer back. Later, another friar, Don Serafino, visited the baker in prison and warned him: "Paulo, watch out, the prior and many friars are totally furious with you [...] [they think] that it was you who revealed those things about them on behalf of Ottavio."[26]

---

[25] Onestà 2, 1579, fols. 22ᵛ, 31ʳ⁻ᵛ.

[26] "parlami qui"; "signor priore io ho inteso che mi volete far fare dispiacere dicendo che io sia stato quello che habbia palesato che Ottavio habbi fatto"; "va fa' bene et attendi a fatti tuoi"; "per stare in quel luogo non volse rispondere altro"; "paulo habbiti l'ochio che il priore et molti frati sono irati molto verso di te [...] che tu sia stato quello habbi palesato i fatti loro per conto d'ottavio"; Onestà 2, 1579, fol. 33ʳ⁻ᵛ.

It seems that it was Ottavio's uncle who had spread the rumour that Paulo the baker was the informer.[27] He admitted that they had quarrelled over a suspected theft by the youth, but he steadfastly insisted to the Officers "that he never told Paulo or others that if he accused his nephew, he would send Ottavio to the Office of Decency to denounce him [too]." However, the uncle mentioned a rumour that Paulo the baker had encouraged all of those who previously had been sexually involved with Ottavio to denounce the youth to the Officers: "Paulo the baker went to tell Michelangelo, the milliner at the *Borgo* gate, and others that if they had had anything to do with Ottavio, they should go and act like him, namely go to the Office to accuse him."[28] The whole sequence of events is complex and hard to grasp. After dismissing the evidence brought against him by torture, Paulo the baker was released on threat of a heavy fine if he took any personal action against Ottavio.[29] There is no further trace of the canons or the prior in the sources.

The trial was conducted by the secular court through the Officers of Decency, apparently without any input from the episcopal justice system. As we have seen, the rule of prevention was applied in cases involving 'mixed jurisdiction' (*mixti fori*) crimes, whereby the legal authority that had first become aware of a violation was entitled to proceed against the accused. It cannot be excluded that the diligent intervention of the Office of Decency in Ottavio's case was a way to purloin control of an important local religious institution from an episcopate that was increasingly inclined to favour the interests of Rome over those of Lucca. Nevertheless, the brutality of the torture inflicted on young Ottavio and the severity of those who interrogated the other defendants suggests that civic institutions had resolved to take a more decisive stance on controlling sexual and religious heterodoxy. It seems, therefore, that this previously unseen force was used to prevent potential internal and external scandals deriving from 'misaligned' ideas or mores. It is highly likely that the regulation of sodomy played a role in bringing San Frediano, the Lucchese bastion of religious dissent, into the fold of post-Tridentine orthodoxy. Excesses were no longer to be tolerated.

---

[27] Onestà 2, 1579, fol. 33[r-v].

[28] "che non ha mai detto a Paulo né ad altri che se accusava suo nipote farebbe andare Ottavio ad accusarlo al'honestà"; "Paulo del fornaio è andato a dire a Michelangelo capellaio a porta di borgho et ad altri che se hanno hauto a fare con ottavio che vadino a fare come lui volendo intendere essere venuto all'offitio ad accusarlo"; Onestà 2, 1579, fol. 34[v].

[29] Onestà 2, 1579, fol. 35[r].

CHAPTER 12

RESISTANCE AND SUBVERSION

It is difficult to define the real impact of Counter-Reformation fervour on societies and daily practices in Catholic countries during the Early Modern Period. Nevertheless, testimonies collected from the mid-seventeenth century
onwards demonstrate that both the clergy and laity saw the Council of Trent
as a watershed moment in the regulation of sexual behaviours. An Inquisition record from 1659 states that Francesco Pavona, "a gentleman by birth
but with ill fortune," claimed that the theologians who assembled at Trent
prohibited "fornication because, being old, they could not do it themselves."[1]
In Venice, in 1688, Fra' Illuminato Festa used similar reasoning in an attempt
to seduce a woman: "before the Council of Trent, carnal sins were not sins,
not even venial ones."[2] In 1711, a priest named Agostino Ciceri maintained
that sexual activity should not be considered sinful if it was conducted to stay
in good physical health. In any case, he continued, "the canon of the Council
of Trent, which forbade the sin of the flesh, had not really been approved."[3]
These statements lead us to believe that Tridentine reforms had a profound
impact. In sixteenth-century Lucca, however, it was still too early for such
levels of awareness, also because the issue was far from settled.

In Lucca, there was resistance to the reforming zeal of Bishop Alessandro I Guidiccioni from every level of society, from the popular classes to the
ruling elite. Although resistance took shape in varying ways in different environments, anti-ecclesiastical themes and feelings were part of a continuum.
People from different social classes shared positions ranging from general
skepticism towards religious institutions to the conscious development of
complex theories on jurisdictionalism, to radical forms of irreligion and social subversion. As Filippo de Vivo has noted, in early modern societies the
handling of public communication in both religious and political matters was

---

[1] "gentiluomo di nascita ma di bassa fortuna […] la fornicatione perché non la pote-
vano esercitare per essere vecchi"; ACAU, 1318, Inquisizione, fasc. 358, act of 9 May 1659,
cited in Rurale, *Ecclesiastico e gentiluomo*, 169–170.

[2] Barbierato, *Inquisitor in the Hat Shop*, 103.

[3] Barbierato, *Inquisitor in the Hat Shop*, 104.

a crucial factor in the management of power and the maintenance of social cohesion. The 'public sphere,' defined by the philosopher Jürgen Habermas as the arena (not a physical space) in which groups and individuals discussed matters of collective and political interest, already existed before the eighteenth century, albeit featuring different dynamics than those of modern, liberal democracies. In republican contexts such as Venice and Lucca, the act of governing was performed by a moderately large-sized political class that exercised authority over a modestly-sized community. A constant flow of information and ideas circulated outward from the centre through formal channels (laws, edicts, and publications of public proclamations), and, above all, in a world dominated by interpersonal relations, informal and unofficial channels. Information also flowed inward from the periphery. The manner in which many of the trials of the Office of Decency started demonstrates that regulated procedures were combined with information leaks, tip-offs, and frequent, corrupt practices.[4]

Cities were lively environments; squares, *botteghe*, and markets offered public spaces where citizens from widely different social backgrounds could interact and debate matters of public interest. During the sixteenth century, the religious question naturally played a central role in such debates; its constituent issues went beyond Protestant and Catholic polemics. However, as we will see, in Lucca, the different factions among the ruling elite and their popular-class supporters splintered when questions concerning the defence of local liberties, which was easily integrated into proto-jurisdictionalist discourse by the political elite, led to popular unrest taking shape as radical unbelief. At the most elementary level, blasphemy and iconoclasm were expressions of a spontaneous, burgeoning reaction from commoners, such as artisans, builders, peasants, and apothecaries, to the moralism and bigotry of the Catholic Church. This reaction was tolerated as long as the commoners showed no awareness of the social and political implications of unbelief. However, when such awareness was apparent — and trial records show that this was not a rare occurrence —, the institutions stepped in brutally. Also in Lucca, where there were no organized displays of radical religious dissent, institutions reacted harshly to blasphemy, iconoclasm, and witchcraft. Both here and elsewhere, irregular sex and unbelief were grouped together not only in the condemnatory rhetoric of preachers, but also in the proliferation of heretical opinions that questioned the foundation of the legitimacy

---

[4] De Vivo, *Information and Communication in Venice.*

of Church authority, starting with criticism of ecclesiastical prescriptions on sexual morality. Inquisition courts and city magistracies abounded with trials against men and women who were convinced that sex between unmarried individuals was not a sin. In the most radical cases, these individuals felt that prohibited acts such as sodomy were among the pleasures provided by a provident Nature to its creatures.[5] Such radical assertions were sometimes accompanied by the proudly proclaimed idea that the precepts that governed rigid Christian sexual morality had been invented by the ecclesiastical elite in order to control the people by instilling in them the fear of hellfire. Individuals who defended such opinions often highlighted the immorality of the clergy and the ruling class, thereby introducing an element of social revanchism by claiming the right to pleasure.[6]

In keeping with the heritage of republicanism in Lucca, the government assumed control of similar, although less articulated, non-normative behaviours through the legal instrument of divine and human *lèse-majesté*. According to well-established legal tradition, sexual violations negated the natural order, the safeguarding of which God had entrusted to sovereigns. The negation of sexual order was thus interpreted as an act of political provocation,[7] a vision shared by the government and understood by those who claimed their right to use pleasure at will. With a value system broadly shared amongst social actors, it seems that both the governors and the governed spoke the same language, albeit in different ways: either to justify, or to evade, control. The non-normative use of sex was both condemned as an expression of political subversion and, although not explicitly, lived as such by those who defended its liceity.

One uncommon feature in Lucca, however, is the absence of documented male-male sodomy in popular subversive discourse. In the legislative rhetoric found across early modern Western Christianity, same-sex relations — especially between men — clearly constituted the most radical form of social and political subversion. In practice, however, it is only among defendants convicted of heterosexual sodomy (often rape) that we find cases in Lucca where sexual non-conformity appears to have embodied a scornful attitude towards institutional authorities. From the archival records

---

[5] The most striking case of such beliefs was Antonio Rocco, see above, Chapter 8, 165. On libertinism and sodomy in Italy: Dall'Orto, "'Nature is a Mother Most Sweet.'"

[6] Barbierato, *Inquisitor in the Hat Shop*. On the sins of the clergy, see Romeo, *Amori proibiti*; Rurale, *Ecclesiastico e gentiluomo*.

[7] See below, 223–226.

examined thus far, it can be supposed once again that, in terms of concrete procedural practice, the institutions of the Republic of Lucca decided neither to embrace the trend of branding male-male desire as heretical nor to interpret it as radically subversive. While in Lucca, during the sixteenth century, a clear association between male-male desire and the crime of *lèse-majesté* seems to have provided the government with a flexible tool for preventing Church institutions from scrutinizing homosexual behaviours, the demonic stereotype of the subversive radical was embodied by the rapist of women and not, as elsewhere, by the homosexual sodomite and heretic.

Resistance to the top-down attempt to reform society was not exclusively focused on sexual matters. In sixteenth-century Lucca, the many episcopal court proceedings to supervise different moral violations by the clergy and laity included the control of behavioural norms in the vicinity of places of worship, with new bans on dancing and games. The records of one such case underline the shocked reactions of believers, who were poorly informed about new orders issued by the bishop and who sometimes genuinely failed to grasp why they had been implemented. After admitting to playing ball in a street adjacent to a church, one man who was on trial at the episcopal court added that "he did not know that the bishop had banned playing there, and 'I have seen playing and dancing there all my life.'"[8] Another defendant expressed his disapproval even more clearly, though he stopped short of directly criticizing the authority of the Church:

> I confess that I have played ball in the public road near the hospital of Segromigno together with Gio. di Paulo, because it has always been normal to play there, just like our elders have always said. I did not know that Mons. Bishop had issued any ban, which, for my part, I would have obeyed out of the respect that we all have, *although we think that we can play there because it is a public street.*[9]

---

[8] "non sapeva che il vescovo havesse proibito di non vi si potesse giocare, et ci ho visto giocare et ballare tutto il tempo della vita mia"; ASDL, Criminale 11, 1578–1579, fol. 176ʳ.

[9] "Io confesso che ho giocato a palla nella strada publica che è in contro all'hospedale di Segromigno insieme con Gio. di Paulo, perché è stato sempre solito giocarsi come hanno detto sempre i nostri vecchi, et non sapevo che Mons. Vescovo havesse fatto alcuna prohibizione, che quanto a me haveria obedito per la reverenza che gli habbiamo tutti, *se bene come strada publica pensiamo di poterci giocare.*" ASDL, Criminale 22, 1578–79, fol. 138ʳ. Emphasis added.

Along with these protests documented by the episcopal court, the records of the Office of Decency show that, also with regard to sexual morality, Lucchese society still featured mores that were far removed from the post-Tridentine ideal, which countered centuries of custom by legitimizing only marital sexual relations. As we will further explore later, towards the end of the sixteenth century the magistrates' interest in male-male sodomy declined and trials increasingly focused on male-female prostitution, concubinage, and other irregular cohabitation arrangements. This change allowed for the emergence of opinions about male-female sexual non-conformity that would otherwise have been condemned to silence, highlighting that people's ethical convictions and practices differed significantly from the moral order enforced by Counter-Reformation Catholicism.

Zabetta di Giovanni da Moriano was a prostitute who increased her earnings by sewing old clothes for a "huckster" (*rivendugliore*) known as Arrigo 'Lombardo.' When Zabetta contracted a serious and disabling rectal infection, Arrigo ended their sexual relationship, perhaps fearing the pox. In 1586, the woman described the previous three years of her life as a terrible ordeal, spent going from one physician to another: "one told me that it's caused by haemorrhoids, one that it was liver flow, one [that it was] a fistula, and one [told me that it was] one disease and someone else another."[10] One witness, however, claimed that he had heard her complain that a man had injured her during sexual relations "against nature" (*contro natura*).[11] The outcome of the trial is not known, but it can be seen once again that prostitution and coupledom were not mutually exclusive. The increasing control of prostitution was one of the elements that affected both Catholic and Protestant Europe. For example, between 1520 and 1590, almost all cities in Germany closed their municipal brothels. Initially developing in Protestant areas, this phenomenon began quietly, but as time passed it was sometimes accompanied by an aggressive campaign against whoredom.[12] Catholic institutions were also committed to controlling and regulating the matter. Once again, it must be underlined that the boundary between prostitutes and women of 'ill repute' was permeable and transient. The discriminating factor was acceptance by the local community; cases such as that of Zabetta and Arrigo were common.

---

[10] "et chi mi ha detto che procede da morice et chi diceva che era flusso di fegato chi una fistola et chi un male et chi un'altro"; Onestà 3, 1586, unnumbered folio (deposition of Zabetta, 3 June 1586).

[11] Onestà 3, 1586, unnumbered folio (deposition of Altobello, 31 May 1586).

[12] Wiesner-Hanks, *Christianity and Sexuality*, 86.

Indeed, such couples could live a peaceful existence and even enjoy a certain level of social integration. The woman, however, was always at risk of being accused of illegal prostitution by anyone wishing to use it against her because of a personal grudge or concerns about the reputation of the neighbourhood.

This flexibility was no longer tolerable in Catholic and Protestant countries alike. Although more extreme measures were sometimes adopted, such as banning and arresting prostitutes, the most common solution was to limit them to certain areas of the city. Only those who were not properly registered were punished.[13] As we have already seen in Chapter 5, from the sixteenth century onward shelters for prostitutes seeking redemption were established throughout Western Europe. Run by congregations and confraternities created *ad hoc* or able to devote substantial energies to the cause, such institutions were supported by noblemen, merchants, prelates, and noblewomen who wanted to invest money and relational resources in charitable establishments that would pay great dividends in terms of patronage and visibility. The institutions soon became multifaceted operations, providing redeemed prostitutes with refuge, penance, and *educat*ion, marketing items produced by their guests, and periodically assigning dowries to add to their reconstituted capital of honour and ability.[14] Sometimes, however, the profile of these institutions was somewhat ambiguous, with disturbing underlying implications. The House of Compassion (*Casa della Pietà*) in Florence, for example, had an extremely high mortality rate, the reasons for which remain unknown.[15] In other cases, such institutions effectively became prisons where forced labour was widely exploited.[16]

Studies conducted on prostitution in Lucca suggest that no such institutions were founded in the Republic.[17] As we saw in Chapter 3, in 1534 the government established the office of the Protectors of Prostitutes (*Protettori delle Meretrici*) in order to stop the abuse of these working women who were deemed a necessary presence in order to limit the spread of sodomy in the city. The office also played a supervisory role by identifying and authorising specific women to practise the profession.[18] Although this procedure could

---

[13] Wiesner-Hanks, *Christianity and Sexuality*, 124–125.

[14] Pelaja and Scaraffia, *Due in una carne*, 182.

[15] Terpstra, *Lost Girls*.

[16] Wiesner-Hanks, *Christianity and Sexuality*, 124–126.

[17] Canosa and Colonnello, *Storia della prostituzione in Italia*, 57–73; Hewlett, "French Connection."

[18] Canosa and Colonnello, *Storia della prostituzione in Italia*, 60.

have been used as a subtle way to underline the boundary separating 'public' women from their 'honest' counterparts, it does not seem that this approach was ever effectively implemented in Lucca. In the 1590s, prostitutes in the city still constituted an outlet not only for unmarried men but also for the expression of sexual desires that had no place in the conjugal bed due to obsequious respect for the sacred bond of marriage. For example, in 1592, a man denounced by the prostitute Margherita claimed that he had wanted to have anal sex with her because "I've got the thing in front at home because I've taken a wife, I want a bit of the other."[19] Another client reported by Margherita said that he had a wife and, perhaps wishing to demonstrate his good conduct, specified on more than four occasions that he did not believe "he had been unfaithful to her in these nine years."[20] The freedom with which these positions were defended before judges suggests that they were not perceived as potentially aggravating circumstances in trials. Despite the post-Tridentine pressure from Church authorities for moral renewal, it seems that Lucchese society continued to recognize the social value of prostitution by protecting its legal form and turning a blind eye when it was practised occasionally. This was in keeping with a centuries-old, highly political, pattern of tolerance in the Christian West that had its theological basis in the work of Saint Augustine of Hippo: just as the cesspit prevented the palace from being soiled with excrement, prostitution limited sexual disorder to only one part of society, thereby constituting a 'lesser' evil that it was better to allow.[21]

Other depositions given to the Office of Decency demonstrate that in the 1590s marriage was still perceived of as a 'process' in the popular mentality, even though, as we saw in Chapter 9, this was one of the features that was targeted for elimination by the Council of Trent. For instance, one defendant claimed that he had "taken a wife in April" but had not yet "married" (*sposata*) her, admitting at the same time that he had recently paid two female prostitutes for sex.[22] Clearly, in his eyes a promise of marriage was equivalent to 'taking a wife.' This demonstrates that despite the efforts of the episcopate to impose the new procedure, marriage was still seen to consist of many

---

[19] "della cosa davanti ne ho a casa che ho preso moglie, io voglio un poco di quello delle altre volte"; Onestà 3, 1592, fol. 37ᵛ.

[20] "in questi nove anni di haverli fatto torto"; Onestà 3, 1592, fol. 38ᵛ.

[21] Augustine of Hippo, *De ordine*, col. 1000. The passage is discussed in Ferrante, "Il valore del corpo," 210–211 n. 12.

[22] "preso moglie da aprile in qua"; Onestà 3, 1592, fols. 38ᵛ–39ʳ.

stages; consecration by a priest was yet to be seen as the determining factor in the creation of a conjugal union.

When, during an interrogation in 1595 Marco di Luca Pardini da Lucca said that he was not married, he was asked whether "he usually goes to prostitutes." He replied "that he is used to going to them sometimes."[23] The relative acceptance of such behaviour was also demonstrated by his subsequent statements; he said that he was a "poor young man" and that "if I wasn't a good man my master wouldn't keep me."[24] In 1595, when the cobbler who had sex with Maria da Pariana[25] defended himself, he stated that when he had sex with her, he "did it as human beings do," also adding that he did so "following the precepts of the law of God."[26] Seeing the confidence with which he invoked divine justice, the secular judges, who had never before commented about the relative liceity of prostitution, now admonished him, asking what he meant by "the law of God, because God does not command you to go whoring."[27] This bewildered the cobbler, who replied: "when someone is before you, my Lords, he gets confused," revealing the gap between their relative value systems.[28] For her part, when the woman who hosted Maria was asked if she had ever reproached her for her behaviour, she replied: "no, my Lord, I didn't scold her because [...] she was a prostitute and by providing a service to those who sought her out, she practised her craft so that she could earn a living."[29]

These cases show the extent to which people were reluctant to internalize the precepts publicized by Tridentine Catholicism. However, there was not only bottom-up opposition to the reformist zeal. The government of Lucca also strenuously opposed it, staying loyal, as we have seen, to the long tradition of political control of matters of faith and morality. The government's defence of the republican model in response to the Holy See's pressure to establish an

---

[23] "se è solito andare alle meretrice"; "che è solito andarvi alle volte"; Onestà 3, 1595, fol. 125ʳ.

[24] "povero giovane"; "se non fossi homo da bene il mio padrone non mi terrebbe"; Onestà 3, 1595, fol. 125ᵛ.

[25] See above, Chapter 5, 105–108.

[26] "come fanno li huomini"; "come comanda la legge di Dio"; Onestà 3, 1595, 127v. Similar opinions were allegedly held by a prostitute in 1597; see above, Chapter 5, 105.

[27] "la legge di Dio perché Dio non comanda si vadi a puttane"; Onestà 3, 1595, fol. 127ᵛ.

[28] "quando uno è davanti voialtri signori, si perde"; Onestà 3, 1595, fol. 127ᵛ.

[29] "signor no, non l'ho ripresa perché [...] era meretrice et facendo servizio a chi la ricercava faceva l'arte sua per poter vivere"; Onestà 3, 1595, fol. 130ʳ.

inquisitorial court in Lucca led to open conflict. While not based on the explicit theoretical formulations that would develop into jurisdictionalism over the following centuries, it was certainly a concrete example of such a policy, being grounded in regular negotiations, relentless diplomatic interplay, and the prompt defence of pre-existing prerogatives that the *civilitas* perceived as under threat from the aggression of the post-Tridentine Church.[30] The turning point in relations between the secular and religious authorities in the Republic came in 1578 with an order that established that a sentence pronounced by an ecclesiastical judge — even if *in absentia* — would make a citizen of Lucca ineligible for any public office. This retroactive law was a harsh blow to republican freedom because it also excluded the children and grandchildren of convicts from public life unless the Holy See decided to restore them "to the pristine state." This was the heavy price that Lucca had to pay to free itself once and for all from the pressure of the Holy Office.[31]

Nevertheless, there was never a decline in the consolidated tradition of Lucchese proto-jurisdictionalism. Indeed, after 1562, the application of Tridentine decrees in Lucca was monitored by an *ad hoc* court — the Office of Jurisdiction (*Offizio sopra la Giurisdizione*) — created by the government to safeguard the prerogatives of its republican institutions. The main aim of this magistracy was to regulate cases of immunity from legal proceedings and the set of exceptions that often brought laymen before the Curia of the Bishop, at the same time allowing clergymen to remain unpunished for various crimes.[32] Established to monitor procedural jurisdiction, the Office of Jurisdiction was essentially a kind of appeal court for cases in which verdicts by "other judges whose jurisdiction is not subject to the Magnificent Council" were deemed to be "against the obligation of reason, or against the regulations of the Statutes of the city of Lucca, or in violation or fraud of the temporal jurisdiction of its judges."[33] Over the decades, the prerogatives of the Office's court expanded, and the Office became one of the most important legal bodies in the Republic. It closely observed the work of the episcopal court (about which many

---

[30] On the republican model as *ante litteram* jurisdictionalism, see Ragagli, "La Coscienza di una Repubblica."

[31] "nel pristino stato"; Ragagli, "La Repubblica e il Sant'Uffizio," 192–193.

[32] Tori, "I rapporti fra lo Stato e la Chiesa a Lucca," 70.

[33] "altri giudici di iurisdizione non suddita al magnifico Consiglio"; "contro il debito di ragione, o contro le disposizioni delli *Statuti della città di Lucca*, o vero in lesione o fraude della temporale iurisdizione delli suoi giudici"; Tori, "I rapporti fra lo Stato e la Chiesa a Lucca," 71.

complaints were made to the General Council) and fought against the fiscal immunity of the clergy, subsequently playing a vital role in regulating relations between the city government and the regular orders. In 1629, it also assumed control of printed works published in the Republic. Although, except in a few cases, the work of the Office of Jurisdiction did not result in legislative proposals, it took shape in a *de facto* form of jurisdictionalism; rather than asserting an official claim, it conducted extensive concrete monitoring in order to protect the autonomy of civil institutions from the control of the Church.[34]

Although the Republic of Lucca never directly denied the prerogatives of the Holy See, it made some extremely radical requests in order to defend the rights of its secular authorities on matters of faith. In 1605 Bernardino Bernardini, the ambassador of Lucca to the Holy See, hoped that the episcopal court would be stripped of its power to impose temporal penalties, such as imprisonment or confiscation, asking that its jurisdiction remain limited to the application of spiritual penalties. This request, which clearly lacked either the support of a jurisprudential tradition or a basis in Canon law, was then reduced to a demand that the court of the vicar be denied the ability to act in secret, obliging it to keep the secular government constantly informed about any citizens being prosecuted before starting formal trials. Even more complex, perhaps, was the ambassador's effort to defend the jurisdiction of Lucca's Office of Religion over matters of faith, even after its legitimacy and very existence had been questioned. These accusations were launched by Pope Paul V and his jurists, who not only criticized the clemency of the Office of Religion in Lucca, but also deemed Lucca's mere presumption to set up an office of religion an insult to the Holy See. In his defence, the ambassador demonstrated a clear awareness of the unique nature of Lucca, emphasizing its difference from other republics, such as Venice and Genoa, as the last city-state in Italy.

On the basis of a shrewd legal consideration, Ambassador Bernardini explained that it was perfectly legitimate for civil institutions to prosecute heresy. It was essentially a question of extending the category of a 'mixed jurisdiction' offence to crimes of faith, which, besides their doctrinal element, over which the State had no prerogative, constituted an evident attack on public order. Because the matter was thus relevant to secular authority, the governing assembly was fully entitled to monitor religious orthodoxy in order to defend the common good. Unlike his previous position, this new stance boasted a long jurisprudential tradition rooted in the late medieval

---

[34] Tori, "I rapporti fra lo Stato e la Chiesa a Lucca," 71–81.

communes and the zealous work of *inquisition*s under the Podestà.[35] On the basis of the same principle, civil statutory legislation had always included laws against blasphemy, iconoclasm, magic, and witchcraft, and, indeed, as we have already seen, sodomy. Any divergent behaviour was essentially perceived to be a political crime because it was an attack on the established order.

The connection is clearly shown by the allegations made against Lorenzo dal Fabbro in the trial discussed in detail in Chapter 8. The witness who denounced the hypocrisy and sexual misconduct of the defendants closed his long tirade by clearly stating that, in his opinion, dal Fabbro should be held accountable not just for religious crimes, but also for political treason.[36] The association between heresy, sodomy, and *lèse-majesté* had long-established roots. During the sixteenth century, *crimen laesae majestatis* was the crime prosecuted most frequently in the court of *Cause Delegate*. In the rankings of offences in the 1446 and 1539 Statutes of Lucca, which were based on a value scale to quantify seriousness, "treason against the city of Lucca" appeared as the worst of the five cases that were the most repugnant crimes targeted by the judicial authorities of the State. Although heresy and sodomy (along with blasphemy, adultery, rape, witchcraft, iconoclasm, and sacrilege) were classed as "*atrocious*" (*atroci*) crimes (still considered extremely serious, but at a slightly lower level), they were compared to political offences and seen as a threat to the safety of the state.[37]

The propensity to 'politicize' crimes against religion or morality was common in the administration of sixteenth-century justice. As legal historian Mario Sbriccoli wrote on the matter, in the system of political crimes the connection between criminal law and the political history of European states was clear; the enormous increase in studies and doctrinal formulations on the subject of *crimen laesae majestatis* in the sixteenth and seventeenth centuries shows the topical nature of the problem and the concern it raised for governments. The obsession with the 'homeland in peril,' which made *crimen laesae majestatis* a separate chapter in the history of legal systems in medieval and early modern Europe, can probably be explained by the certainty that no power was eternal and the fear that inevitably derived from this.[38]

---

[35] This extremely important episode was brought to light by Ragagli, "La repubblica e il Sant'Uffizio," 328–355.

[36] "d'offesa maiestà"; "d'heresia"; Adorni-Braccesi, "Una città 'infetta'," PhD thesis, 528.

[37] "tradimento contro la città di Lucca"; Adorni-Braccesi, "La magistratura," 277.

[38] Sbriccoli, '*Crimen laesae majestatis*', 6–7.

The scope of political crime gradually broadened to cover an increasing number of offence types. Through this development, the judgement of the intention behind the crime made *lèse-majesté* a potential supplementary accusation in every case, working on the supposition that any violation of the law contained an element of 'provocation to the State' that could be interpreted as an affront to its authority.[39] The most significant outcome of this gradual evolution was the coining of the judicial category of *crimen laesae majestatis divinae*' (an offence against the majesty of God), although it was complex to interpret. '*Majestas divina*' (the majesty of God) and *ordo religionis* (the order of religion) became stronger key elements in the general ideological context framing 'the system of power'; defending them was the direct equivalent of safeguarding the State.[40]

There is sufficiently reliable evidence that shows that in fifteenth-century Lucca sodomy was already perceived as a crime associated with treason. On 18 April 1483, the General Council (*Gran Consiglio*) decided that, for the next three years, at least once during their two-month period of office, every member of the College of Elders (*Anziani*) had to provide slips bearing the names (up to a maximum of three each) of those suspected of indulging in the 'unmentionable sin.' Clerks were supposed to count these slips in secret and inform the General Council of the three most frequently denounced individuals, as long as they had been named at least fifteen times.[41] The first victims of this measure were announced during the same session, and two of the three who had obtained more than fifteen denunciations were banished: Giovanni di Andrea Neroni and Salvatore di Antonio di Giovanni.[42] Although few people were convicted through this procedure,[43] the many extensions to the measure granted over the years show the scope of the focus on

---

[39] Sbriccoli, '*Crimen laesae majestatis*', 263.

[40] Sbriccoli, '*Crimen laesae majestatis*', 346.

[41] Those who had obtained three quarters of the assembly votes were to be exiled for five years. Those who violated banishment were liable to the penalties imposed by law unless they had been summoned to the city to appear before the Podestà. The order concluded by prohibiting the Elders and clerks from revealing the names of those who were denounced on the slips against whom no action was taken.

[42] ASL, CG 21488–490 (18 June 1483).

[43] On 19 March 1488, Francesco, a cooper, known as "Fallo a tutti" ("Do it to everyone") was banished; Bartolomeo di Antonino da Carrara was handed over to the Podestà because he was a minor and *patiens* (a passive partner) so that he could be held in the city prison for two months and receive twenty-five lashes in public.

the matter.[44] As proof of the link between sodomy and treason, there was an antecedent to this 1483 special law on sodomy in terms of form and method precisely in the *discolato*, a procedure to ostracize reprobates who posed a threat to the State, which was introduced by an edict of 31 July 1482. The edict established that members of the General Council would periodically adopt a similar procedure: during sessions of the Council they would write down the names of four citizens whose presence was believed to constitute a risk to the political and civic life of the Republic.[45] Like the 1483 law on sodomy, this measure was also supplemented in the latter part of the century with repeated extensions.[46] The decision to establish the *discolato* in 1482 was the result of a coherent government policy created to defend republican liberty; although it was undoubtedly detrimental to the freedom of public debate, it also aimed to guarantee domestic stability, which became an indispensable condition for the survival of Lucca's political independence.[47] Blasphemers and profaners were also to be banished "as reprobates" in a provision that obliged the Office of Blasphemy (*Officio sopra la Blasfemia*) to record in registers "the names of delinquents and their fathers and surnames, and number of times, so that they can easily be recognized." These registers had to be stored in a secret room, the *tarpea*, "under the same penalties to which the Office of Decency is bound." The identity of anyone mentioned in the registers several times had to be announced "in the Magnificent Council that is usually held for reprobates every year in the month of March." These individuals were to be considered *ipso iure* and *ipso facto* banished "from the city and territory

---

[44] The first relevant measure reduced the incisiveness of the law, increasing the necessary number of denunciations from fifteen to twenty-five. In 1486 it was then extended for two years via a resolution that lowered the figure back to twenty denunciations. (ASL, CG 21, 727, 17 March 1486). A subsequent extension in 1488 introduced a clause protecting the secrecy of the vote, whereby every councillor had to write down something, even when he had no one to accuse, so that the identity of the denouncers was not revealed when the slips were delivered. It was also established that the penalty of banishment would be imposed only on those older than eighteen years; for those younger than eighteen, discussions would be held to decide a suitable punishment (ASL, CG 22, 154, 19 March 1488). Finally, in 1494 the law was extended for a further ten years, without any further amendments (ASL, CG 21, 510, 27 August 1483).

[45] As in the 1483 measure, after a secret count, the four most frequently denounced individuals were to be judged again; if three quarters of those present voted for them, they were banished for three years on pain of death (ASL, CG 21, 371–374, 31 July 1482).

[46] Salerni, "Una repubblica cittadina," 109–112 and 99–109.

[47] Berengo, *Nobili e mercanti*, 21–22.

of Lucca for three years." and "all of the laws and statutes that speak out against reprobates" would be used against them.[48] While the association that linked sodomy and blasphemy to political crime was evident, the law also cited the Office of Decency as the model reference institution for controlling orthodoxy. The magistracy responsible for monitoring deviant sexuality had indeed been established almost a century before bodies such as the Office of Blasphemy, founded in the 1530s,[49] or the Office of Religion, created in its image in 1545.

From the 1570s onward, in Lucca sodomy was more often directly associated with blasphemy and sacrilege than with heresy. Given that religious heterodoxy not only guided the inner lives of some of the ruling class but also influenced different forms of civic life, it was other forms of 'non-conformity' that alarmed civil institutions. Since blasphemy and sacrilege expressed the total rejection of all of the values on which social cohabitation and civic life were based, sodomy was strictly suppressed when it became associated with them, assuming the character of a subversive choice.[50] Although the city had long protected dissenters who embraced doctrinally formulated heresies, the justice system set severe measures against unbelief and the radical denial of God, and was even more unnerved by the invocation of demonic forces. In 1574, a bell ringer at the cathedral of San Martino was convicted of stealing a consecrated host for his military friend, who wanted to take it into battle. Both were burnt at the stake in the public square. Not long after, the same fate befell Polissena and Margherita, two suspected witches who confessed that they had "ravaged children," animals, and adults and had signed a pact with the devil, with whom they also claimed to have had sexual intercourse.[51]

---

[48] "come discoli"; "li nomi dei delinquenti e de' padri loro et cognomi et le volte, di sorte che chiaramente si cognoschino"; "sotto le medesime pene a che è tenuto l'Offizio del'Honestà"; "nel Magnifico Consiglio che si suol fare per li discoli ogni anno del mese di marzo"; "dalla città et territorio di Lucca per anni tre more discolorum"; "tutte le leggi et statuti che parlano contra de' discoli"; ASL, Libri di corredo alle carte della Signoria 1, fol. 104[r-v].

[49] Adorni-Braccesi, "La repubblica di Lucca e 'l'aborrita' Inquisizione," 247.

[50] On blasphemy, see Prosperi, *Tribunali della coscienza*, 352–367; Loetz, *Dealings with God*; Nash, *Blasphemy in the Christian World*; Barbierato, *Inquisitor in the Hat Shop*.

[51] "guastato bambini"; Ragagli, "La Repubblica e il Sant'Uffizio," 129–131. For a brief overview of witchcraft trials in Lucca, see Antonelli, *Lucca, processi di stregoneria*; for more in-depth analysis, see Antonelli, *La stregoneria in Lucca*; Galasso Calderara, Sodini, *Abratassà*.

The fear of the demonic increased in tandem with profound changes in popular religiosity, which increasingly tended to put faith in superstitious beliefs during collective worship. On 30 March 1588, a young soldier was gambling near an icon of the Virgin Mary at the Borgo gate in Lucca. When he violently flung down the dice after his umpteenth loss, crying out "whore of God," he dislocated his arm to the amazement of those present, who immediately thought that the painted Madonna had miraculously intervened.[52] The site soon became a place of pilgrimage; as the number of visiting devotees increased, the first cases of miraculous healings and exorcisms occurred. After a cult was established, there was also a proliferation of accounts of supposed apparitions seen in the surrounding countryside.

At the same time, a new confraternity, called the "Madonna dei Miracoli," was founded in order to worship the image and preserve it for posterity. The phenomenon started to create public order problems, so the government intervened by handing the matter over to Lucca's Office of Religion. The latter acted in conjunction with the bishop, who, for his part, had already launched an inquiry to assess the reliability of the miraculous events. In the end, it was decided that the icon should be removed from the wall at the city gate and taken to the Palace of the Podestà, the symbolic centre of civic power, showing the government's desire to maintain control over matters of faith. At the same time, a crowd that had gathered in front of the Palace was satisfied by the swift recognition of the new cult: after just five days, the sacred image was made available for popular worship in the church of San Pietro in Cortile (tellingly under the strict control of the republican government). All the clergy in the city took part in a solemn procession headed by the Canons Regular of the Mother of God, also attended by the Standard-Bearer of Justice and two Elders (*Anziani*).[53] A year later, in 1589, there was another witchcraft trial that ended with the death of two more women. The main defendant died under torture, while the other was found hanged in prison; she might have been killed, since her interrogations may have compromised certain influential figures of the Lucchese elite with whom she was involved.[54]

The interest of the Office of Decency in cases where sodomy was associated with violent expressions of 'demonic' unbelief typified the new climate in the Republic of Lucca towards the end of the sixteenth century. It is difficult,

---

[52] "puttana di Dio"; ASL, Offizio sopra la Biastima 1, unnumbered folio, 2 April 1588.
[53] Ragagli, "La Repubblica e il Sant'Uffizio," 240–246.
[54] Ragagli, "La Repubblica e il Sant'Uffizio," 246–261.

however, to establish whether this occurred because of greater institutional diligence or a real proliferation of wild and irrational heterodox behaviour. On 21 August 1570, Maria di Agostino della Marca came before the Officers to denounce her abusive husband. She recounted that "from the first night that he took her," he had

> almost always had sex with her in the wrong way [...] and because it hurt her a lot and seemed like something that Turks and beasts would do [she rebelled]. When she did not want to consent, he beat her soundly, telling her that if she ever spoke about it, he would kill her [...] and would set fire to the house.[55]

When threatened with a court appearance, the husband reacted contemptuously, saying that he had nothing to fear from justice and boasting that in several previous dealings the authorities had failed to break him. His cruelty was accompanied by a scornful attitude towards God and the sacraments: he forced Maria to eat meat on Fridays, blasphemed, and beat her if he discovered that she had been to confession, a sacrament that he had rejected ten years before. When he found her saying the rosary one day, he threatened her and "wanted her to call the devil loudly three times, and she was forced to do this so as not to be beaten."[56] After an unproductive interrogation, Maria was brought before her husband to repeat her many accusations. Given his reluctance to admit to the allegations, the Officers ordered that he be tortured. Although he tenaciously denied 'the truth,' extended torture eventually drew out a confession.[57] He was initially sentenced to perpetual banishment, but when the case was transferred to the Office of Religion various attenuating circumstances were recognized, even though some of the prosecution's case was confirmed; for example, the Office believed his denial that he had forbidden his wife to confess. While he admitted to avoiding the sacrament himself, he said that this had been for only a year as a result of some ongoing disputes that prevented him from revealing his secrets. Similarly, he portrayed eating

---

[55] "Dalla prima notte che la prese"; "quasi sempre usata a mal modo [...] et perché li faceva molto male, et parendoli cosa da turchi et bestie [lei si ribellava] et quando non li voleva consentire la batteva molto bene dicendoli che se lo dicesse mal per lei l'ammasserebbe [...] et li attaccherebbe fuoco in casa." ASL, Onestà 1, 1570, fol. 15ʳ⁻ᵛ.

[56] "volse che chiamasse tre volte il diavolo forte et così fu forzata per non toccare delle busse"; ASL, Onestà 1, 1570, fol. 15ʳ⁻ᵛ.

[57] ASL, Onestà 1, 1570, fols. 17ᵛ–18ʳ.

meat on Fridays as the result of a short-lived moral capitulation, rather than a real desire to show contempt for the Christian precept. This milder admission of guilt led to the partial mitigation of the original sentence: the Office of Decency's strict punishment of perpetual banishment was replaced by the Office of Religion with an — admittedly steep — fine of one hundred *scudi*, commutable to six months' imprisonment.[58]

In February 1572, a seventeen-year-old girl, Faostina, went to the Office to denounce another instance of domestic male-female sodomy with descriptions of violence extremely similar to those in Maria and her husband's case, supplemented with some acts of unbelief. Faostina said that her husband, Vincenzo, "took some consecrated candles with a certain disdain, put them in his mouth and gnawed at them. He then put the gnawed candles under his feet and stamped on them repeatedly." Some time before this incident, at the dinner table, after "dropping a bowl on the floor," Vincenzo took a crucifix "and gnawed on it with his teeth, and then put it under his feet and stamped on it repeatedly." On another occasion, "about two or three months ago, one Saturday evening, he flew into a rage and said 'Christ, it's Saturday evening and I haven't got two pennies to rub together'. He went to a painting of the Apostles at the Last Supper that was there in the house, saying 'Oh my Christ' [...] and spat in [Christ's] face again and again."[59]

Vincenzo had also attempted to kill his father on several occasions and tried to do the same to his wife when she refused to consent to his sexual desires. The questioning followed the same procedure employed in the previous trial of Maria and her husband, with counter interrogations and torture, although many testimonies were also provided by relatives and those with knowledge of the couple's everyday life (perhaps because the investigators were more thorough in their truth-seeking or because of the diligence of the notaries in providing a more complete record of the proceedings). Faostina and Vincenzo's case also ended with a confession and a conviction; on this

---

[58] ASL, Cause Delegate 13, 1481–1482, cited in Ragagli, "Esami per inosservanza," 319.

[59] "per certo sdegno prese alcune candele benedette se le cacciò in bocca et le ciancicò, et poi così ciancicate, se le mise sotto i piedi et le scalciò più volte"; "cascandoli una scodella in terra"; "et lo ciancicò con i denti, et poi se lo mise sotto i piedi et lo scalciò più volte"; "circa 2, o, 3 mesi sono, un sabbato sera, levandosi in collera disse: 'e Cristo che un sabbato sera io non habbi se non sei quattrini', et andò alla volta di una cena di apostoli dipinta che era li in casa, dicendo: 'hai Cristo' [...] et li sputò più volte nella faccia"; Onestà 2, 1572, fols. 18ʳ.

occasion, however, the sentence was in keeping with the standard practice of the Office, namely, a choice between a fine of twelve and a half *scudi* or two months' imprisonment.[60]

In April 1591, Caterina da Menabbio and Zabetta di Vincentone da San Concordio reported that they had been brutally raped by Lorenzo Pieri. Caterina was the first to testify, explaining that Lorenzo's assault had followed a lengthy harassment. She had even tried moving to a different house to escape him but to no avail; after discovering where she was, Lorenzo broke into her new home at night (an aggravating circumstance in cases of carnal violence)[61] and raped her viciously: "he took me forcibly in bed by the hair, and used his teeth and his hands to strike me. Then he positioned himself, wanting [carnal] knowledge of me from behind." Lorenzo was probably a painter of sacred images, given that Caterina had warned him that "there was no point in him making pious panels if he made that other mistake." When threatened with a denunciation at the Palace of the Podestà, he also displayed his contempt for the political and legal authorities by brazenly stating "that they were a bunch a shit."[62] The rapist did not act alone, but sent away his accomplices just before committing the crime so that he could be alone with the woman, who nevertheless managed to resist him. Caterina's statement to the Officers also documents his wild blaspheming: "when I shouted at Lorenzo, telling him not to kill me, he said: 'Whore of God, I'm not going to kill anyone. I just want to do it my way.'"[63]

Lorenzo Pieri's second victim, Zabetta, was less fortunate. She testified that she had been unable to fight him off because of the effects of medication and that, consequently, he had sodomized her three times while he "blasphemed, treating God like mud."[64] Because he had caused a "rupture" (*rottura*) in her anus, and also, perhaps, because of the aggravating circumstances of the domestic break-in and defamation of God, Lorenzo was placed

---

[60] Onestà 2, 1572, fols. 18r–27v.

[61] *Gli Statuti della città di Lucca*, Book IV, Chap. 105, Della pena di coloro che intrassero nell'altrui casa occultamente, et dolosamente, per cagione di commettere adulterio, o stupro, o altro delitto.

[62] "mi prese per forza nel letto per i capelli et con li denti et con le mani mi schiantava et poi si mise per volermi conoscere per dietro"; "non li varrebbe fare le taulette divote se facesse quest'altro errore"; "che li havea tutti nel culo"; Onestà 3, 1591, fol. 1r.

[63] "gridando al detto Lorenzo che non mi dovesse assassinare, egli disse: 'puttana di Dio, non assassino nessuno, voglio solo fare a mio modo'"; Onestà 3, 1591, fol. 1v.

[64] Onestà 3, 1591, fol. 12r.

in the custody of the Podestà, who was called to impose the penalty in the Statutes in accordance with the new rigorous policy: Lorenzo was decapitated and his corpse was burnt at the stake.[65]

In 1593, a woman accused her husband, a policeman (*birro*) named Altobello from Brescia, of anal rape. Both the accusation and defence statements are full of contradictions. The woman, Maria, complained that he regularly betrayed her with a prostitute, Angelica; he told Maria that he loved the latter so much that he would marry her if she, Maria, would die. Furthermore, he refused to have vaginal intercourse with Maria, and sought sexual contact only in order to sodomize her. When she refused to consent to this, except on one occasion, Altobello violently beat and bullied her. Like other women documented in the Office of Decency's records, Maria also sought comfort in relatives, friends, confidants, and her confessor. Her sister told the Officers that she had once seen Altobello stab Maria in the thigh when he lost his temper.[66] For her part, the maintained prostitute Angelica told a story of extreme poverty, saying that she had often wanted to end her relationship with Altobello and leave Lucca but, in the end, had always yielded to his requests because of her destitution. She admitted that on many occasions over the past three years, he had taken her to his house to eat and sleep while his wife was present.[67]

A neighbour, Fello da Siena, said that he had heard about Altobello's blasphemy,[68] while his wife, Diamante, knew from her conversations with Maria that he often beat her when he arrived home drunk. One curious detail that emerged was that Diamante envied her friend, despite her knowledge of the beatings, because she could enjoy herself since she had no children. Clearly not wanting to reveal the reasons for the barrenness of her marriage, Maria simply provided her confidant with a reality check, responding laconically: "everyone knows his own business best."[69] Strangely enough, although Maria doggedly accused her husband, she refused to substantiate conjecture about his unbelief despite her sister's insistence on this point in her statements.[70] Indeed, throughout the latter's dealings with the Officers, she strongly underlined that Altobello tended to express contempt for both holy

---

[65] "biastimava facendo di Dio come del fango"; Onestà 3, 1591, fol. 3[r-v].
[66] Onestà 3, 1591, fol. 67[r]–68[v].
[67] Onestà 3, 1591, fols. 68[v]–69[r].
[68] Onestà 3, 1591, fol. 70[v].
[69] "ognuno sa i fatti suoi"; Onestà 3, 1591, fol. 71[r-v].
[70] Onestà 3, 1591, fol. 76[r].

things and established power: "and she launched into a tirade, saying many things about the wicked life of her brother-in-law, as prone to blasphemy as to ill-will towards the Most Illustrious Lords."[71] The outraged woman described an episode that for her clearly summed up the accused's immorality and indifference towards public affairs: when the Palace of the Podestà was set on fire one night by conspirators, he lay in a drunken stupor in his bed while the rest of the city rushed from their slumber to douse the flames:

> I went to see him because he didn't get up, as I felt was appropriate, to go like the others to help and be of service in what was needed. When I approached him, imploring him to get up, he stretched out his hands to grab hold of me and embrace me, saying "these are the flames."[72]

The series of inconsistencies in the witness statements led the magistrates to exonerate Altobello of sodomy and hand him back to the Office of Blasphemy,[73] although his wife continued to defend him against the accusations of profanity.[74] Toward the end of January, Altobello was interrogated and denied all allegations: he had called his wife a whore and a slut, but had never added "of God" (*di Dio*) or reviled any sacred images. He was subjected to excruciating, lengthy torture: three quarters of an hour of repeated jerks (*squassi*) of the rope. He immediately tried to minimize the seriousness of the accusations by referring to his weakness for alcohol, perhaps more as a clever strategy than out of any real humility: "I'm a man who eats little and drinks a lot, and sometimes when I go to dinner, wine has a bad effect on me, and at times I've given her light slaps."[75] In the end, his perseverance paid off and he was acquitted. While the government policy maintained a relatively protective stance towards citizens who had embraced Reformed ideas, civic institutions were concerned with the most explosive, irreverent, and popular

---

[71] "et proruppe in dire molte cose della mala vita di questo suo cugnato, tanto pronto di biastima quanto per mala volontà verso gli Illustrissimi signori"; Onestà 3, 1591, fol. 68ʳ.

[72] "andando io a trovarlo perché non si levava come mi pareva debito per andare come li altri per aiutare et servire in quello occorresse, et essendomi accostata pregandolo che si levasse, stese le mani per pigliarmi et abbracciarmi dicendo "queste son le fiamme." Onestà 3, 1591, fol. 74ᵛ.

[73] Onestà 3, 1591, fol. 96ᵛ.

[74] ASL, Offitio sopra la bestemmia 1, unnumbered folio, 13 January 1594.

[75] "io sono huomo che mangio poco et bevo assai et vado alle volte a cena che il vino mi ha fatto male, et li ho dato alle volte de' buffetti"; Onestà 3, 1591, fol. 96ʳ.

forms of unbelief fuelled by contempt for the established order and socially shared moral values. It is important to underline, however, that in Lucca, unlike elsewhere, these forms of non-conformity were associated with male-female sodomy and men's violence against women, rather than homosexual sex. Although the sources do not offer any explanation on the matter, the most likely hypothesis is that the Republic preferred to direct its attention elsewhere, partly to prevent the persecution of homosexual practices from creating scandal in an increasingly claustrophobic and repressive climate. However, it might also have been because, except in cases that involved violence or created scandal, male same-sex intercourse was perceived as only a minor problem.

As we have seen, the application of the decrees of the Council of Trent and the increasing attempts of the Roman Curia to extend its political control over the entire peninsula were widely opposed in Lucca at both ends of the social spectrum. The civic government developed complex resistance strategies that met precise practical needs but that also were inspired by theoretical and legal considerations. Nevertheless, there was a high price to pay for maintaining independence. As far as the regulation of sexual non-conformity was concerned, sodomy progressively became a hushed topic. At the end of the sixteenth century, the work of the Office of Decency shrank almost to the point of disappearance, although the documentation for each trial grew significantly in length. In the meantime, the prosecution of heterosexual sodomy rose steeply in comparison (Table 7). In 1589, 1591, and 1592, the few trials that were held were related exclusively to illicit relations between a man and a woman; as was the case for the majority of cases investigated by the Office from 1589 onwards. Although the sources do not provide reasons for the trend reversal, it is unlikely that it was due to a sudden change in social customs; it seems more probable that the Office redirected its efforts towards this form of infraction. While the thorny issue of sodomy had previously been tackled by institutions through judicial surveillance, compromising between the need to moralize and pragmatic toleration, it later became an object of scandal that was simply no longer mentioned, especially in its homosexual form. The climate of the Counter-Reformation, which is palpable in the rhetoric of the trial records, finally implemented the decree of silence that had accompanied the age-old condemnations of practices 'against nature.' Centuries after it was first used, the term 'unmentionable sin' now ceased to be just a metaphor and became a descriptor of a factual reality.[76] In the political and religious

---

[76] On the unspeakable nature of the 'nefarious sin,' see Chiffoleau, "Dire l'indicible."

turmoil of the sixteenth century, the many changes adopted by the Republic of Lucca in order to maintain institutional continuity included modifying its traditional strategies for limiting same-sex sexual practices, which at the time were persistent and widespread in urban societies. Homosexual desire was not, however, extirpated, but relegated to the ambiguous prison of the closet, the position it would thenceforth occupy in Western Christianity.

CLOSING NOTE

The gradual decline of the Office of Decency is illustrated by the final chapter in its long history. Although its seventeenth-century trials have yet to be studied in detail, we know that in 1649 the Office's jurisdiction was assigned to the Magistracy of Secretaries (*Magistrato dei Segretari*). This provision was intended as only the start of a mutual-cooperation mechanism and did not initially remove all of the Office's responsibilities. However, although the purpose of adding another legal authority to find and punish sodomy was to "increase diligence in identifying delinquents," it effectively signalled a jurisdictional transfer.[1] The provision also acknowledged the excessive tolerance of the sentences given by the Office of Decency, imposing a further authoritarian shift in the statutory provisions after the turning point of 1583: "and for this reason it is deemed to be beneficial and expedient that even the first time that those older than eighteen fall into this nefarious sin, they should be banished from this city or state, and the second time they should be punished by death until the soul separates from the body." It was also established that the names "of all those who had been denounced" had to be made public in the *discolato* sessions, even if they had not yet been investigated or convicted.[2] However, the trial records collected in the *Cause Delegate* archive show that, in practice, the Magistracy of Secretaries did not adapt to the tightening of laws. Out of the nine cases from the eighteenth century, three have no reported conclusion, one was suspended, three concluded with an acquittal, one ended with a month's imprisonment of an eighteen-year-old youth, and the one resulted in the five-year banishment from the Republic of Lucca of Lazzaro Pollastrini, a *bottegaio* (store keeper) from Gragnano.[3]

---

[1] "moltiplicare le diligenze per rinvenire i delinquenti"; ASL, CG 128, Riformagioni, 9 February 1649; see also Bongi, *Inventario*, vol. I, 105. On the Magistracy of the Secretaries, see Montauti, "Le cause delegate," 82–84.

[2] "et per questo stimerebbero utile, ed espediente, che anche per la prima volta che i maggiori di 18 anni incorressero in questo nefando vitio, dovessero bandirsi da questa città o stato, e nella seconda volta punirsi con la pena della vita affinché muoiano, et l'anima dal corpo si separi"); "di tutti quelli che fossero stati denunziati"; ASL, CG 128, Riformagioni, 9 February 1649. On the *discolato* sessions, see Chapter 12, 224–226.

[3] Montauti, "Le cause delegate," table 2 in the appendix. The trials collected in the *Cause Delegate* archive were all held during the eighteenth century (43–44).

CONCLUSION

The last section has shown that by focusing on sexuality, the observer is placed in a vantage point from which to investigate the social impact of the Protestant Reformation and the Catholic response to it, moving beyond doctrinal disputes and political controversies. Working with criminal sources dealing with sexual infractions allows for an exploration of the complex interactions between the top-down attempt of religious authorities to extend their control over society and the multiple forms of negotiation and resistance at both an institutional and a popular, informal level.

Until the 1560s, when the local Church in Lucca accepted the decrees of the Council of Trent, the Office of Decency embodied a strategy of regulating sexual desires that was typical of the late medieval and early modern pattern shared by urban societies across Italy and Europe. Lay people were widely involved in the administration of religious matters in a context in which managing the spiritual life of the community assured its members stability, a sense of belonging, conviviality, and communal participation. Because forms of religiosity were an essential part of collective identity, political institutions and lay associations governed along with local religious hierarchies that were often an emanation of the city's ruling classes. Social stability was a religious value to be pursued. Avoiding the spread of sexual sins was considered an indispensable task in order to ensure God's protection of the community. A pragmatic approach, however, led to constant negotiation between the moral injunctions of the Church and the complex needs of a multifaceted society. Many lay people, both men and women, had to delay marriage or were unable (and sometimes, unwilling) to marry. However, the reason for this matter-of-fact attitude, as we have seen, was not justified only in light of material and practical needs. Indeed, the sources have revealed that, in these societies, different ethical codes coexisted with the official moral teachings of the Church in a complicated, but not impossible, relationship.

As a response to the emphasis of the Reformation on marriage, the conciliar sessions at Trent profoundly changed the approach of the Catholic Church to the sacramental nature of marriage and, as a consequence, to human sexuality as a whole. A revaluation of marriage as a form of Christian vocation brought about a relative reconsideration of the role of sex not just as a means of reproduction — which, however, never ceased to be considered its main purpose — but also as a way to cement the intimacy of the couple.

Spouses were increasingly made to feel responsible for fulfilling a life of Christian perfection within marriage. However, with responsibility came burden. Sex outside of wedlock increasingly became a source of embarrassment that was easier to deal with by pushing it into the closet rather than facing it directly. While in the seventeenth century preachers were asked to be more cautious than they had been in the past when dealing with sexual sins, the casuistry for confessors multiplied its interest in non-conforming sex, favouring a problematic proliferation of sexual discourses that called for institutional regulation. Despite this control, which was to be exerted through censorship, a dichotomy was established. A radical fracture was created between the public sphere, where sex became unmentionable, and the internal tribunal of the individual conscience, increasingly subject to the discipline of confession, where multilayered sexual discourses bloomed in secret.

In Lucca, the controlling efforts of the Church encountered many forms of resistance. On an institutional level, the republican ruling class remained attached to the civic religion model that characterized many Italian city-states between the Middle Ages and the beginning of the Early Modern Period. Paradoxically, sympathy for the Reformation among a large part of the elite was consistent with their inclination to preserve this tradition. Rather then being an element of change, many perceived the Reformed *credo* as the accomplishment of a long-established approach to civil and religious matters that was deeply influenced by the humanistic ideals cultivated by the elites. The civil institutions of Lucca fought a local Church that, since Guidiccioni's bishopric, increasingly privileged the interests of the Holy See over the priorities of the local government. The documented changes in the activities of the Office of Decency prove that the regulation of sexuality was one of the contested fields over which the Republic agreed to give way to the Church, although only partially. The progressive shift in the focus of the Officers from male same-sex to different-sex sodomy shows that the government was willing to adopt an original strategy to respond to the pressures of the Papal Curia. On the one hand, the policing of different-sex sodomy can be read as a counterpart to the new emphasis on spousal relationships. On the other hand, it can be interpreted as a way to preserve a moderate approach to the regulation of male same-sex behaviours. In the new climate of severe control that the Church was establishing across the Italian peninsula, it would have been increasingly harder to justify dozens of trials resolved through expedite negotiations and relatively lenient penalties. Silence on the matter was seen as a preferable solution. This silence, however, resulted in increasingly fewer archival sources documenting past homoeroticism.

In the light of these considerations, we can appreciate the extent to which sexuality was considered a highly charged political issue. The juridical definition of *lese majesté* (treason) indeed played a crucial role in the process that led a civil institution to be entrusted with the regulation of non-normative sexual behaviours. Moreover, it seems that, beyond judicial theory and practice, common people understood to some degree the political implications of non-conforming sex. Some of the defendants refused to repent and viscerally confronted the Officers' authority in matters of sexual behaviour, with equal, overarching contempt for the civil and religious authorities of the Republic. At the same time, others engaged in unreproductive intercourse while questioning God's authority through outbursts of blasphemy and devil worship. We cannot ignore the fact that the reports of these cases involve an element of manipulation. However, it is noteworthy that the stereotypical construction of the diabolical sodomite in Lucca appears to have been developed in purely heterosexual terms. This exception can be interpreted as further proof that the strategy adopted by the government involved simply turning away from male same-sex behaviour, scaling down its previous level of attention in a context that was becoming increasingly less oriented towards the social negotiation of morality policies.

This book, however, is more than a study of the relations between the sixteenth-century religious conflicts and the history of sexuality. The archival series of the Office of Decency is one of the richest sources for reconstructing the social practices, performances, and perceptions of non-normative sexual behaviours in early modern Italy that have thus far been analyzed. Through thorough investigation, we have managed not only to obtain a more nuanced picture of the practice of and attitudes towards homoerotic relationships in the Early Modern Period, but also to uncover some of the most meaningful pages in the as-yet unexplored history of heterosexual sodomy. As far as male same-sex sodomy is concerned, this study has taken a step forward in understanding the complex range of attitudes, behaviours, values, and emotional performances attached to male-male sex and intimacy. The study of the Iberian world and its colonies has already shown the extent to which male same-sex practices were experienced in manifold ways, stretching from the abuse of male authority over younger subordinates to relationships based on love and affection. It has also uncovered the existence of complex networks of semi-clandestine homoerotic sociability, as well as the interplay of gender and sexual performances, with attributes of effeminacy often associated with the receptive partner in male same-sex intercourse in both cultural constructs and social habits. Despite these historiographical achievements, the history of male homosexuality in medieval and early modern Italy is, however, still predominantly anchored to the idea of the ubiquity of a pederastic model reminiscent of Classical Antiquity. Although, especially in Anglophone scholarship, much has happened thanks to the contribution of cultural historians and queer literary scholars, these innovative approaches have mostly been disconnected from the thorough investigation of judicial archives. Because criminal sources are the only available gateway to the sexual and emotional experiences of common people, this progress has thus occurred at the expense of a bottom-up approach to the history of sexuality that focuses on the grassroots of society. Obviously, documents of this type need to be carefully handled, insofar as they reflect the unbalanced power relations between authorities and subjects. However, a multilayered methodological approach has allowed this study to observe the source material from different perspectives. While trial reports have been used to explore the difficult power struggles that enlivened the community of Lucca, selective reading has also revealed clues that have shed light on the everyday life experiences of diverse historical actors across the social spectrum.

Blind spots in the sources have been as relevant as the manifest interests of notaries and judges. As we have seen, consensual sex and relationships between (predominantly young) peers did not attract any particular attention and were regulated through recourse to practices of expedite justice that resulted in negotiated, relatively lenient, penalties. This tendency occasioned concise judicial reports that do not contain enough details to explore the subjective perception and life experiences of the defendants. In these cases, the use of a quantitative approach has uncovered patterns that elucidate the dynamics of homoeroticism in juvenile clandestine sociabilities. The succinct information was collected by notaries following a relatively consistent template that reported the age of the defendants, their occupations, the number of their partners, the number of sexual acts, and whether they played an 'active,' 'passive,' or 'reciprocal' role in intercourse. After compiling a database and processing the series, the data has led to conclusions that go against the grain of established opinions about male same-sex practices in early modern Italy. While the pederastic model seems to be at play after the age of twenty-five, the young male population engaged in consensual sexual acts that were often characterized by a predominance of sexual versatility. Sexual roles were not dependent on an age gap, and the insertive partner did not always occupy a position of social dominance over the receptive one.

However, there were exceptions to this model. For example, seventy-two-year-old Girolamo Nucchelli was a member of the ruling class who dared to allow young, working class men to sodomize him. It is significant that his case became caught up in the mesh of criminal justice when he attempted to seduce the young son of one the most prominent families in Lucca. This element may suggest that he could have avoided criminal prosecution if he had kept paying young men of low social background to satisfy his sexual desires. Once the proceedings started, the judges acted with a severity that was rarely displayed in other circumstances. An adult member of the ruling class who subverted the unspoken sexual template that allowed adult men to exert their authority over young subjects by sexually submitting them to their desires was a threat to the honour of the Republic and thus called for a clear, strict response. The attention of the judges, demonstrated by longer and more detailed reports, was thus primarily focused on cases that transgressed the unspoken norm that permitted young men to freely explore their sexuality until they reached the age of marriage. The same unspoken norm allowed older men to enjoy many possibilities of sexual satisfaction while maintaining the position of dominance that society granted to and expected of them. Finally, the Officers of Decency were particularly concerned with cases in which brutal and blatant violence occurred.

The need to conform to the moral commands of the Church in matters of sexual mores was thus informally negotiated with different ethical codes. Behaviours and desires were not just 'repressed' and 'controlled', but creatively regulated. Even after the Council of Trent, when the Church attempted to aggressively control the life of believers through a hierarchical restructuring of its local and central institutions, there was not a shift from regulation to repression but, instead, a change in the strategies of surveillance. While previously, forms of social containment were privileged previously, after the Council of Trent Catholic authorities endeavoured to turn regulation inward, favouring the internalization of piety through the frequent practice of the sacraments, especially confession. Even though scholars of the history of sexuality have been extremely attentive to the dynamics of this historical shift since the reception of the Foucauldian revision of the 'repressive hypothesis', the influence of the Foucauldian paradigm in the past somewhat narrowed our understanding of this ground-breaking historical moment. It is now clear that the proliferation of discourses on sex has helped to imprint the conflicts created by sexuality at the core of individual subjectivity. However, the excessive focus on sources that are relevant to the history of epistemology (medical, juridical, and theological) has favoured a top-down approach that has completely underestimated the creative capacities of people to adapt established systems of belief to their needs and to the coexistence of multiple interpretative paradigms at the same moment in time. The substantial history of resistance to the changes brought about by the application of the decrees of the Council of Trent in Lucca is a clear sign that, beyond the learned discourses of atheists and libertines, common people were also able to readapt dominant discourses to their needs through processes of resourceful negotiation that must not be neglected.

The first wave of studies on the history of male same-sex sexuality focusing on judicial sources tended to repeat the mechanistic obsession of the judges with the sexual acts performed by suspects and defendants. This book attempts to integrate the new achievements in cultural studies, queer theories, and the history of emotions into a tradition of social history that still has much to offer scholars and readers. Insights from the history of emotions have been particularly helpful in reinterpreting criminal archives. Chapter 7 reflects a diversified theoretical approach to emotions in history. First, rather then abandoning the exploration of clandestine homosexual cultures based on occasional sexual exchanges, I have tried to analyze their internal dynamics in light of historian of emotions Monique Scheer's reinterpretation of Pierre Bourdieu's theories on social habitus. No act that is repeated in a ritualized and socialized fashion is merely mechanical, nor is it devoid of repercussions in the structuring of the social self of those performing it. Within their semi-clandestine networks and in order to satisfy their desires, sodomites in Lucca had to learn an unspoken language that, when enacted with the body, called for the acquisition of a set of social skills requiring an informal initiation process. This was but one of the many social performances people had to enact in a society in which personal experiences and self-perception were shaped by belonging to multiple groups that were rigidly structured by ritual. Cultural and counter-cultural social scripts were cemented by the collective repetition of gestures and symbolic rites that favoured the internalization of socially shared values on a semi-conscious, and therefore powerfully influential, level. Even in a context like Lucca, where the overt expression of male same-sex desires through literature and art did not have a chance to flourish, participating in a sociability that focused on sexual encounters and was regulated by informal rules and encrypted languages cannot be considered a neutral activity.

The tools used by scholars of the history of emotions have been deployed not just to make sense of recurring patterns, but also to analyze the scattered traces of homoerotic emotional bonds. In order to make sense of them, these fragments have been contextualized in the wider framework of the history of friendship and the family. This perspective has proven to be beneficial in manifold ways. Especially where there is no evidence of conscious celebrations of homoerotic love, such as those that historians have uncovered in cities like Venice and Florence, putting aside the counter-cultural model and interpreting non-normative sexual behaviour along with other forms of social and affective bonding leads to a deeper understanding of the complex nature of past homoeroticism. When male-male sex was integrated into the wider picture of male sociability, it was often shaped against the model of same-sex friendship. However, male homoeroticism, like other sexual non-conformities such as concubinage and prostitution, also had a place within the confines of the household. Analyzing homoeroticism and its links to male friendship together with — rather than opposed to — the history of the family and household helps to revise our understanding of homoerotic bonds, which increasingly appear to have been located along a spectrum ranging from social seclusion to organic integration into wider circles of sociability. Furthermore, it also allows a reconsideration of the quality of the emotional bonds within the premodern family itself. Rather than creating a contrast between the contemporary nuclear elective family as a highly emotional site and the premodern household dominated by material interests and hierarchical relationships, we are now able to appreciate the complexity of affective bonds structured along axes that were radically different from those familiar to a twenty-first-century Western observer. Although there is still much to be done, the inclusion of male same-sex desire in this picture broadens our understanding of the complexity at play in the extended networks associated with households and of the inventiveness with which historical actors adapted available social scripts to their needs.

This invitation is consistent with a revision of the traditional liberal historiography on the family that started two decades ago, but which has gained new momentum as the analysis of past emotional lives became sharper. Some elements of present research, however, seem to confirm one of the core theses of the now outdated 'liberal' historiography on the family: the lack of sensitivity towards childhood and the tendency to consider the most vulnerable component of society exclusively as adults-in-training, devoid of specificity. Indeed, as we have seen, there was a propensity in the sodomy trials in Lucca to recognize the accountability of children involved in episodes of abuse: they were not exempt from punishment unless, like adults, they had accused themselves and denounced their partners/abusers to gain impunity. These considerations, however, need to be contextualized in a wider framework in which cases of child abuse raised the increasing concern of the Office of Decency. This concern is demonstrated not only by the lengthy reports of these cases but also by the proliferation of laws and decrees promulgated in the second half of the sixteenth century to discipline the matter. Punishments were probably imposed on young victims as a preventive disciplinary measure meant to discourage them from continuing to indulge in a practice that was often seen as a 'contagious' disease that was potentially transmitted through the sexual act, whether consensual or not. It is even more interesting to notice, however, that children and adolescents were recognized to have an independent form of sexual agency. They were seen as subjects with desires, not just objects of desire. Some elements from the source material seem to suggest that the same negative stereotypes attributed to lustful women were projected onto the sinful child and teenager. What has emerged is a paradigm in which sexual passivity, whether ascribed to women, children, or young adolescents, was charged with negative connotations that included a disconcerting, insatiable desire seen as irrepressible and uncontrollable. While the 'unruliness' of cisgender young men was tolerated, the feared 'hunger' of sexually-receptive subjects called for a stronger moral reaction. Besides the cultural constructs of the time, however, women, abused children, and sexually-receptive teenagers revealed another form of agency, one that the records of the time documented only indirectly. These socially 'weaker' subjects sometimes reacted to the systemic abuse they were forced to endure from male power. It is quite likely, and sometimes demonstrated in the sources, that women and young servants used accusations of sodomy to throw off the yoke of patriarchal authority that was often exercised with unbelievable cruelty. As far as women are concerned, the increasing representativeness of cases of heterosexual sodomy in the documents produced by the Office of Decency during the sixteenth century provides us with vibrant testimony to their ability to create networks of support that helped them face the everyday struggles posed by living in a violent, male-dominated society.

This study has attempted to show the benefits of a holistic approach to the study of sexuality and gender. The history of the family, the study of homoeroticism, institutional and religious history, social and cultural history, and the histories of emotions, gender, childhood, and youth are all part of a kaleidoscopic picture in which each element sheds light on the others. I hope that this multifaceted approach has allowed the vibrant life captured in the sources to shine once again through the written words on these pages.

Appendix

Table 1
1539 Statutes

Offender's Age	First Sentence	Second Sentence	Third Sentence
under 14	At the discretion of the court		
14–17	25–50 lashes	lashes (number at the discretion of the court) 1-year imprisonment	
18–30	1-year imprisonment 50-florin fine	2-year imprisonment 100-florin fine	Death penalty
31–50	Pillory 2-year imprisonment 100-florin fine	Death penalty	
51 and over	Death penalty		

Table 2
Penalties Usually imposed by the Officers

Age of Convicted	Corporal Punishment	Fine	Jail	Banishment
10–13	12–25 lashes	4 *scudi*	15 days	6 months
14–17	25 lashes	4–8 *scudi*	1 month	6 months — 1 year
18–25		12.5 *scudi*	2 months	2 years
26–35		12.5 *scudi*	2 months	2 years

Table 3
Profession of the Accused and Summoned

Weaver	179	Servant	14
Various	113	Goat butcher (*beccai*)	12
Baker	57	Woodcutter	12
Spinner	33	Apothecary	8
Soldier	31	Broker	7
Butcher	30	Envoy	7
Tailor	29	Mattress maker	7
Cheesemaker	27	Cobbler	6
Shoemaker	27	Donzel	6
Barber	24	*Strinaporci*[1]	6
Clergyman	23	Bath keeper	5
Innkeeper	21	Dyer	5
Shop boy	17	Hat maker	5
Construction worker	15	Miller	5
Prostitute	15	Oil maker	5

Table 4
Age of the Accused and Summoned

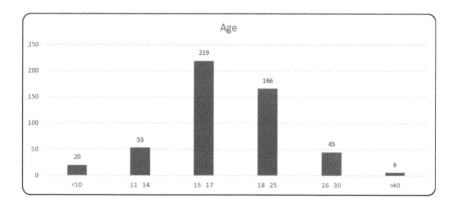

---

[1] A strinaporci probably refers to the person who removed the bristles from pork rind by burning them off.

Table 5
Defendants and Convicts

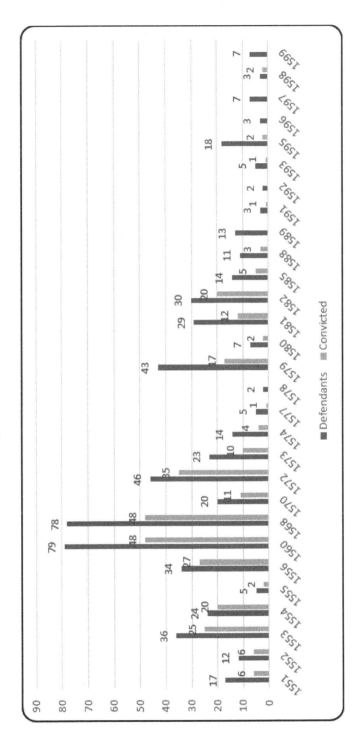

■ Defendants ■ Convicted

Table 6
1539 and 1583 Statutes

Age	Age	First Conviction		Second Conviction		Third Conviction	
1539	1583	1539	1583	1539	1583	1539	1583
Under 14	under 14	At the discretion of the court	At the discretion of the court		Doubled		
14–17	14–17	Lashes	30-day imprisonment	1-year imprisonment	60-day imprisonment		
18–30	18–25	1-year imprisonment 50 florins	2-month imprisonment 2-year banishment	2-year imprisonment 50 florins	1-year imprisonment 2-year banishment	Death penalty	Death penalty
30–50	25–50	Pillory 2-year imprisonment 100 florins	1-year imprisonment 10-year banishment	Death penalty	Death penalty		
50 and older	50 and older	Death penalty	Death penalty				

Table 7
Heterosexual Sodomy

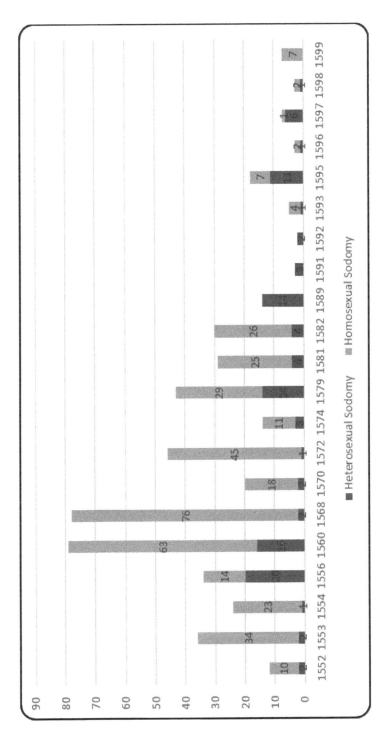

GLOSSARY

Anziani (Elders): Lucca's main executive body; it consisted of ten members: the *Gonfaloniere di Giustizia* (Standard-Bearer of Justice), who chaired meetings, and nine other men elected every two months by thirty-six constituents.

Balìa: an *ad hoc* committee entrusted with extra-ordinary powers to deal with an emergency or special situation.

Bolognino (pl. *bolognini*): a coin issued in Bologna from the twelfth to the eighteenth century. Coins called *bolognini* were also issued by mints of other communes, including Lucca.

Cadastre, see *Catasto*

Capitano di Custodia (Custody Captain): in Lucca, the Custody Captain was part of the *podestà*'s retinue (*famiglia*). His responsibility were the supervision and protection of the city and its villages, which he carried out with his own staff of gatekeepers and guards carried out night patrols, guarded against gambling and the possession of prohibited weapons. When necessary, the *Capitano di Custodia* also assembled citizen militias.

Catasto (cadastre): real estate register for tax purposes.

Collegium Subdomitarum (Committee on Sodomites): a committee constituted in Venice in 1418 within the "Council of Ten" in order to investigate and prosecute sodomy. The Council of Ten, consisting of ten regularly elected particians, was one of the main governing bodies of the Republic. It was entrusted with overseeing corruption, intelligence services, and military affairs and, in general, maintaining peace within the state. The fact that this body elected a committee of selected citizens to prosecute sodomy is proof of the political relevance of governing sexual morality in early modern Italian states.

Committee on Sodomites, see *Collegium Subdomitarum*.

Consiglio Generale (General Council): Lucca's main legislative body. It consisted of ninety members, thirty for each of the three subdivisions (*terzieri*) in which the city was divided, chosen annually, for a one-year term, by the *Anziani* (Elders) and a committee of twelve citizen. Despite the increasing power of the executive branch, the Council, which met up to three times a week, always remained the true heart of republican life. Actively involved in legislation, it also appointed ordinary and special courts.

Custody Captain, see *Capitano di Custodia*

Ducato (pl. *ducati*; English, ducat): a coin issued by various jurisdictions. The first *ducati* in Italy were issued in silver by King Roger II of Sicily in the mid twelfth century, soon followed by the Republic of Venice with silver ducats in 1202 and gold ducats in 1284. Subsequently, gold ducats were issued by the Papal States, the Holy Roman Empire, and many other jurisdictions both in Italy and abroad.

Fiorino (pl. *fiorini*; English, florin): a Florentine coin first issued in silver then, from 1253, in gold. On the obverse it was engraved with the Florentine lily and on the reverse with St John the Baptist in a hair shirt. Several variants were subsequntly issued and identified by their size and weight (*largo, leggero, stretto, di grosso, di buon peso, di suggello*). The florentine coin was widely used for commercial transactions, and it was adopted by other jurisdictions, among them Lucca, Milan, and the Papal dominions.

General Council, see *Consiglio Generale*.

Gonfaloniere di Giustizia (Standard-Bearer of Justice): originally, the keeper of the commune's standard (flag); eventually, the magistrate who was the head of government and in charge of the commune's military. In Lucca, he chaired the sessions of the General Council.

Grosso (pl. *grossi*): the most widespread coin in Europe. It was made of silver and its weight and value changed depending on where it was produced.

Lira (pl. *lire*): originally a widespread money of account across medieval Europe; in the fifteenth century it became a coined currency.

Lords of the Night, see *Signori di Notte*.

Maggiore Esattore: the chief tax collector.

Magistracy of Secretaries, see *Magistrato dei Segretari*.

Magistrato dei Segretari (Magistracy of Secretaries): founded in Lucca in 1371, when the General Council approved a proposal to appoint one or more men responsible for receiving secret information from scouts regarding the security of the Republic and passing it on to the government. In time, the provisions of the Statutes were modified by decrees issued by the General Council, which assumed control of the election of the Secretaries and sometimes increased their number. Among other duties, the *M.d.S.* was responsible for monitoring female monasteries; punishing those who threatened the chastity of the girls and women in almshouses; investigating and punishing those who disclosed state secrets, authors of slanderous pamphlets or anonymous letters, and defilers of houses.

Mazziere (pl. *mazzieri*; English, macebearer): in Lucca, gatekeepers at the Palace of the Government.

Night Officers, see Ufficiali di Notte.

Office of Blasphemy, see *Officio sopra la Blasfemia*.

Office of Decency, see *Offizio sopra l'Onestà*.

Office of Religion, see *Offizio sopra la religione*.

Officio sopra la Blasfemia (Office of Blasphemy): founded in Lucca in 1531 to prosecute the widespread practice of blasphemy. It was one of the measures taken by the government to contain the circulation of religious dissent while firmly keeping the hands of the episcopal justice off its control.

Offizio sopra la religione (Office of Religion): founded in Lucca in 1545 in the wake of the spread of the Protestant Reformation, it was a special civic tribunal exclusively devoted to the control of religious dissidence in the territories of the Republic. The magistracy, which was establish to limit the interference of the Roman Holy Office in the internal affairs of the city-state, was structured on the model of the Office of Decency.

Offizio sopra l'Onestà (Office of Decency): a magistracy founded in Lucca in 1448 to prosecute sodomy. Its activity reached its peak in the sixteenth century and declined in the seventeenth. It was eventually suppressed and, in 1649, its jurisdiction transferred to the Magistracy of Secretaries.

Podestà: the chief magistrate of Italian communes. Term and obligations varied from place to place, but in Lucca he was appointed for a period of six months and chosen from the aristocracy of a city at least sixty miles away. He was the head of the judicial power, and presided over the legislative branch and had an important role as supervisor of the military. Although by 1372 he had lost the political power he had enjoyed in the thirteenth century, he remained the major judicial authority and police official in Lucca until the early modern period.

Protectors of Prostitutes, see *Protettori delle Meretrici*.

Protettori delle Meretrici (Protectors of Prostitutes): founded in Lucca in 1534 to protect public prostitutes from abuses. Among other reasons, the General Council justified the decision by stating that prostitution was an instrument to prevent men from indulging in worse sins, including sodomy.

Scudo (pl. *scudi*): a gold or silver coin minted by almost all Italian states. Golden *scudi* imported from France started circulting in Italy at the beginning of the sixteenth century; once introduced, the *scudo* competed with the *ducato*.

Signori di Notte (Lords of the Night): a Venetian criminal court already active in the twelfth century. It was charged with patrolling the streets at night in order to prevent crimes from being committed.

Standard-Bearer of Justice, see *Gonfaloniere di Giustizia*.

Statuti (Statutes): collections of norms regulating the activity of political bodies and public and private institutions. Starting from the thirteenth century they became increasingly systematized bodies of legislation in Italian communes. In Lucca, the process of codification reached its peak in the sixteenth century, with the publication in 1539 of a printed version of the new statutes in the Tuscan vernacular. This was both a celebration of Lucca's republican ideals and an attempt to reinforce the internal cohesion of its political body.

Targetto (pl. *targetti*): a messenger with a badge (*targa*). In Lucca, *targetti* were messengers and servants of the courts and city-magistrates.

Ufficiali di Notte (Night Officers): a court dedicated to the control of sodomy in Florence. Active from 1432 to 1502, it served as a model for Lucca's Office of Decency.

Cited Works

Abbreviations

ACAU   Archivio della Curia Arcivescovile di Udine
AHN   Archivo Histórico Nacional, Madrid
ASDL   Archivio Storico Diocesano di Lucca
ASL   Archivio di Stato di Lucca
ATL   *Anziani* al tempo delle libertà [Archivio di Stato di Lucca]
CD   Cause Delegate [Archivio di Stato di Lucca]
CG   Consiglio Generale [Archivio di Stato di Lucca]
Onestà *Offizio sopra l'Onestà* [Archivio di Stato di Lucca]

Manuscript Sources

Lucca. Archivio di Stato di Lucca (ASL)
    Anziani al tempo delle libertà (ATL)
    Capitoli della Confraternita della Madonna della Stiava.
    Cause Delegate (CD) 12, 13.
    Consiglio Generale (CG) 5, 7, 16, 17, 18, 21, 22, 42, 44, 50, 51, 56, 57, 58,
       63, 65, 66, 70, 73, 74, 79, 100, 128.
    Diplomatico, San Frediano, 13 February 1396.
    Libri di corredo alle carte della Signoria 1
    Libro d'oro della nobiltà lucchese, 1826–1847.
    Offizio sopra l'Onestà (Onestà) 1–6.
    Offizio sopra la Biastima 1.
    Offizio sopra la Giurisdizione 68.
    Podestà. Sentenze e Bandi 264, 286.
    Riformagioni, armario 45, n. 18.
    Statuti 4, 10, 17.

Lucca. Archivio Storico Diocesano di Lucca (ASDL)
    Criminale 11, 14, 22, 113
    Criminale (numero provvisorio): 78, 108, 109)

Venice. Biblioteca Marciana
    Cod. Marc., It. 234–922

Printed Sources

Adorni-Braccesi, Simonetta. "Le carte lucchesi del processo inquisitoriale di Alessandro Diodati (aprile 1959 – aprile 1560)." *Annali della Scuola Normale Superiore di Pisa. Classe di Lettere e Filosofia* 5.1 (2009): 363–386.

————. "Guidiccioni, Alessandro." In *Dizionario Biografico degli Italiani*, 61. Rome: Istituto dell'Enciclopedia Italiana, 2004), s.v. Online at: https://www.treccani.it/enciclopedia/alessandro-guidiccioni_(Dizionario-Biografico).

————. "Tra fuga e partita: Italiani a Ginevra nel Cinquecento." In Adriano Prosperi, Massimo Donattini, Gian Paolo Brizzi, eds. *Il piacere del testo. Saggi e studi per Albano Biondi*. Rome: Bulzoni, 2001, 23–44.

————. "La magistratura delle *Cause Delegate* nella Repubblica di Lucca: eresia e stregoneria (secoli XVI-XVIII)." In Andrea Del Col and Giovanna Paolin, eds. *L'Inquisizione Romana: metodologia delle fonti e storia istituzionale. Atti del seminario internazionale, Montereale Valcellina, 23 e 24 settembre 1999*. Trieste: Edizioni dell'Università di Trieste, 2000, 273–294.

————. "Strategie politiche e proselitismo religioso degli esuli lucchesi tra confessionalismi e libertà di coscienza nella seconda metà del XVI secolo." In Susanna Peyronel Rambaldi, ed. *Circolazione di uomini e d'idee tra Italia ed Europa nell'età della Controriforma: Atti del XXXVI Convegno di studi sulla Riforma e i movimenti ereticali in Italia (Torre Pellice, 1–3 settembre 1996)*. Torre Pellice: Società di Studi Valdesi, 1997, 13–39.

————. *«Una città infetta». La Repubblica di Lucca nella crisi religiosa del Cinquecento*. Florence: Leo S. Olschki, 1994.

————. "Le Nazioni lucchesi nell'Europa della Riforma." *Critica storica* 3 (1991): 363–426.

————. "La repubblica di Lucca e «l'aborrita» Inquisizione: istituzioni e società." In Andrea del Col, Giovanna Paolin, eds. *L'inquisizione romana in Italia nell'età moderna. Archivi, problemi di metodo e nuove ricerche. Atti del seminario internazionale, Trieste, 18–20 maggio 1988*. Rome: Ministero per i beni culturali e ambientali, Ufficio centrale per i beni archivistici, 1991, 233–262.

————. "Una città 'infetta': Lucca nei contrasti religiosi del '500. Unpublished PhD thesis. Pisa and Florence, University of Pisa and University of Florence, 1986.

_____. "Giuliano da Dezza, *caciaiuolo*. Nuove prospettive sull'eresia a Lucca nel XVI secolo." *Actum Luce* 9 (1980): 89–139.

Aldrich, Robert and Garry Wotherspoon. *Who's Who in Gay and Lesbian History. From Antiquity to the Mid-Twentieth Century*. London: Routledge, 2001.

Alfieri, Fernanda. "Impossibili unioni di uguali. L'amore fra donne nel discorso teologico e giuridico (secoli XVI–XVIII)." *Dimensioni e problemi della ricerca storica* 2 (2012): 105–125.

Andreucci, Salvatore. "Momenti e aspetti del moto penitenziale dei disciplinati nella città di Lucca." *Actum Luce* 1 (1973): 53–80.

Anonymous. *I Germini sopra quaranta meritrice della Città di Fiorenza,* ed. Danilo Romei. [Florence]: Nuovo Rinascimento, 2020. Online at: http://www.nuovorinascimento.org/n-rinasc/testi/pdf/germini/germini_nr.pdf

Antonelli, Vittorio. "Lucca, processi di stregoneria." In Adriano Prosperi, Vincenzo Lavenia, John Tedeschi, eds. *Dizionario storico dell'Inquisizione*. Pisa: Edizioni della Normale, 2010.

_____. "La stregoneria in Lucca." In Giovanna Bosco e Patrizia Castelli, eds. *Stregoneria e streghe nell'Europa moderna. Convegno internazionale di studi, Pisa, 24–26 marzo 1994*. Rome: Ministero per i beni culturali e ambientali, Ufficio centrale per i beni librari, le istituzioni culturali e l'editoria. Pisa: Pacini, 1996, 409–423.

Aquinas, Thomas. *S. Thomae Aquinatis Liber de veritate catholicae fidei contra errores infidelium, qui dicitur Summa contra Gentiles*, ed. by Ceslao Pera, Pietro Caramello, and Marc Paul. Turin: Marietti, 1961.

_____. *Summa theologica*, trans. by the Fathers of the English Dominican Province, New York: Benziger Bros., 1947–48.

_____. *Scriptum super Sententiis magistri Petri Lombardi,* ed. Pierre Mandonnet, 2 vols. Parma: Fiaccadori, 1858.

Ariès, Philippe. *Centuries of Childhood: A Social History of Family life*, trans. Robert Baldick. New York, Knopf, 1962.

Ariosto, Ludovico. *The Comedies of Ariosto*, ed. and trans. Edmond M. Beame and Leonard G. Sbrocchi. Chicago and London: The University of Chicago Press, 1975.

_____. *Commedie e satire*, ed. Giovanni Tortoli. Florence: Barbèra, Bianchi e comp., 1856.

Arondekar, Anjali R. *For the Record: On Sexuality and the Colonial Archive in India*. Durham: Duke University Press, 2009.

Augustine of Hippo. "De ordine." In Jacques-Paul Migne, ed. *Patrologiae cursus completus* 32 (Paris, 1841), col. 977–1020.

Azpilcueta, Martin de. *Manuale de' confessori et penitenti*. Venice: Gabriel Giolito di Ferrarii, 1569 [1557].

Baldassari, Marina. *Bande giovanili e «vizio nefando». Violenza e sessualità nella Roma barocca*. Rome: Viella, 2005.

Barbierato, Federico. *The Inquisitor in the Hat Shop: Inquisition, Forbidden Books, and Unbelief in Early Modern Venice*. Farnham and Burlington: Ashgate, 2012.

Barclay, Katie, Kimberley Reynolds and Ciara Rawnsley, eds. *Death, Emotion and Childhood in Premodern Europe*. London: Palgrave Macmillan, 2016.

Barclay, Katie. "The Emotions of Household Economics." In Andrew Lynch and Susan Broomhall, eds. *The Routledge History of Emotions in Europe, 1100–1700*. London and New York: Routledge, 2020, 185–199.

————. *Love, Intimacy and Power: Marriage and Patriarchy in Scotland, 1650–1850*. Manchester / New York: Manchester University Press, 2011.

Barsanti, Paolo. *Il Pubblico insegnamento in Lucca dal secolo XIV alla dine del secolo XVIII*. Lucca: Marchi, 1905.

Barton, Florence Whitfield. *Calvin and the Duchess*. Louisville, KY: J. Knox Press, 1989.

Bennassar, Bartolomé. "Le modèle sexuel: L'Inquisition d'Aragon et la répression des péchés 'abominables.'" In Bartolomé Bennassar, ed. *L'Inquisition espagnole, V^e–XIXe siècle*. Paris: Hachette, 1979, 339–69.

Bennett, Judith M. *History Matters: Patriarchy and the Challenge of Feminism*. Philadelphia: University of Pennsylvania Press, 2006.

Berco, Cristian. *Sexual Hierarchies, Public Status: Men, Sodomy, and Society in Spain's Golden Age*. Toronto: University of Toronto Press, 2007.

————. "Social Control and its Limits: Sodomy, Local Sexual Economies, and Inquisitors during Spain's Golden Age." *The Sixteenth Century Journal* 36.2 (2005): 331–358.

Berengo, Marino. *L'Europa delle città: Il volto della società urbana europea tra Medioevo ed Età Moderna*. Turin: Einaudi, 1999.

————. *Nobili e mercanti nella Lucca del Cinquecento*. Turin: Einaudi, 1999 [1965].

Bernardino da Siena. *Le prediche volgari*, ed. Ciro Cannarozzi, vol. 4, *Quaresimale del 1425*, t. 2. Florence: Libreria editrice fiorentina, 1940.

Biagioni, Mario. *Radical Reformation and the Making of Modern Europe: A Lasting Heritage.* Leiden: Brill, 2017.

Black, Christopher F. *Italian Inquisition.* New Haven: Yale University Press, 2009.

Blackmore, Josiah and Gregory S. Hutcheson, eds. *Queer Iberia: Sexualities, Cultures, and Crossings from the Middle Ages to the Renaissance.* Durham: Duke University Press, 1999.

Boddice, Rob. *The History of Emotions.* Manchester: Manchester University Press, 2018.

Boer, Wietse de. *The Conquest of the Soul: Confession, Discipline, and Public Order in Counter-Reformation Milan.* Leiden: Brill, 2001.

Bongi, Salvatore. *Inventario del Regio Archivio di Stato in Lucca.* Lucca: Istituto Storico Lucchese, 1872–1888.

_____. *Bandi lucchesi del secolo decimoquarto.* Bologna: Tipografia del Progresso, 1863.

Boone, L.J. "Those Damned Sodomites: Public Images of Sodomy in the Eighteenth Century Netherlands." In Kent Gerard and Gert Hekma, eds. *The Pursuit of Sodomy: Male Homosexuality in Renaissance and Enlightenment Europe.* New York: Harrington Park Press, 1989, 237–248.

Bossy, John. *Christianity in the West, 1400–1700.* Oxford and New York: Oxford University Press, 1985.

Boswell, John. *Christianity, Social Tolerance, and Homosexuality: Gay People in Western Europe from the Beginning of the Christian era to the Fourteenth Century.* Chicago: University of Chicago Press, 1980.

Bray, Alan. *The Friend.* Chicago: University of Chicago Press, 2003.

_____. *Homosexuality in Renaissance England.* New York: Columbia University Press, 1995 (first edition 1982).

Broomhall, Susan, ed. *Early Modern Emotions: An Introduction.* London and New York: Routledge: 2017.

Broomhall, Susan, Jane W. Davidson and Andrew Lynch, eds. *A Cultural History of the Emotions.* 6 vols. London/Oxford/New York/New Delhi/Sydney: Bloomsbury, 2019.

Burger, Glenn and Steven F. Kruger, eds. *Queering the Middle Ages.* Minneapolis: University of Minnesota Press, 2001.

Burke, Peter. "Humanism and Friendship in Sixteenth-Century Europe." In Julian Haseldine, ed. *Friendship in Medieval Europe.* Gloucestershire, UK: Sutton, 1999, 251–61.

Cadden, Joan. *Nothing Natural is Shameful: Sodomy and Science in Late Medieval Europe*. Philadelphia: University of Pennsylvania Press, 2013.

Canepari, Eleonora. "Civic Identity, 'Juvenile' Status and Gender in Sixteenth-Century Italian Towns." In Deborah Simonton, ed. *The Routledge History Handbook of Gender and the Urban Experience*. London, New York: Routledge, 182–194.

Canosa, Romano. *La restaurazione sessuale. Per una storia della sessualità tra Cinquecento e Settecento*. Milan: Feltrinelli, 1993.

_____. *Storia di una grande paura. La sodomia a Firenze e Venezia nel Quattrocento*. Milan: Feltrinelli, 1991.

_____ and Isabella Colonnello. *Storia della prostituzione in Italia: dal Quattrocento alla fine del Settecento*. Rome: Sapere 2000, 1989.

Cantarella, Eva. *Bisexuality in the ancient world*, trans. Cormac Ó Cuilleanáin. New Haven: Yale University Press, 2002.

_____ and Andrew Lear, eds. *Images of Ancient Greek Pederasty: Boys Were Their Gods*. London, New York: Routledge, 2008.

Cantarella, Glauco M. "Pier Damiani, il *Liber Gomorrhianus* e Leone IX." In Maria C. De Matteis, ed. *Ovidio Capitani: Quaranta anni per la storia medievale*, 2 vols. Bologna: Patron, 2003, 117–125.

Caponetto, Salvatore. *The Protestant Reformation in Sixteenth-Century Italy*, trans. Anne C. Tedeschi and John Tedeschi. Kirksville, MO: Thomas Jefferson University Press, 1999.

_____. "La repubblica di Lucca nelle orazioni di Aonio Paleario." *Actum Luce* 1.2 (1986): 7–16.

Carrasco, Rafael. *Inquisición y represión sexual en Valencia. Historia de los sodomitas (1565–1785)*. Barcelona: Laertes, 1985.

Cavaillé, Jean-Pierre. *Les déniaisés. Irréligion et libertinage au début de l'époque modern*. Paris: Classiques Garnier, 2013.

_____. "Alcibiade enfant à l'école. Clandestinité, irréligion et sodomie." *Tangence* 81 (2006): 15–38.

Centrone, Bruno, ed. *Studi sui* Problemata *physica aristotelici*. Naples: Bibliopolis, 2011.

Chiang, Howard, ed. *Revisiting* The History of Sexuality: *Thinking with Foucault at Forty*. Special issue of *Cultural History* 5.2 (2016).

Chiffoleau, Jacques. "Dire l'indicible. Remarques sur la catégorie du nefandum du XIIᵉ au XVᵉ siècle. *Annales* 45.2 (1990): 289–324.

Civitale, Giuseppe. *Historie di Lucca*, ed. Mario F. Leonardi. Rome: Istituto storico italiano per l'Età moderna e contemporanea, 1988.

Cohen, David. "Law, Society and Homosexuality in Classical Athens." In Mark Golden and Peter Toohey, eds. *Sex and Difference in Ancient Greece and Rome*. Edinburgh: Edinburgh University Press, 2003, 151–166.

Corbin, Alain, ed. *Violences sexuelles*. Paris: Editions Imago, 1989.

_____, Jean-Jacques Courtine and Georges Vigarello, eds. *Histoire des émotions*. 3 vols. Paris: Éditions du Seuil, 2016–2017.

Corpus Iuris Canonici, vol. 2, *Decretalium collections*, ed. Emil A. Friedberg. Graz: Akademische Druck/u. Verlagsanstalt, 1959.

Covarrubias y Orozco, Sebastian de. *Tesoro de la lengua castellana, o Española*. Madrid: Luis Sanchez, 1611.

Cozzi, Gaetano. *Una vicenda della Venezia barocca. Marco Trevisan e la sua 'eroica amicizia'*. Venezia: Fondazione Giorgio Cini, 1960.

Crompton, Louis. *Homosexuality & Civilization*. Cambridge, MA: Belknap Press of Harvard University Press, 2003.

_____. "The Myth of Lesbian Impunity: Capital Laws from 1270 to 1791." *Journal of Homosexuality* 6.1–2 (1981): 11–25.

Crouzet-Pavan, Elizabeth. "A Flower of Evil: Young Men in Medieval Italy." In Giovanni Levi and Jean-Claude Schmitt, eds. *A History of Young People in the West*, vol. 1, *Ancient and Medieval Rites of Passage*, trans. Camille Naish. Cambridge, MA: Harvard University Press, 1997, 173–221.

Cryle Peter and Lisa O'Connell, eds. *Libertine Enlightenment: Sex, Liberty, and Licence in the Eighteenth Century*. New York: Palgrave Macmillan, 2004.

Cunningham, Andrew and Ole Peter Grell. *The Four Horsemen of the Apocalypse: Religion, War, Famine, and Death in Reformation Europe*. Cambridge and New York: Cambridge University Press, 2000.

Dall'Orto, Giovanni. "'Nature is a Mother Most Sweet': Homosexuality in Sixteenth- and Seventeenth-Century Italian Libertinism." In Gary P. Cestaro, ed. *Queer Italia: Same-Sex Desire in Italian Literature and Film*, New York: Palgrave Macmillan, 2004, 83–104.

_____. "'Adora più presto un bel putto, che Domenedio'. Il processo a un libertino omosessuale: Francesco Calcagno (1550)." *Sodoma* 5 (1993): 43–55.

_____. "'Socratic Love' as a Disguise for Same-Sex Love in the Italian Renaissance." In Kent Gerard and Gert Hekma, eds. *The Pursuit of Sodomy: Male Homosexuality in Renaissance and Enlightenment Europe*. New York: Harrington Park Press, 1989, 33–65.

Damiani, Pier. *The Book of Gomorrah and St. Peter Damian's Struggle Against Ecclesiastical Corruption*, ed. and trans. Matthew Cullinam Hoffman. New Braunfels: Ite and Thoman Books and Media, 2015.

_____. *Die Briefe des Petrus Damiani*, ed. Kurt Reindel. 4 vols. Munich: Monumenta Germaniae Historica, 1983–1993.

Darnton, Robert. "Sex for Thought." In Kim M. Phillips and Barry Reay, eds. *Sexualities in History: A Reader*. New York: Routledge, 203–221.

Davidson, James N. *The Greeks and Greek Love: A Radical Reappraisal of Homosexuality in Ancient Greece*. London: Weidenfeld and Nicholson, 2008.

Davidson, N.S. "Sex, Religion, and the Law: Disciplining Desire." In Bette Talvacchia, ed. *A Cultural History of Sexuality in the Renaissance*. Oxford and New York: Berg 2011, 95–111.

_____. "Sodomy in Early Modern Venice." In Tom Betteridge, ed. *Sodomy in Early Modern Europe*. Manchester and New York: Manchester University Press, 2002, 65–81.

Derrida, Jacques. *Archive Fever: A Freudian Impression*, trans. Eric Prenowitz. Chicago: University of Chicago Press, 1996.

De Vivo, Filippo. *Information and Communication in Venice: Rethinking Early Modern Politics*. Oxford and New York: Oxford University Press, 2007.

Delicado, Francisco. *La Lozana andalusa*, ed. Luisa Orioli. Milan: Adelphi, 1970.

Dezza, Ettore. *Accusa e inquisizione dal diritto comune ai codici moderni*. Milan: Giuffrè, 1989.

Dinshaw, Carolyn. "Touching on the Past," in Mathew Kuefler, ed. *The Boswell Thesis: Essays on Christianity, Social Tolerance, and Homosexuality*. Chicago: University of Chicago Press, 2006, 57–73.

_____. *Getting Medieval: Sexualities and Communities, Pre- and Postmodern*. Durham: Duke University Press, 1999.

Donoghue, Emma. *Passions Between Women: British Lesbian Culture 1668–1801*. London: Scarlet Press, 1993.

Dover, Kenneth J. *Greek Homosexuality*. Duckworth: London, 1978.

Edelman, Lee. *No Future: Queer Theory and the Death Drive*. Durham: Duke University Press, 2004.

Eichhorn, Kate. *Archival Turn in Feminism: Outrage in Order*. Philadelphia: Temple University Press, 2013.

Eisenbichler, Konrad, ed. *A Companion to Medieval and Early Modern Confraternities*. Leiden: Brill, 2019.

_____. *The Boys of the Archangel Raphael: A Youth Confraternity in Florence, 1411–1785*. Toronto and Buffalo: University of Toronto Press, 1998.

Elias, Norbert. *Civilizing Process*, trans. Edmund Jephcott. Oxford and Cambridge, MA: Blackwell, 1994 [1939].

Epistola de morte Paulii Tertij Pont. Max. deque iis quae ei post mortem eius acciderunt. Piacenza: n.p., 1549 [but probably Basel: Oporinus, 1549].

Erasmus of Rotterdam. *On Good Manners for Boys*. In Erasmus of Rotterdam, *Collected Works*, vol. 25, trans. Brian McGregor. Toronto: University of Toronto Press, 1985, 269–289.

_____. *De Ratione studii*. In *Opera Omnia Desiderii Erasmi Roterodami*, ed. Jean-Claude Margolin, vol. 1.2. Amsterdam: North Holland, 1971, 152–579.

Eribon, Didier. *Insult and the Making of the Gay Self*, trans. Michael Lucey. Durham: Duke University Press, 2004 [1999].

_____. *Réflexions sur la question gay*. Paris: Fayard, 1999.

Eusebius of Caesarea. *Chronicon*, ed. Johannes Multivallis. Paris: Henri Estienne and Jodocus Badius Ascensius, 1512.

Faderman, Lillian. *Surpassing the Love of Men: Romantic Friendship and Love between Women from the Renaissance to the Present*. New York: Morrow, 1981.

Faggioni, Maurizio P. "L'atteggiamento e la prassi della Chiesa in epoca medievale e moderna sull'omosessualità." *Gregorianum*, 91.3 (2010): 478–509.

Fasoli, Paolo. "Bodily 'Figurae': Sex and Rhetoric in Libertine Venice, 1642–1651." *Journal for Early Modern Cultural Studies* 12.2 (2012): 97–116.

Feci, Simona and Laura Schettini, eds. *La violenza contro le donne nella storia: contesti, linguaggi, politiche del diritto (secoli XV–XXI)*. Rome: Viella, 2017.

Felici, Lucia. *Giovanni Calvino e l'Italia*. Turin: Claudiana, 2010.

Ferrante, Lucia. "Il valore del corpo, ovvero la gestione economica della sessualità femminile." In Angela Groppi, ed. *Il lavoro delle donne*. Rome: Laterza, 1996, 206–228.

Fiorelli, Piero. *La tortura giudiziaria nel dritto comune*. 2 vols. Milan: Giuffrè, 1953–1954.

Firpo, Massimo. *Juan de Valdés and the Italian Reformation*, trans. Richard Bates. Farnham, UK: Ashgate, 2015.

_____. *Dal sacco di Roma all'Inquisizione. Studi su Juan de Valdés e la Riforma italiana*. Alessandria: Edizioni dell'Orso, 1998.

_____. *Riforma protestante ed eresie nell'Italia del Cinquecento.* Rome: Laterza, 1993.

Foucault, Michel and James O'Higgins. "Sexual Choice, Sexual Act: An Interview with Michel Foucault." *Salmagundi,* 58–59 (1982–1983): 10–24.

Foucault, Michel. *Archaeology of Knowledge,* trans. A.M. Sheridan Smith. London: Routledge, 2002.

_____. *The Will to Knowledge,* trans. Robert Hurley. London: Penguin, 1998 [1976].

_____. *Dits et Écrits (1954–1988),* vol. 4, eds. Daniel Defert, François Ewald and Jacques Lagrange. Paris: Gallimard, 1994.

_____. *The History of Sexuality,* vol. 2, *The Use of Pleasure,* trans. Robert Hurley. New York: Vintage Book, 1990.

_____. *The History of Sexuality,* vol. 3, *The Care of the Self,* trans. Robert Hurley. New York: Vintage Book, 1990.

Franco, Niccolò. *Rime di Nicolo Franco contro Pietro Aretino,* ed. Enrico Sicardi. Lanciano: Carabba, 1916.

Freccero, Carla. *Queer / Early / Modern.* Durham: Duke University Press, 2006.

Freeman, Elizabeth. *Time Binds: Queer Temporalities, Queer Histories.* Durham: Duke University Press, 2010.

Gagliardi, Isabella. *Li trofei della croce: l'esperienza gesuata e la società lucchese tra Medioevo ed età moderna.* Rome: Edizioni di Storia e Letteratura, 2005.

Galasso Calderara, Estella, Carla Sodini, eds. *Abratassà. Tre secoli di stregherie in una libera Repubblica.* Lucca: Maria Pacini Fazzi, 1989.

Gandolfi, Emiliano. "La riforma a Lucca. Un quadro dell'origine e della diffusione del movimento riformatore." *Actum Luce* 1.2 (1980): 31–65.

Garza Carvajal, Federico. *Butterflies Will Burn: Prosecuting Sodomites in Early Modern Spain and Mexico.* Austin: University of Texas Press, 2003.

Ghirardo, Diane Y. "The Topography of Prostitution in Renaissance Ferrara." *Journal of the Society of Architectural Historians* 60.4 (2001): 402–431.

Gilmour-Bryson, Anne. "Sodomy and the Knights Templars." *Journal of the History of Sexuality* 7.2 (1966): 152–183.

Ginzburg, Carlo and Lucio Biasiori, eds. *A Historical Approach to Casuistry: Norms and Exceptions in a Comparative Perspective.* London: Bloomsbury Academic, 2019.

Gli Statuti della città di Lucca nuovamente corretti, et con molta diligentia stampati. Bologna: Giovan Battista Faello, 1539.

Goldberg, Jonathan, ed. *Queering the Renaissance*. Durham: Duke University Press, 1994.

————. *Sodometries: Renaissance Texts, Modern Sexualities*. Stanford: Stanford University Press, 1992.

————. and Madhavi Menon. "Queering History." *PMLA* 120.5 (2005): 1608–1617.

Golden, Mark and Peter Toohey, eds. *A Cultural History of Sexuality in the Classical World*. Oxford: Berg 2011.

Goodich, Michael. *The Unmentionable Vice. Homosexuality in the later Medieval Period*. Santa Barbara: ABC/CLIO, 1979.

Gowing, Laura, Michael Hunter, and Miri Rubin, eds. *Love, Friendship and Faith in Europe, 1300–1800*. Basingstoke: Palgrave Macmillan, 2005.

Grafton, Anthony. *Defenders of the Text: The Traditions of Scholarship in an Age of Science, 1450–1800*. Cambridge, MA: Harvard University Press, 1991.

Grassi, Umberto. "Emotions and Sexuality: Regulation and Homoerotic Transgression." In Andrew Lynch and Susan Broomhall, eds. *The Routledge History of Emotions in Europe, 1100–1700*. London: Routledge, 2020, 133–150.

————. *Sodoma. Persecuzioni, affetti, pratiche sociali*. Rome: Carocci, 2019.

————. "Sex and Toleration: New Perspectives of Research on Religious Radical Dissent in Early Modern Italy." *Intellectual History Review* 29.1 (2019): 129–144.

————. "Acts o Identities? Rethinking Foucault on Homosexuality." *Cultural History* 5.2 (2016): 200–221.

————. "Shame and Boastfulness in Early Modern Italy: Showing Off Masculinity and Exposing Sexual Submission in Class and Age Competitions." In Anna Foka, Jonas Liliequist, Lewis Webb, eds. *Gender and Status Competition in Premodern Societies*. Turnhout: Brepols, forthcoming.

Grell, Ole Peter. *Brethren in Christ: A Calvinist Network in Reformation Europe*. Cambridge, UK: Cambridge University Press, 2011.

Grendler, Paul F. *Schooling in Renaissance Italy: Literacy and Learning, 1300–1600*. Baltimore: Johns Hopkins University Press, 1989.

Gruzinski Serge. "The Ashes of Desire: Homosexuality in Mid-Seventeenth-Century New Spain." In Pete Sigal, ed. *Infamous Desire: Male Homosexuality in Colonial Latin America*. Chicago: The University of Chicago Press, 2003, 197–214.

Guglielmi, Nilda. *Il Medioevo degli ultimi: emarginazione e marginalità nei secoli XI–XIV*. Rome: Città nuova, 2001.

Guglielmi, Pietro. *I canonici regolari lateranensi. La vita comune nel clero*. Vercelli: [s.n.], 1992.

Guidiccioni, Alessandro I. *Regole per le classi de' sacerdoti, e per ogn'altro chierico della città, e diocesi di Lucca. Con alcuni avvertimenti al popolo. Del molto illustre, & reverendissimo monsignor Alessandro Guidiccioni vescouo di Lucca*. Lucca: Vincenzo Busdraghi, 1588.

_____. *Alli sacerdoti della sua diocesi salute nel Signore*. Lucca: Vincenzo Busdraghi, 1567.

Haas, Louis. *The Renaissance Man and His Children: Childbirth and Early Childhood in Florence, 1300–1600*. New York: St. Martin's Press, 1998.

Halperin, David M. *One Hundred Years of Homosexuality and other essays on Greek love*. New York: Routledge, 1990.

_____. *How to Do the History of Homosexuality*. Chicago: The University of Chicago Press, 2002.

Hergemöller, Bernd-Ulrich. *Sodom and Gomorrah: On the Everyday Reality and Persecution of Homosexuals in the Middle Ages*, trans. John Phillips. London: Free Associations Books, 2001.

Herlihy, David and Christiane Klapisch-Zuber. *Tuscans and Their Families: A Study of the Florentine Catasto of 1427*. New Haven: Yale University Press, 1985.

Hewlett, Mary. "Fortune's Fool: The Influence of Humanism on Francesco Burlamacchi, 'Hero' of Lucca." In Konrad Eisenbichler and Nicholas Terpstra, eds. *The Renaissance in the Streets, Schools, and Studies: Essays in Honour of Paul F. Grendler*. Essays and Studies, 16. Toronto: Centre for Reformation and Renaissance Studies, 2008, 125–156.

_____. "The French Connection: Syphilis and Sodomy in Late-Renaissance Lucca." In Kevin Siena, ed. *Sins of the Flesh: Responding to Sexual Disease in Early Modern Europe*. Essays and Studies, 7. Toronto: Centre for Reformation and Renaissance Studies, 2005, 239–260.

Himes, Norman E. *Medical History of Contraception*. New York: Schocken Books, 1970 [1936].

Hsia, R. Po-chia. *Social Discipline in the Reformation: Central Europe, 1550–1750*. London: Routledge, 1989.

Huizinga, Johan. *The Autumn of the Middle Ages*, trans. Rodney J. Payton and Ulrich Mammitzsch. Chicago: University of Chicago Press, 1996 [1919].

Hunt, Lynn, ed. *The Invention of Pornography: Obscenity and the Origin of Modernity, 1500–1800.* New York: Zone, 1993.

Hurteau, Pierre. "Catholic Moral Discourse on Male Sodomy and Masturbation in the Seventeenth and Eighteenth Centuries." *Journal of the History of Sexuality* 4.1 (1993): 1–26.

Imbasciati, Bianca Rosa. "Lucca e la repressione dell'omosessualità: i procedimenti penali del 1382." MA thesis. Pisa, University of Pisa, 1986–87.

Johnson, Harold and Francis A. Dutra, eds. *Pelo Vaso Traseiro. Sodomy and Sodomites in Luso-Brazilian History.* Tucson: Fenestra Books, 2007.

Jordan, Mark D. *The Invention of Sodomy in Christian Theology.* Chicago: The University of Chicago Press, 1997.

Kaplan, Benjamin J. *Divided by Faith: Religious Conflict and the Practice of Toleration in Early Modern Europe.* Cambridge, MA: Belknap Press of Harvard University Press, 2007.

Karras, Ruth Mazo. *From Boys to Men. Formations of Masculinity in Late Medieval Europe.* Philadelphia: University of Pennsylvania Press, 2003.

_____. *Common Women: Prostitution and Sexuality in Medieval England.* New York: Oxford University Press, 1996.

Kirby, Torrance, et al., eds. *A Companion to Peter Martyr Vermigli.* Brill's Companions to the Christian Tradition, 16. Leiden: Brill, 2009.

Klapisch-Zuber, Christiane. "Il bambino, la memoria e la morte." In Egle Becchi and Dominique Julia, eds. *Storia dell'infanzia*, vol. 1, *Dall'antichità al seicento.* Rome: Laterza, 1996, 155–181.

Kłosowska, Anna. *Queer Love in the Middle Ages.* New York: Palgrave Macmillan, 2005.

Langbein, John H. *Torture and the Law of Proof.* Chicago: The University of Chicago Press, 1977.

Lear, Andrew. "Ancient Pederasty: An Introduction." In Thomas K. Hubbard, ed. *A Companion to Greek and Roman Sexualities.* Chichester, UK: Blackwell, 2014, 102–127.

Leggi e decreti dell'eccellentissimo consiglio generale aggiunti alli statuti del quarto libro. Lucca: Vincenzo Busdraghi, 1589.

León, Pedro de. *Grandeza y miseria en Andalucia. Testimonio de una encrucijada historica (1578–1616)*, ed. Pedro Herrera Puga. Granada: Facultad de Teologia, 1981 (original manuscript XVII sec.).

Lithgow, William. *Totall discourse of the rare adventures & painefull peregrinations of long nineteene yeares travayles from Scotland to the most famous kingdomes in Europe, Asia and Affrica.* London: Nicholas Okes, 1632; reprint, Glasgow: J. MacLehose, 1906.

Loetz, Francisca. *Dealings with God: From Blasphemers in Early Modern Zurich to a Cultural History of Religiousness.* Aldershot, UK: Ashgate, 2009.

Lombardi, Daniela. *Storia del matrimonio. Dal Medioevo a oggi.* Bologna: Il Mulino, 2008.

Lotz-Heumann, Ute. "The Concept of 'Confessionalization': A Historiographical Paradigm in Dispute." *Memoria y Civilización* 4 (2001): 93–114.

Lucà Trombetta, Pino. *La confessione della lussuria: definizione e controllo del piacere nel cattolicesimo.* Genoa: Costa & Nolan, 1991.

Lucensis ecclesiae constitutiones synodales. Adiecti sunt canones poenitentiales, sanctorumque apostolorum. Praefixo indice locupletissimo rubricarum, seu titulorum, capitumque, & locorum maxime insignium. Lucca: Vincenti Busdraghi, 1571.

Luzzati, Michele "Michele Burlamacchi." In *Dizionario Biografico degli Italiani* 15. Rome: Istituto dell'Enciclopedia Italiana, 1972. Online at: http://www.treccani.it/enciclopedia/michele-burlamacchi_%28Dizionario-Biografico%29/

Lynch, Andrew and Susan Broomhall, eds. *Routledge History of Emotions in Europe, 1100–1700.* Abingdon, UK: Routledge, 2019.

MacCulloch, Diarmaid. *The Reformation.* New York: Viking, 2004.

Manlio, Fulvio. *Lucca, le sue corti, le sue strade, le sue piazze.* Empoli: Barbieri, Noccioli & Co., 1968.

Manselli, Raoul. *La Repubblica di Lucca.* Turin: UTET, 1986.

Mantecón Movellan, Tomás A. "Beyond Repression: Gender Identities and Homosexual Relations between Muslims and Christians in 16th- and 17th-Century Spain." In Umberto Grassi, ed. *Mediterranean Crossings: Sexual Transgressions in Islam and Christianity (10th–18th Centuries).* Rome: Viella, 2020.

————. "Los mocitos de Galindo: sexualidad contra natura, culturas proscritas y control social en la temprana edad moderna." In Tomás A. Mantecón Movellan, ed. *Bajtín y la historia de la cultura popular.* Santander: Ediciones de la Universidad de Cantabria, 2008, 209–240.

Martini, Gabriele. *Il «vitio nefando» nella Venezia del Seicento. Aspetti sociali e repressione di giustizia.* Rome: Jouvance, 1988.

Matt, Susan J. and Peter N. Stearns, eds. *Doing Emotions History.* Urbana: University of Illinois Press, 2014.

McCall, Andrew. *Medieval Underworld*. London: H. Hamilton, 1979.

McLaren, Angus. *History of Contraception: From Antiquity to the Present Day*. Oxford: Blackwell, 1990.

McLelland, Joseph C., ed. *Peter Martyr Vermigli and Italian Reform*. Waterloo (ON): Wilfried Laurier University Press, 1980.

McNair, Philip M.J., *Peter Martyr in Italy: An Anatomy of Apostasy*. Oxford: Oxford Clarendon Press, 1967.

Merrick, Jeffrey and Michael Sibalis, eds. *Homosexuality in French History and Culture*. New York: Harrington Park Press, 2001.

Mills, Robert. *Seeing Sodomy in the Middle Ages*. Chicago: The University of Chicago Press, 2015.

Moeller, Bernd. *Imperial Cities and the Reformation: Three Essays*, trans. H. C. Erik Midelfort and Mark U. Edwards, Jr. Philadelphia: Fortress Press, 1972 [1962].

Mommsen, Wolfgang J., Peter Alter and Robert W. Scribner, eds. *Stadtbürgertum und Adel in der Reformation: Studien zur Sozialgeschichte d. Reformation in England u. Deutschland. The Urban Classes, the Nobility and the Reformation: Studies on the Social History of the Reformation in England and Germany*. Stuttgart: Klett-Cotta, 1979.

Montauti, Amelia. "Le cause Delegate. Un tribunale straordinario a Lucca nell'età moderna." MA thesis. Pisa, University of Pisa, 1979–80.

Monter, William. *La otra Inquisición: la Inquisición española en la Corona de Aragón, Navarra, el País Vasco y Sicilia*. Barcelona: Crítica, 1992.

Mott, Luiz and Aroldo Assunção. "Love's Labors Lost: Five Letters from a Seventeenth-Century Portuguese Sodomite." In Kent Gerard and Gert Hekma, eds. *The Pursuit of Sodomy: Male Homosexuality in Renaissance and Enlightenment Europe*. New York: Harrington Park Press, 1989, 91–101.

Mott, Luiz. "My Pretty Boy: Love Letters from a Sodomite Friar, Lisbon (1690)." In Harold Johnson and Francis A. Dutra, eds. *Pelo Vaso Traseiro. Sodomy and Sodomites in Luso-Brazilian History*. Tucson: Fenestra Books, 2007, 231–261.

_____. "Pagode português: a subcultura gay em Portugal nos tempos inquisitoriais." *Ciência e Cultura* 40 (1988):120–139.

Naphy, William G. "Sodomy in Early Modern Geneva: Various Definition, Diverse Verdict." In Tom Betteridge, ed. *Sodomy in Early Modern Europe*. Manchester: Manchester University Press, 2002, 94–111.

Nash, David. *Blasphemy in the Christian World: A History.* Oxford: Oxford University Press, 2007.

Niccoli, Ottavia. *La vita religiosa nell'Italia moderna. Secoli XV–XVIII.* Rome: Carocci, 2008.

_____. *Rinascimento anticlericale. Infamia, propaganda e satira in Italia tra Quattro e Cinquecento.* Rome: Laterza, 2005.

_____. *Il seme della violenza. Putti, fanciulli e mammoli nell'Italia tra Cinque e Seicento.* Rome: Laterza, 1995.

_____. *Prophecy and People in Renaissance Italy,* trans. Lydia G. Cochrane. Princeton: Princeton University Press, 1990 [1987].

_____. "Istituzioni ecclesiastiche e vita religiosa tra Quattro e Cinquecento." In Nicola Tranfaglia and Massimo Firpo, eds. *La storia. I grandi problemi dal Medioevo all'età contemporanea,* vol. 4, *L'età moderna.* T. 2, *La vita religiosa e la cultura.* Turin: UTET, 1986, 105–134.

Norton, Rictor. *Mother Clap's Molly House: The Gay Subculture in England, 1700–1830.* Brimscombe Port: Chalford Press, 2006.

_____. *The Myth of the Modern Homosexual: Queer History and the Search for Cultural Unity.* London: Cassell, 1997.

O'Malley, John W. *Trent and All That: Renaming Catholicism in the Early Modern Era.* Cambridge, MA: Harvard University Press, 2000.

_____. *First Jesuits.* Cambridge, MA: Harvard University Press, 1993.

Oestreich, Gerhard. *Neostoicism and the Early Modern state,* ed. Brigitta Oestreich and H.G. Koenigsberger, trans. David McLintock. Cambridge, UK: Cambridge University Press, 1982 [1969].

Olsen, Glenn. W. *Of Sodomites, Effeminates, Hermaphrodites, and Androgynes: Sodomy in the Age of Peter Damian.* Toronto: Pontifical Institute of Medieval Studies, 2011.

Ozment, Steven E. *Ancestors: The Loving Family in Old Europe.* Cambridge, MA: Harvard University Press, 2001.

Pascal, Arturo. *Da Lucca a Ginevra. Studi sulla emigrazione religiosa lucchese nel secolo XVI.* Pinerolo: Unitipografia Pinerolese, 1932.

Pastore, Stefania, Adriano Prosperi, and Nicholas Terpstra, eds. *Brotherhood and Boundaries: Fraternità e barriere.* Pisa: Edizioni della Normale, 2011.

Pelaja, Margherita and Lucetta Scaraffia, *Due in una carne. Chiesa e sessualità nella storia.* Rome: Laterza, 2008.

Perry, Mary Elizabeth. "The 'Nefarious Sin' in Early Modern Seville." In Kent Gerard and Gert Hekma, eds. *The Pursuit of Sodomy: Male*

Homosexuality in Renaissance and Enlightenment Europe. New York: Haworth Press, 1989, 67–90.

Pertile, Antonio. *Storia del diritto penale.* Padova: Tipografia Salmin, 1892.

Pezzini, Domenico. "Aelred's Doctrine of Charity and Friendship." In Marsha L. Dutton, ed. *A Companion to Aelred of Rievaulx (1110–1167).* Leiden: Brill, 2017, 221–245.

Plamper, Jan. *History of Emotions: An Introduction,* trans. Keith Tribe. Oxford: Oxford University Press 2015.

Po-Chia Hsia, Ronnie. "Looking back from the Reformation." In John Arnold, ed. *Oxford Handbook of the Middle Ages.* Oxford: Oxford University Press, 2014, 550–562.

Priuli, Girolamo. *I diarii di Girolamo Priuli (1494–1512),* ed. Roberto Cessi and Arturo Segre. Città di Castello: Lapi, 1912–1938.

Prodi, Paolo. *Papal Prince. One Body and Two Souls: The Papal Monarchy in Early Modern Europe,* trans. Susan Haskins. Cambridge, UK: Cambridge University Press, 1987 [1982].

_____ and Carla Penuti, eds. *Disciplina dell'anima, disciplina del corpo e disciplina della società tra medioevo ed età moderna.* Bologna: Il Mulino, 1994.

Prosperi, Adriano. *Tribunali della coscienza: Inquisitori, confessori, missionari.* Turin: Einaudi, 1996.

Puff, Helmut. "Early Modern Europe: 1400–1700." In Robert Aldrich, ed. *Gay Life and Culture: A World History.* London: Thames and Hudson, 2006, 78–101.

_____. *Sodomy in Reformation Germany and Switzerland: 1440–1600.* Chicago: The University of Chicago Press, 2003.

_____. "Female Sodomy: The Trial of Katherina Hetzeldorfer (1477)." *Journal of Medieval and Early Modern Studies* 30.1 (2000): 41–61.

Pugh, Tison. *Queering medieval genres.* New York: Palgrave Macmillan, 2004.

Quantin, Jean-Louis. "Le Saint-Office et le probabilisme (1677–1679). Contribution à l'histoire de la theologie morale à l'époque moderne." *Mélanges de l'École Française de Rome* 114 (2000): 875–960.

Ragagli, Simone. "L'Inquisizione della Repubblica. Conflitti di giurisdizione e coscienza nella Lucca del primo Seicento. *Rivista Storica Italiana* 3 (2020): 786–826.

_____. "La coscienza di una Repubblica. Le radici del giurisdizionalismo lucchese nell'età della crisi religiosa." *Actum Luce* 47.2 (2018): 7–70.

_____. "La Repubblica e il Sant'Uffizio. Il controllo delle coscienze nella Lucca del secolo di ferro." Ph. D. thesis. Pisa, Scuola Normale Superiore di Pisa, 2008–09.

_____. "Esami per inosservanza dei decreti sulla religione a Lucca dal 1562 al 1572." MA thesis. Pisa, University of Pisa, 1999–2000.

Reddy, William M. *Navigation of Feeling: A Framework for the History of Emotions*. Cambridge, UK: Cambridge University Press, 2001.

Reinhard, Wolfgang. "Reformation, Counter-Reformation, and the Early Modern State. A Reassessment." *Catholic Historical Review* 75 (1989): 383–404.

_____ and Heinz Schilling, eds. *Die katholische Konfessionalisierung. Wissenschaftliches Symposion der Gesellschaft zur Herausgabe des Corpus Catholicorum und des Vereins für Reformationsgeschichte*. Gütersloh: Gütersloher Verlagshaus, 1995.

Rich, Adrienne. "Compulsory Heterosexuality and Lesbian Existence." *Signs* 5.4 (1980): 631–660.

Rocco, Antonio. *L'Alcibiade fanciullo a scola*, ed. Laura Coci. Rome: Salerno Editrice, 1988 [XVII century].

Rocke, Michael J. *Forbidden Friendships. Homosexuality and Male Culture in Renaissance Florence*. New York: Oxford University Press, 1996.

_____. "Sodomites in Fifteenth-Century Tuscany: The Views of Bernardino da Siena." In Kent Gerard and Gert Hekma, eds. *The Pursuit of Sodomy: Male Homosexuality in Renaissance and Enlightenment Europe*. New York: Harrington Park Press, 1989, 7–31.

Romei, Danilo. *Da Leone X a Clemente VII. Scrittori toscani nella Roma dei papati medicei (1513–1534)*. Manziana (Rome): Vecchiarelli, 2007.

_____. "Introduzione." In Francesco Berni, *Rime*, ed. Danilo Romei. Milan: Mursia, 1985, 5–18.

Romeo, Giovanni. *Amori proibiti. I concubini tra Chiesa e Inquisizione*. Rome: Laterza, 2008.

_____. *L'Inquisizione nell'Italia moderna*. Rome: Laterza, 2004.

Rosenwein, Barbara H. *Generations of Feeling: A History of Emotions, 600–1700*. Cambridge, UK: Cambridge University Press, 2016.

_____. *Emotional Communities in the Early Middle Ages*. Ithaca.: Cornell University Press, 2006.

Rossiaud, Jacques. *Medieval Prostitution*, trans. Lydia G. Cochrane. New York: Blackwell, 1988.

Rublack, Ulinka. *Reformation Europe*. Cambridge, UK: Cambridge University Press, 2005.

Ruggiero, Guido. "Prostitution: Looking for Love." In Bette Talvacchia, ed. *A Cultural History of Sexuality in the Renaissance*. Oxford: Berg 2011, 157–174.

_____. *The Boundaries of Eros: Sex Crime and Sexuality in Renaissance Venice*. New York: Oxford University Press, 1985.

Rurale, Flavio. *Ecclesiastico e gentiluomo. Clero, sesso e politica nella prima età moderna*. Viterbo: Sette città, 2018.

Salerni, Alessandro. "Una repubblica cittadina: la giustizia criminale a Lucca nel secondo Quattrocento." MA thesis. Pisa, University of Pisa, 1983–84.

Sanudo, Marin. *I diarii di Marino Sanuto (MCCCCXCVI–MDXXXIII) dall'autografo Marciano ital. cl. VII codd. CDXIX–CDLXXVII*, ed. Rinaldo Fulin, et al.. Regia Deputazione Veneta di Storia Patria, 58 vols. Venice: Visentini, 1879–1903.

Sardi, Cesare. *I capitani lucchesi del secolo XVI*. Lucca: Giusti, 1902.

Savigni, Raffaele. "Le confraternite lucchesi (secc. XIV–XVI) e l'evoluzione della religione civica: relazioni tra chierici e laici e ridefinizione dei confini." In Stefania Pastore, Adriano Prosperi, and Nicholas Terpstra, eds. *Brotherhood and Boundaries: Fraternità e barriere*. Pisa: Edizioni della Normale, 2011, 423–446.

Sbriccoli, Mario. 'Crimen laesae majestatis'. *Il problema del reato politico alle soglie della scienza penalistica moderna*. Milan: Giuffré, 1974.

Scaramella, Pierroberto. "Sodomia." In Adriano Prosperi, Vincenzo Lavenia, John Tedeschi, eds. *Dizionario storico dell'Inquisizione*. 4 vols. Pisa: Edizioni della Normale, 2010. 3:1145–1150.

Scheer, Monique, "Are Emotions a Kind of Practice (and Is That What Makes Them Have a History)? A Bourdieuian Approach to Understanding Emotions." *History and Theory* 51 (2012): 192–220.

Schilling, Heinz, ed. *Religion, Political Culture, and the Emergence of Early Modern Society: Essays in German and Dutch History*. Leiden: Brill, 1992.

_____. "Confessional Europe." In Thomas A. Brady, Jr., Heiko A. Oberman, and James D. Tracy, eds. *Handbook of European History, 1400–1600: Late Middle Ages, Renaissance and Reformation*, vol. 2, *Visions, Programs and Outcomes*. Leiden: Brill, 1995, 641–675. Sedgwick, Eve Kosofsky. *Epistemology of the Closet*. Berkeley: University of California Press, 1990.

Seidel Menchi, Silvana. "Italy." In Robert Scribner, Roy Porter, and Mikuláš Teich, eds. *The Reformation in National Context.* Cambridge, UK: Cambridge University Press, 1994, 181–201.

Sergent, Bernard. *Homosexuality in Greek Myth,* trans. Arthur Goldhammer. Boston: Beacon Press, 1986.

Shorter, Edward. *The Making of the Modern Family.* New York: Basic Books, 1975.

Sigal, Pete, ed. *Infamous Desire: Male Homosexuality in Colonial Latin America.* Chicago: The University of Chicago Press, 2003.

Simons, Patricia. "Lesbian (In)Visibility in Italian Renaissance Culture." *Journal of Homosexuality* 27.1 (1994): 81–122.

Skinner, Marilyn B. *Sexuality in Greek and Roman Culture.* Hoboken: Wiley-Blackwell, 2013.

Solomon, Robert C. *True to Our Feelings: What Our Emotions Are Really Telling Us.* Oxford: Oxford University Press, 2007.

Soyer, François. *Ambiguous Gender in Early Modern Spain and Portugal: Inquisitors, Doctors and the Transgression of Gender Norms.* Leiden: Brill 2012.

Spector, Scott, Helmut Puff, and Dagmar Herzog, eds. *After the History of Sexuality: German Genealogies with and beyond Foucault.* New York: Berghahn Books, 2012.

Statuto del 1308: Statutum Lucani Communis an. MCCCVIII, ed. Salvatore Bongi and Leone Del Prete, *Memorie e documenti per servire alla storia di Lucca,* vol. 3, part 3. Lucca: Giusti, 1867.

Stearns Peter N. and Carol Z. Stearns. "Emotionology: Clarifying the History of Emotions and Emotional Standards." *The American Historical Review* 90.4 (985): 813–836.

Stone, Lawrence. *The Family, Sex and Marriage in England 1500–1800.* London: Weidenfeld & Nicolson, 1977.

Stone, Martin. "Scrupolosity and Conscience: Probabilism in Early Modern Scholastic Ethics." In Harald E. Braun and Edward Vallance, eds. *Contexts of Conscience in Early Modern Europe, 1500–1700.* New York: Palgrave Macmillan, 2004, 1–16.

Tabacchi, Stefano. "Giova, Giuseppe." In *Dizionario Biografico degli Italiani* 55 (2001). Online at: http://www.treccani.it/enciclopedia/giuseppe-giova_ (Dizionario-Biografico)/

Taddei, Ilaria. "*Puerizia, adolescenza* and *giovinezza*: Images and Conceptions of Youth in Florentine Society during the Renaissance." In Konrad

Eisenbichler, ed. *The Premodern Teenager: Youth in Society, 1150–1650.* Toronto: Centre for Reformation and Renaissance Studies, 2002, 15–26.

Talvacchia, Bette. "Introduction: The Look and Sound of Sexuality in the Renaissance." In Bette Talvacchia, ed. *A Cultural History of Sexuality in the Renaissance.* Oxford: Berg 2011, 1–33.

Tedallini, Sebastiano di Branca. *Il Diario Romano dal 3 maggio 1485 al 6 giugno 1524,* ed. Paolo Piccolomini. Città di Castello: Lapi, 1907.

Terpstra, Nicholas. "Civic Religion." In John H Arnold, *Oxford Handbook of Medieval Christianity.* Oxford: Oxford University Press, 2014, 148–165.

_____. *Lost Girls: Sex and Death in Renaissance Florence.* Baltimore: The Johns Hopkins University Press, 2010.

_____. *The Art of Executing Well: Rituals of Execution in Renaissance Italy.* Kirksville, MO: Truman State University Press, 2008.

_____. *Abandoned Children of the Italian Renaissance: Orphan Care in Florence and Bologna.* Baltimore: Johns Hopkins University Press, 2005.

_____. *Lay Confraternities and Civic Religion in Renaissance Bologna.* Cambridge: Cambridge University Press, 1995.

Thomas de Chobham. *Summa de arte praedicandi,* ed. Franco Morenzoni. Turnhout: Brepols, 1988.

Thomas K. Hubbard, ed. *A Companion to Greek and Roman Sexualities.* Chichester, UK: Blackwell, 2014.

Todeschini, Giacomo. "'Soddoma e Caorsa'. Sterilità del peccato e produttività della natura alla fine del medioevo cristiano." In Umberto Grassi, Giuseppe Marcocci, eds. *Le trasgressioni della carne. Il desiderio omosessuale nel mondo islamico e cristiano, secc. XII–XX.* Rome: Viella, 2015, 53–80.

Tommasi, Girolamo. *Sommario della storia di Lucca.* Bologna: Arnaldo Forni, 1975 [1874].

Tori, Giorgio. "I rapporti fra lo Stato e la Chiesa a Lucca nei secoli XVI–XVIII." *Rassegna degli Archivi di Stato* 26.1 (1976): 37–81.

Tortorici, Zeb. *Sins Against Nature: Sex and Archives in Colonial New Spain.* Durham: Duke University Press, 2018.

Toscan, Jean. *Le carnaval du language: le lexique érotique des poètes de l'équivoque de Burchiello à Marino (XVᵉ–XVIIᵉ siècles).* Lille: Presses universitaires de Lille, 1981.

Traub, Valerie. "The New Unhistoricism in Queer Studies." *PMLA* 128.1 (2013): 21–39.

_____. *The Renaissance of Lesbianism in Early Modern England.* Cambridge, UK: Cambridge University Press, 2002.

_____. "The (In)Significance of 'Lesbian' Desire." In Jonathan Goldberg, ed. *Queering the Renaissance.* Durham: Duke University Press, 1994. 61–83.

Trexler, Richard C. *Public Life in Renaissance Florence.* New York: Academic Press: 1980.

_____. *Church and Community 1200–1600: Studies in the History of Florence and New Spain.* Rome: Edizioni di storia e letteratura, 1987.

_____. *Sex and Conquest: Gendered Violence, Political Order, and the European Conquest of the Americas.* Ithaca: Cornell University Press, 1995.

Trinkaus, Charles and Heiko A. Oberman, eds. *The Pursuit of Holiness in Late Medieval and Renaissance Religion: Papers from the University of Michigan Conference.* Leiden: Brill, 1974.

Trumbach, Randolph. "The Transformation of Sodomy from the Renaissance to the Modern World and its General Consequences." *Signs* 37.4 (2012): 832–848.

_____. *Sex and the Gender Revolution,* vol. 1, *Heterosexuality and the third Gender in Enlightenment* London, Chicago: University of Chicago Press, 1998.

_____. "London Sapphists: From Three Sexes to Four Genders in the Making of Modern Culture." in Gilbert Herdt, ed. *Third Sex, Third Gender: Beyond Sexual Dimorphism in Culture and History.* New York: Zone Books, 1993, 111–136.

_____. *The Rise of the Egalitarian Family: Aristocratic Kinship and Domestic Relations in Eighteenth-Century England.* New York: Academic Press, 1978.

Vainfas, Ronaldo. "The Nefarious and the Colony." In Harold Johnson and Francis A. Dutra, eds. *Pelo Vaso Traseiro. Sodomy and Sodomites in Luso-Brazilian History.* Tucson: Fenestra Books, 2007, 337–367.

_____. *Trópico dos pecados: Moral, sexualidade e Inquisição no Brasil.* Rio de Janeiro: Campus, 1989.

Velasco, Sherry. *Lesbians in Early Modern Spain.* Nashville: Vanderbilt University Press, 2011.

White, Hayden V. *Metahistory: The Historical Imagination in Nineteenth-Century Europe.* Baltimore: Johns Hopkins University Press, 2014 [1973].

Wickersham, Jane K. *Rituals of Prosecution: The Roman Inquisition and the Prosecution of Philo-Protestants in Sixteenth-Century Italy.* Toronto: University of Toronto Press, 2012.

Wiesner-Hanks, *Merry E. Christianity and Sexuality in the Early Modern World: Regulating Desire, Reforming Practice.* London: Routledge, 2000.

Williams, Craig A. *Roman Homosexuality: Ideologies of Masculinity in Classical Antiquity.* New York: Oxford University Press, 1999.

Williams, George Huntston. *Radical Reformation.* Philadelphia: Westminster Press, 1962.

Winkler, John J. "Laying Down the Law: The Oversight of Men Sexual Behavior in Classical Athens." In David M. Halperin, John J. Winkler, and Froma I. Zeitlin, eds. *Before Sexuality: The Construction of Erotic Experience in the Ancient Greek World.* Princeton: Princeton University Press, 1990, 171–205.

Zeeden, Ernst W. *Konfessionsbildung. Studien zur Reformation, Gegenreformation und katholischen Reform.* Stuttgart: Klett-Cotta, 1985.

Zorzi, Andrea. "Justice." In Andrea Gamberini and Isabella Lazzarini, eds. *The Italian Renaissance State.* Cambridge: Cambridge University Press, 2012, 497–498.

INDEX